Laws of War and 21st Century Conflict

Laws of War and 21st Century Conflict

E. L. Gaston, editor

International Debate Education Association

New York, London & Amsterdam

Published by
International Debate Education Association
400 West 59th Street
New York, NY 10019

This book is published with the generous support of the Open Society Foundations.

Rebecca Agule contributed significant writing, research, and other assistance that allowed this book to be completed. Additional editing and research contributed by Samantha Schott. Special thanks to Clif Gaston, Bill Abresch, Niko Grubeck, Bonnie Docherty, and Chris Rogers for their helpful comments, suggestions, and support.

Library of Congress Cataloging-in-Publication Data
Laws of war and 21st century conflict / E.L. Gaston, editor.
   p. cm.
 ISBN 978-1-61770-026-2
1. War (International law) 2. Humanitarian law. I. Gaston, E. L.
 KZ6385.L393 2012
 341.6--dc23
                      2011051292

Typeset by Richard Johnson
Printed in the USA
IDEBATE Press

Contents

Introduction

Since 2001, many commentators have begun to describe modern conflict as a new era of warfare. The landscape of war has changed: a modern battlefield might as easily be found in an urban shopping mall, or the frontline trenches in a failed state. Weaponry that once populated science-fiction novels and movies is now a reality, with unmanned aerial vehicles used against military targets in several countries, and automated robots taking over some soldiers' roles on the battlefield. The diffusion of telecommunications technology and the Internet put new weapons in the hands of individuals and networks unaffiliated with state actors, fundamentally changing the calculus of armed conflict. A remote-controlled bomb can be activated with the touch of a button from an ordinary, commercial mobile phone. A devastating cyber attack against military facilities could be launched from a home computer by a hacker on the other side of the world. As American legal scholars Laurie Blank and Amos Guiora describe:

> Gone are the days of soldiers facing each other across large battlefields, tanks shelling tanks, and fighter jets engaging in dogfights. War, or armed conflict, to use a more precise legal term, now takes place *everywhere*— in cities, refugee camps and other historically non-military areas—and involves or affects nearly everyone in the area.[1]

Yet despite how different modern warfare appears on its face, is it so fundamentally different from wars of the past? Surely every era of warfare has appeared dramatically different from past ones. Is the newness of 21st century warfare any greater than the paradigm shifts in warfare in the past, as societies went from spear- or arrow-based fighting to gunpowder; from military tactics based on the use of cavalry and single-shot rifles to those dominated by automated weapons and trench warfare; from armored tanks and air battles to a "Cold War" in which deterring attacks often resulted in a greater strategic advantage than fighting them.

Further, while new, more lethal weaponry and unconventional tactics may color our perception that we are engaged in fundamentally new warfare, in fact, many of the dominant modes of 21st century warfare, including terrorism, guerilla warfare, and counterinsurgency, have long existed. Globalization and technological changes have certainly made these forms of warfare more deadly and more difficult to contain, but many of the essential features of armed conflict remain. Perhaps today's "new warfare" is not so new after all.

Even if modern warfare does not present such unique or unparalleled challenges as we might think at first glance, it still has been different enough to complicate the application of existing international law. Can the same international rules that have been developed and used since the mid-19th century still apply to 21st century warfare? Authors in this book debate this core question, with some arguing that existing international law is outdated and irrelevant to modern conflict, and others taking a more conservative approach by identifying gaps or ambiguities that must be filled or clarified, but still keeping the existing body of law.

Background on the Laws of War

Modern attempts to regulate warfare have generally fallen into two main categories: efforts to limit states' resort to war (often referred to as *jus ad bellum*) and efforts to constrain state conduct during warfare (referred to as *jus in bello*). The rationale for separating the rules and rationales was the hope that even if warring parties violated international law in commencing an armed conflict, they would still act justly and according to humanitarian restraints once war had begun. This book will focus on the latter category, examining the way that "new" warfare has complicated determinations of what is or is not lawful in the conduct of war.[2]

The modern body of international law regulating state conduct during armed conflict is referred to alternately as the law of armed conflict (LOAC), the "laws of war," or international humanitarian law (IHL).[3] While it has earlier roots, this modern body of law began to take form in the mid- to late-19th century. Early efforts included the 1863 Lieber Code, developed at the request of Abraham Lincoln during the Civil War.[4] One of the first codified standards of battlefield conduct for soldiers, it also established the principle that the means and methods of warfare are not unlimited. The 1864 Geneva Convention for the Amelioration of the Condition of the Wounded in Armies in the Field stood for the principle that war-wounded may receive treatment, and established protections for those providing aid;[5] and the 1868 St. Petersburg Declaration, the first international agreement prohibiting certain weapons of war, also established the principle that superfluous injury and unnecessary suffering should be prevented in war.[6]

The principles established in these early documents heavily influenced the subsequent development of IHL. The sources of IHL can be diverse—ranging from treaty instruments to state practice to general principles. However, the two most significant codified sources of IHL, discussed frequently by authors in this compendium, are referred to as Hague and Geneva Law. These are the collective provisions resulting from the legal instruments leading up to and resulting from the Hague conferences of 1899 and 1907;[7] and the four 1949 Geneva Conventions[8] and their two Additional Protocols of 1977.[9] Although specific principles will be introduced in each of the relevant chapters, a shorthand for thinking about these two main sources of law is that Hague Law establishes limitations on the conduct of war, while Geneva Law deals with the privileges of protected persons in warfare.

The Hague Conferences reinforced the principle that the means and methods of warfare are not unlimited, and that warring parties should only cause destruction that is militarily necessary. The conferences drew a distinction between combatants and civilians, and affirmed that warring parties should weigh the benefits of a military action against the potential harm to civilian persons or property. The Hague Conferences also included a provision known as the Martens Clause, which has often been interpreted as providing that any situations or future developments in warfare not covered by a specific provision of IHL should still be bound by customary international law and by "the laws of humanity and the requirements of the public conscience."[10]

The Geneva Conventions and their two Additional Protocols of 1977, further clarified the specific privileges for combatants and civilians in warfare that now form the core of modern IHL. The 1949 Geneva Conventions negotiated after World War II were in many ways a response to the atrocities that occurred in the two world wars following the Hague Conventions. In order to ensure better protection for victims of conflict, the four conventions enumerated specific protections and privileges for those not taking part in combat, including civilians, and combatants who were wounded, shipwrecked, taken prisoner, or otherwise taken out of the fighting. The two subsequent Additional Protocols of 1977 further codified and developed protections for civilians in international conflict (Protocol I), and the rules governing noninternational (internal) conflicts (Protocol II). Many of the provisions of Hague and Geneva Law have risen to the level of customary international law, meaning that they are binding even on those states that are not a party to those treaties.[11]

As this brief history of IHL development makes clear, the basic framework and early rules of IHL were negotiated by states, often with a presumption of regulating state-on-state conflicts (though certain provisions have always clearly presaged some conflicts involving nonstate actors, for example internal conflicts). As such, the traditional IHL framework relied, in part, on the expectation of reciprocity. States agreed to be bound by these rules, though they might result in tactical disadvantages, because they knew the other side would also be bound. However, as a legal matter, IHL obligations do not depend on the other side following them. IHL rules operate on a principle of the equal application of the law, which means they apply in the same way to all warring parties regardless of their compliance with either jus ad bellum or jus in bello principles, regardless of whether they are a state or nonstate actor, and regardless of any other power or status differences. Some commentators have questioned this principle of equal application more frequently in the past decade as insurgent and terrorist fighters have frequently ignored, and often deliberately flouted international law.

The rules of IHL often take the form of flexible principles or standards, rather than outright rules. (There are, however, some specific prohibitions in IHL, often regarding certain types of weapons.)[12] When applying these principles, what is or is not lawful may depend on the situation and the surrounding facts. For example, one key principle common to many IHL treaties and customary international law is that warring parties must avoid intentionally causing harm to civilians, and unintentional harm to civilians—often referred to as "collateral damage"—must be limited to the extent possible. While this principle may seem simple enough, in practice when civilians are killed it may be more difficult to determine whether the harm was intentional or avoidable, in which case it would likely be unlawful, or whether it was lawful collateral damage. Many of the challenges of "new warfare" discussed in this compendium relate to how new dynamics or tactics in warfare complicate application of these standards.

In general though, the heavy reliance on situation-dependent standards and principles has made IHL flexible enough to apply in a variety of conflict scenarios, and to accommodate new types of warfare over time. For example, IHL requirements against targeting civilians and for limiting the risk of collateral damage apply whether the weapon at issue is an artillery cannon or laser weapons from drones. These same principles may also apply by analogy to new technologies that seem completely different from traditional warfare, like "information" warfare, or cyber war.[13]

Where analogizing to existing provisions is not as clear, or controversy exists over limitations for particular weapons or means of warfare, states have negotiated new treaties or provisions of treaties.[14] For example, two of the most recent treaties are the 1997 treaty banning the use, stockpiling, and production of landmines[15] and a 2008 treaty banning the use, stockpiling, and production of cluster munitions (mini-bomblets dropped in the thousands over an area the size of a football field, which may act like mini-landmines if they fail to explode on contact).[16]

"NEW" WARFARE, "NEW" RULES FOR IHL?

It is remarkable that a regulatory framework that originated at a time when cavalry units were still relevant and hot-air balloons were used for surveillance, has successfully evolved to deal with threats stemming from the development of air power; trench warfare; weapons of mass destruction, including chemical, biological, and nuclear weapons; laser weapons; landmines; precision-guided munitions; drones and robotics; and cyber warfare. Despite these achievements, many of the authors in this book focus on the ways that IHL has failed to keep pace, with some suggesting that we are a seeing a "new" era of warfare that merits new rules for armed conflict.

Much of IHL was designed to address a conflict involving one or more states. At the time when many IHL treaties were ratified, states generally controlled the deployment of military force and were the primary actors in war. The state was the only unit with sufficient and sustained resources to support warfare to develop and train large numbers of fighters into cohesive forces, and with the manufacturing and production capabilities to supply them with adequate weaponry.

However, with technological and economic developments, the field of war became open to nonstate actors as well. Though few actors today possess the most state-of-the-art, lethal tools of war, a lot of damage can be done with assault rifles, homemade explosive devices, or even a few box cutters and knowledge of how to fly a plane (in the case of the terrorist who perpetrated the September 11, 2001 attacks on the United States). Small arms like AK-47s, rocket-propelled grenades, or shoulder-fired missiles are cheap, easy to use, and readily transportable. Globalization has helped increase the flow of these small arms, estimated to kill hundreds of thousands worldwide annually. These weapons not only enable nonstate actors such as terrorist groups to inflict significant blows against states but also fuel local or regional conflicts such as those in the Democratic Republic of Congo and in Sudan.

As a result of these and other factors, state-on-state conflicts have been increasingly rare since the late 1970s, while internal conflict, including civil wars and insurgency, continue to be common and now represent the major sources of conflict.[17] Globalization has also made transnational threats more frequent and more potent by limiting states' ability to control the spread of violence. With the increasing interconnectedness of economies and communities, global risks spread more quickly, from financial panics, to criminal networks, to health pandemics, to attacks with weapons of mass destruction. Advances in transportation and communications have shrunk global distances, and further enabled irregular warfare. Threats may arise anywhere, and strike with a global reach. A major terrorist threat could originate in Yemen, or from a suburban garage in the United States.

While these dynamics have been in place at least since the end of the Cold War (if not before), it was the Al Qaeda attacks of September 11, 2001, that catalyzed debate, particularly in the United States, about whether IHL was still relevant to modern security challenges. As one American legal scholar, Rosa Brooks (whose other work features later in this book), described:

> [W]e simply lack an adequate international legal paradigm for thinking about the changes brought about by the rise of global terrorism. The analytical underpinnings of the core distinctions drawn by the laws of armed conflict have broken down, and as a result, this body of law is no longer of much practical use in allowing us to determine which rights and persons merit protection. [18]

The question of how to deal with global terrorism is not the only issue that has triggered debate over the relevance of IHL in recent years. The blurring of lines between civilians and combatants, the mismatch between IHL's state-centric framework with the prevalence of nonstate threats and actors, and the rapid transformation of 21st century conflict due to technological change have all sparked proposals for reinterpreting, reforming, or otherwise clarifying existing IHL. The article collections in this book will discuss these and other issues in turn.

Part 1 explores the history of developing laws of war and the impact of the humanitarian movement. For many, efforts to justify war may seem not only immoral, but quixotic. Nonetheless, efforts to regulate war are almost as old as warfare itself. Gary D. Solis explores historical attempts to regulate war, and though he admits that most of these efforts have failed (many catastrophically), he asserts that the importance of limiting the effects of war are so important that the attempt is still worthwhile even if the results are imperfect. Chris af Jochnick and Roger Normand are more negative about the impact of the humanitarian movement. They argue that modern IHL was crafted by states, for states, and only serves to legitimate—not stop—the violence of war.

Part 2 offers a snapshot of some of the legal debates sparked by the September 11 attacks on the United States and the subsequent U.S. military responses in Afghanistan, Iraq, and globally. Is IHL sufficient to meet the challenges posed by asymmetric warfare such as global terrorism or insurgent campaigns, or should it be significantly revised or abandoned altogether? Commentator Patrick J. Buchanan questions the principle that IHL should be applied equally given modern insurgent tactics. He argues that states engaged in conflicts with nonstate actors who do not abide by IHL should not have to follow the rules either. Rosa Brooks argues that warfare has changed enough to justify a rethinking of IHL, but this must be done in ways that balance new security threats against existing rights protections. Rebutting post–September 11 arguments that IHL is out of date for 21st century conflict, Jakob Kellenberger, president of the International Committee for the Red Cross argues that IHL is flexible enough to respond to different threats and modalities of warfare, and recommends better clarification and compliance with existing IHL. Kenneth Roth, executive director of Human Rights Watch, writes that the U.S. framing of global terrorist threats as a "global war" (rather than dealing with them through law enforcement) may erode right protections under both IHL and traditional domestic laws. Legal scholar David P. Fidler argues that some trends in modern warfare, like counterinsurgency theory, may lead to greater, not lesser IHL compliance.

Part 3 takes a closer look at challenges to applying one of IHL's most important principles—protection of civilians. As Laurie Blank and Amos Guiora illustrate, in irregular warfare, nonstate actors often blend with the population, complicating the application of IHL principles that warring parties distinguish and protect civilians. Both the Blank and Guiora excerpt and the article by Charli Carpenter, explore ways that IHL rules might be clarified to enable state parties to operate in such environments while still respecting IHL.

Modern asymmetric tactics are not the only feature of "new warfare" that have affected the protection of civilians. Carpenter's article also engages the role of technological advances in the protection of civilians. Carpenter argues that while technology has increased the destructive force used in war, it has also enabled greater precision and control over uses of force, which has resulted in greater protection for civilians. Commentator Max Boot objects that expectations of the precision capabilities of modern military forces such as those of the United States are unrealistic, and as a result they are held to an impossibly high (and unfair) standard of no civilian casualties.

Continuing on the theme of distinguishing and protecting civilians in warfare, Part 4 explores the blurring of lines between civilians and combatants. Andreas Wenger and Simon J. A. Mason point to the "civilianization" of conflict as one of the most significant sources of legal ambiguity in modern conflict. It is not just that nonstate actors blend in with the population (often purposely); civilians have become increasingly involved in developing, maintaining, and even exercising the tools of warfare. As civilian fields such as communications or economic development become more central to fighting wars, some warring parties have argued that traditionally civilian objects might become legitimate military targets. Amnesty International examines a NATO bombing of a Serbian television station by NATO forces in April 1999, and whether its use for propaganda purposes might be a legitimate rationale for NATO's airstrike. Dapo Akande explores U.S. suggestions that it might treat supporting activities such as producing propaganda, providing financial support, or drug trafficking as combatant activities in Afghanistan. Finally, the Program on Humanitarian Policy and Conflict Research delves into one of the most complex legal debates, how this blurring of the lines complicates an already ambiguous provision of IHL that makes it legal for a warring party to target a civilian who directly participates in hostilities.

Many of the themes of previous sections intersect over the practice of targeted killings, discussed in Part 5. The American Civil Liberties Union (ACLU) questions argues that a law-enforcement rather than wartime targeted killings would be more appropriate when those suspected of terrorism are far from a "hot" battlefield. The ACLU also raises a concern that distinguishing civilians from combatants and ensuring that those targeted are really combatants or civilians directly participating in hostilities might be difficult in places where targeted killings are used. Harold Hongju Koh, the chief legal adviser for the U.S. State Department, defends the U.S. right to use targeted killings wherever members of Al Qaeda or affiliates are found because the United States is in an armed conflict with them. Gabriella Blum and Philip Heymann argue that states will and must use targeted killings in the context of global terrorism, but only as an exceptional tactic. Philip Alston explores particular issues raised by the use of civilian intelligence officers to carry out these wartime killings, and additional concerns about the use of unmanned aerial vehicles (or drones) to carry out targeted killings.

Finally, in Part 6, the authors take a step back from the challenges posed by terrorism and insurgency, and explore how underlying global political, economic, and technological changes are impacting the regulation and control of armed conflict. Moisés Naím describes some of the other "global wars" that have arisen due to globalization, including transnational crime and the war on drugs. He argues that comparing these "wars" with the war on terrorism illustrates how globalization has more fundamentally undermined state abilities to respond to global threats. E. L. Gaston reexamines ongoing debates about the use of private military and security companies (PMSCs), often likened to "mercenaries," in modern warfare. She argues that the real danger behind the expansion of these PMSCs, or the broader trend toward privatization of war, is that it de-links state responsibility from certain actions in warfare, thus undermining broader international controls on armed conflict. Finally, Robert Sparrow gets into the most futuristic discussion of the book—the emerging issues related to increased use of robotics in war. As robotics become more integrated in war, and assume increasingly autonomous functions, can they be programmed to comply with IHL? Even if so, how would the inevitable mistakes be dealt with under international or criminal responsibility frameworks? More broadly, does the increasing automation of warfare undermine more fundamental human controls on war?

Although each author deals with separate responsibility and enforcement issues in turn, taken together the authors in this final chapter raise the question whether any "rewrite" of the laws of war could successfully control 21st century threats. What mechanisms or rules could be effectively enforced given that globalization, technology, and other changing global dynamics have eroded the international system's ability to contain and enforce international law?

Conclusion

Regulating warfare has never been easy, or as some would argue, all that successful. Constant changes in global power balances, weaponry, and military tactics have made it difficult to develop rules with any staying power. IHL provisions have at times been out of date no sooner than they were developed. Even where this not the case, rules will always be broken in war.

This book is fundamentally a story about law, but it is not designed to be particularly legal in nature. It should be accessible for those with no background in international law, or more specifically, the laws pertaining to armed conflict. The introduction to each chapter and many of the articles themselves give background information on the international laws or principles at issue. Nonetheless, it is not a textbook. These introductory materials are only designed to offer enough grounding for readers to be able to engage with the materials. They would not in themselves give the reader a strong understanding of the legal issues involved.

Though some of the articles deal with technical legal issues, the underlying debates are those that everyone can, and should, be engaging with. Ongoing debates about how the international system deals with 21st century threats involve some of the most critical questions of law and policy: Not every harmful act is an act of war, but where should the international system draw the line? Should threats by a state be treated differently than threats by individuals or networks (often called "nonstate actors") and why? What rights must be preserved in wartime, and for whom? How far must states go to protect innocent civilians when national security questions are at issue? Even where the exact legal language is unclear, readers should try to identify the core arguments and disagreements between the articles, and decide which positions they find most convincing.

As you read through the following chapters, keep in mind the larger theme of this book, which is how IHL engages with 21st century warfare. Are claims that we are in a "new" era of warfare exaggerated? Or, is 21st century conflict so "new" that IHL is outdated, to the point of being completely irrelevant for regulating it?

NOTES

1. Laurie Blank and Amos Guiora, "Teaching an Old Dog New Tricks: Operationalizing the Law of Armed Conflict in New Warfare," *Harvard National Security Journal* 1 (2010): 45.

2. An entire book might equally be devoted to "jus ad bellum" concepts that are being challenged by the dynamics of 21st century warfare, including questions of the legitimacy of preventive or preemptive war, and the interrelation (as posited by some state parties) between the *jus ad bellum* justification and the *jus in bello* requirements. These discussions will largely be avoided for this compendium. Discussion will also largely focus on so-called kinetic actions in warfare—those that involve direct fighting. A large portion of international law related to armed conflict deals with the privileges and restrictions related to the detention of suspected enemy combatants. Though these provisions, and debates surrounding them, play a role in many of the issues discussed in this chapter, they will not be dealt with separately. A full treatment of how the laws of war deal with these issues in the 21st century would merit an entire book in itself.

3. Although there are some historical distinctions, the terms are generally used interchangeably in current literature. Some have argued that the conflation of these terms, and the increased use of the term "international humanitarian law," reflects the influence of those in the humanitarian community who wish to emphasize humanitarian concerns in evaluating conduct in war. Gary D. Solis, *The Law of Armed Conflict: International Humanitarian Law in War* (New York: Cambridge University Press, 2011), 23, 24.

4. Instructions for the Government of Armies of the United States in the Field (24 Apr. 1863), reproduced in D. Schindler and J. Toman, *The Laws of Armed Conflicts* (The Netherlands: M. Nijhoff Publishers, 1988), 3.

5. Geneva Convention for the Amelioration of the Condition of the Wounded in Armies in the Field, August 22, 1864. It was later revised several times, and following the last revision in 1949 it now stands as the first of the four Geneva Conventions of 1949.

6. Declaration Renouncing the Use, in Time of War, of Explosive Projectiles under 400 Grams Weight, opened for signature November 29, 1868 [1901], ATS 125 [1] (entered into force December 11, 1868).

7. The most relevant conventions resulting from the Hague Conference for modern IHL interpretation include: Hague Convention II with Respect to the Laws and Customs of War on Land, and Its Annex: Regulation Concerning the Laws and Customs of War on Land, July 29, 1899, 32 Stat. 1803, 1 Bevans 247, 26 Martens Nouveau Recueil (ser. 2) 949, 187 Consol. T.S. 429, entered into force September 4, 1900; Hague Convention II—Limitation of Employment of Force for Recovery of Contract Debts: October 18, 1907, 36 Stat. 2241, 1 Bevans 607, entered into force January 26, 1910; Hague Convention IV—Laws and Customs of War on Land, October 18, 1907, 36 Stat. 2277, 1 Bevans 631, 205 Consol. T.S. 277, 3 Martens Nouveau Recueil (ser. 3) 461, entered into force January 26, 1910; Hague Convention V—Rights and Duties of Neutral Powers and Persons in Case of War on Land, October 18, 1907, 36 Stat. 2310, 1 Bevans 654, 205 Consol. T.S. 299, 3 Martens Nouveau Recueil (ser. 3) 504, entered into force January 26, 1910; Hague Convention VIII Relative to the Laying of Automatic Submarine Contact Mines, 3 Martens Nouveau Recueil (ser. 3) 580, 205 Consol. T.S. 331, entered into force January 26, 1910; Hague Convention IX Concerning Bombardment by Naval Forces in Time of War, 3 Martens Nouveau Recueil (ser. 3) 604, 205 Consol. T.S. 345, entered into force January 26, 1910. These and other instruments from the Hague Conferences can be found in Adam Roberts and Richard Guelff, eds., *Documents on the Laws of War*, 3d ed. (Oxford: Oxford University Press, 2000).

8. Geneva Convention for the Amelioration of the Condition of the Wounded and Sick in Armed Forces in the Field, August 12, 1949, art. 3, 6 U.S.T. 3114, 3116–18, 75 U.N.T.S. 31, 32–34; Geneva Convention for the Amelioration of the Condition of the Wounded, Sick and Shipwrecked Members of the Armed Forces at Sea, August 12, 1949, art. 3, 6 U.S.T. 3217, 3220–22, 75 U.N.T.S. 85, 86–88; Geneva Convention Relative to the Treatment of Prisoners of War, Aug. 12, 1949, art. 3, 6 U.S.T. 3316, 3318–20, 75 U.N.T.S. 135, 136–38; Geneva Convention Relative to the Protection of Civilian Persons in Time of War, August 12, 1949, art. 3, 6 U.S.T. 3516, 3518–20, 75 U.N.T.S. 287, 288–90.

9. Protocol Additional to the Geneva Conventions of August 12, 1949, and Relating to the Protection of Victims of International Armed Conflicts, June 8, 1977, 1125 U.N.T.S. 4; Protocol Additional to the Geneva Conventions of August 12, 1949, and Relating to the Protection of Victims of Non-International Armed Conflicts, June 8, 1977, 1125 U.N.T.S. 609.

10. Preamble, 1907 Hague Convention (IV) respecting the laws and customs of war on land, reprinted in A. Roberts and R. Guelf, *Documents on the Laws of War*, 2nd ed., (Clarendon Press, Oxford, 1989) 45. For a general discussion of the original purpose of the Martens clause and the subsequent, varied interpretations, see Rupert Ticehurst, "The Martens Clause and the Laws of Armed Conflict," *International Review of the Red Cross* 317 (1997).

11. States are bound under international law in two ways: (1) They are bound to provisions of international treaties that they have agreed to; (2) all states are generally bound by what is called "customary international law." Principles of customary international law may not be written down in any treaty (although often they are) but they are rules that are generally accepted by the international community as law. A rule may be considered customary depending on how widespread state practice is, as well as whether states are following that rule out of a sense of obligation (*opinio juris*). For more on customary international law and IHL, see the Web site of the International Committee for the Red Cross, "Customary International Humanitarian Law," October 29, 2010, http://www.icrc.org/eng/war-and-law/treaties-customary-law/customary-law/overview-customary-law.htm.

12. Although less prominent in discussions in this compendium, it is worth noting that IHL specifically prohibits certain types of weapons. For example, the Convention on the Prohibition of the Development, Production, Stockpiling and Use of Chemical Weapons and on their Destruction, otherwise known as the Chemical Weapons Convention, bans the production, stockpiling, and use of chemical weapons. Other IHL instruments ban the use under any circumstances of biological weapons, nuclear weapons, landmines, exploding bullets, cluster munitions, or other specific weapons use.

13. Web site of the International Committee for the Red Cross, "Information Warfare," October 29, 2010, http://www.icrc.org/eng/war-and-law/conduct-hostilities/information-warfare/overview-information-warfare.htm. See also Knut Dörmann, "Applicability of the Additional Protocols to Computer Network Attacks," November 19, 2004, http://www.icrc.org/eng/resources/documents/misc/68lg92.htm.

14. The Convention on Conventional Weapons (CCW) entered into force in 1983 and serves as the umbrella treaty body for protocols on specific weapons regulation under IHL. The convention currently comprises five protocols dealing with weapons usage including mines, incendiary weapons, blinding laser weapons, explosive remnants of war, and others. The 109 states that are members to the CCW meet regularly and periodically negotiate new protocols or amendments to deal with evolving practice and usage of weapons in warfare.

15. Convention on the Prohibition of the Use, Stockpiling, Production and Transfer of Anti-Personnel Mines and on their Destruction, September 18, 1997, art. 1(1)(a), 2056 U.N.T.S. 241, 242.

16. Diplomatic Conference for the Adoption of a Convention on Cluster Munitions, *Convention on Cluster Munitions*, 30 May 2008, CCM/77, http://www.unhcr.org/refworld/docid/4843e59c2.html.

17. For more on changing dynamics of warfare, in particular in relation to intra-state and civil wars, see Human Security Report Project, *Human Security Report 2009/2010: The Causes of Peace and The Shrinking Costs of War* (Oxford University Press: August 2011); Human Security Centre, *Human Security Report 2005: War and Peace in the 21st Century* (Oxford University Press: 2005); Stathis N. Kalyvas, "The Changing Character of Civil Wars, 1800–2009," in Hew Strachan and Sibylle Scheipers (eds.), *The Changing Character of War* (Oxford: Oxford University Press, 2011).

18. Rosa Ehrenreich Brooks, "War Everywhere: Rights, National Security Law, and the Law of Armed Conflict in the Age of Terror," *University of Pennsylvania Law Review* 153 (2004): 675.

Part 1: Regulating War

A central premise of the humanitarian movement is that war can and should be constrained. Humanitarians involved in the development of the laws of war since the mid-19th century have pushed to ensure the basic humanitarian treatment of combatants, and to minimize the impact of war on civilians. While such efforts may be laudable, they can also seem quixotic. As stated by Cicero in 50 BCE, "In time of war, the laws are silent." Others may object that because efforts to regulate war implicitly accept and legitimate some acts of war, including killing and destruction, they are far from "humanitarian" and are in fact immoral. The selections in this section deal with the question of what it means to try to regulate war. How have states regulated war historically? What have been some of the key historical developments in efforts to constrain warfare? Have they been effective, or is the mere idea of trying to regulate warfare futile?

DEVELOPMENT OF MODERN INTERNATIONAL HUMANITARIAN LAW

Many of the articles throughout this book deal with the success or failure of international law to regulate harm inflicted by warring parties in conflict. Efforts to regulate or moderate the effects of warfare are not exclusive to the modern international system. The excerpt from Gary D. Solis's book *The Law of Armed Conflict: International Humanitarian Law in War* describes early guidelines on the conduct of war in Egypt as early as 1400 BCE, in China by the 6th century, up to codes of chivalry in medieval Europe.

Modern efforts to constrain war fall within the "just war" tradition, which can be traced to Christian thinkers like St. Augustine, Thomas Aquinas, and Hugo Grotius.[1] War is seen as a necessary evil. Thus, though war may be morally abhorrent, "just war" ethicists accept that it may happen and try to limit unnecessary resort to war (*jus ad bellum*) or unnecessary suffering or killing once war has commenced (*jus in bello*). This creates a tension: those who claim to speak on behalf of "humanity" push for rules and frameworks that permit and justify the taking of life. This would run directly counter to some religious or philosophical frameworks, for example, pacifist arguments that war is never justified.

Though the precursors for many principles of international humanitarian law (IHL) may have dated back to this older "just war" tradition, many trace the development of the modern international humanitarian law framework to the mid-19th century. The brutality of warfare in such conflicts as the American Civil War, the Franco-German Wars, the Boer War, and others, as well as discomfort with increasingly lethal and inhumane weaponry, often pushed states to limit unnecessary harm during conflict (provided it did not unduly disadvantage their war-making efforts).[2]

One of the most notable early codifications was the Lieber Code.[3] In 1863, Abraham Lincoln tasked scholar Francis Lieber with developing a code of conduct for Union soldiers during the American Civil War. The Lieber Code required prisoners of war to be treated humanely: they must be given adequate food and care, must not be tortured or publicly humiliated. The Lieber Code reflected a mix of moral and pragmatic rationales. Its provisions respected the humanity of those captured but also advanced the interests of the Union, which hoped that the South would reciprocate by treating Union prisoners humanely. The Lieber Code also set forth the principle of "military necessity," which has since become one of the two bedrock balancing principles (along with the principle of humanity) for limiting the effects of war. The principle of military necessity, as it is interpreted now, requires that warring parties attack targets only military objectives.[4] Lieber's rationale for this principle was as pragmatic as it was humanitarian: "Military necessity," he said, "does not include any act of hostility which makes the return to peace unnecessarily difficult."[5]

Subsequent attempts to codify restrictions on tactics and weaponry were similarly a balance between humanitarian and self-interested motivations. The Russian government initiated the conference that led to the St. Petersburg Declaration of 1868, the first formal agreement prohibiting the use of certain weapons in war, because it had developed "exploding bullets" (bullets that explode upon impact, and tend to cause more serious damage to flesh than regular bullets) and decided that they were too inhumane for either it or any other government to use. The St. Petersburg Declaration set the "technical limits at which the necessities of war ought to yield to the requirements of humanity."[6]

Subsequently, the 1899 and 1907 Hague Conferences further codified restrictions on weapons deemed to cause inhumane suffering, for example, by prohibiting weapons that use "asphyxiating" or poisonous gases, and exploding bullets.[7] The Hague Conventions also prohibited attacks that were not required by military necessity. For example, attacking troops who have laid down their arms, or undefended towns or property, were deemed examples of acts that were not militarily necessary, and thus would represent an inhumane or excessive act of war prohibited by the Hague Conventions.[8]

Many of these early instruments were instigated and organized in part on the urgings of private citizens, those advocating for greater limits on the suffering and inhumanity of war. In June 1859, while on a business trip in northern Italy, a Swiss merchant named Henry Dunant witnessed the aftermath of the bloody Franco-Austrian Battle of Solferino.[9] He was appalled that thousands of wounded soldiers were left to die because of a lack of basic care. His reaction to what he saw, memorialized in a pamphlet, *A Memory of Solferino*, led to the formation of relief societies to provide impartial care to all war wounded, and eventually the more than 150 International Red Cross and Red Crescent societies worldwide. In 1863, Dunant, along with other activists, formed the International Committee of the Red Cross (ICRC), which played a critical role in pushing governmental actors to convene many of the early conferences and instruments that led to the early development of IHL.[10] Since that time, non-governmental advocacy by the ICRC and other organizations—now described more generally as the "humanitarian movement"—have played an equally active role in the development and codification of international humanitarian law.

Sadly, few of these early codifications were respected during World War I, and a new treaty process was under way when interrupted by World War II. Targeting of civilians and civilian properties during World War II was common. The massive Luftwaffe air raids on Britain and edges of the eastern and western German fronts, as well as the carpet-bombing of German cities and the first use of atomic weapons in Hiroshima and Nagasaki in Japan resulted in devastating civilian losses. The February 1945 bombing of Dresden, for example, killed almost 25,000 civilians over two days.[11]

In reaction to the carnage of World War II, warring parties negotiated a new series of treaties, which focused more on the protection of civilians and others not taking part in hostilities. The four 1949 Geneva Conventions negotiated, and their two Additional Protocols of 1977, now form the core of modern IHL.

EFFECTIVENESS OF IHL AT REGULATING WARFARE

The various treaties and "customary" law provisions that make up IHL are among the most widely adopted principles in international law. One hundred and ninety-four countries are party to the Geneva Conventions. IHL provisions have been widely integrated into the military manuals and practice of state parties. Further, IHL principles are far more commonly espoused by states than other principles of international law.

Yet, despite these outward signs of progress, many would argue that the humanitarian project has been a failure, if not misguided from the outset. As the above overview of the development of IHL suggests, the only consistency in past IHL practice has been states' tendency to violate them. Despite the growing entrenchment of IHL, civilians today are harmed in conflict more than ever before.[12]

The second excerpt in this section, "The Legitimation of Violence: A Critical History of the Laws of War," by Chris af Jochnick and Roger Normand, puts the blame for failed compliance with IHL directly on the instruments of modern IHL. The problem, they argue, is that those drafting the laws of war—the warring parties themselves—were biased by sovereign interests. Instead of creating a system that would legitimately constrain the costs of war, they created a legal system "formulated deliberately to privilege military necessity at the cost of humanitarian values."[13] In this way, they argue, the current body of IHL may actually be harmful by legitimating the violence of war.

Going even further than Jochnick and Normand, many scholars remain skeptical that war can be regulated at all. Realist scholars, who believe that states are driven to act out of rational self-interest, argue that nations will follow international legal norms only when it is in their interest to do so, particularly in areas like peace and warfare, which touch at the essential survival and power balance of states.[14] The frequent violations of IHL by state parties engaged in warfare would seem to support such theories.

In response to such skeptics, Solis (quoting historian Geoffrey Best) notes "we should perhaps not so much complain that the law of war does not work well, as marvel that it works at all."[15] He agrees with realists that, of any area of international law, we would most expect IHL to fail. "In a sense, its goal is virtually impossible: to introduce moderation and restraint into an activity uniquely contrary to those qualities."[16] But he comes to a conclusion shared by many scholars and activists in the field: that the issue of constraining harm caused by war, or succeeding in stopping the resort to war, is so important that even imperfect progress is worth the effort.

As you read through the two excerpts in this part, consider some of the following questions:
- Solis references the maxim "All's fair in love and war." But the humanitarian movement has historically tried to set outer bounds on what is fair in war. Do you think this approach is realistic? If so, what type of conduct would be acceptable or unacceptable in your view?
- The Jochnick and Normand piece argues that the influence of states in shaping the laws of war have led it to be biased in favor of their inter-

ests rather than humanitarian needs. But states obviously must "buy in" to the laws to some extent if they are to respect them. Are there ways to make sure that IHL treaties negotiated by states will protect civilians in war?

• Even if compliance with IHL will never be perfect, some argue that given the consequences of unfettered war, any amount of violence that is restricted is a significant achievement. Do you think that IHL has played any role in restricting or deterring wartime atrocities? How would you measure or evaluate whether it has done enough to restrict war versus (as Jochnick and Normand claim) that it has possibly done more harm than good?

NOTES

1. The modern seminal text on 'just war' is Michael Walzer's *Just and Unjust Wars: A Moral Argument with Historical Illustrations* (New York: Basic Books, 1977).

2. Michael Howard, "Constraints on Warfare," in *The Laws of War: Constraints on Warfare in the Western World*, ed. Michael Howard, George J. Andreopoulos, and Mark R. Shulman (New Haven: Yale University Press, 1994), 1–10 (describing the push for constraints on warfare in the nineteenth and twentieth centuries); Claude Bruderlein and Jennifer Leaning, "New Challenges for Humanitarian Protection," *British Medical Journal* 319 (August 1999): 430–35 (noting that warring parties were willing to establish such firm protections for civilians because those proposed largely did not interfere with what they saw as tactical and strategic priorities, military assets).

3. Instructions for the Government of Armies of the United States in the Field (24 Apr. 1863), reproduced in D. Schindler and J. Toman, *The Laws of Armed Conflicts* (The Netherlands: M. Nijhoff, 1988), 3. Though the Lieber Code is the most commonly cited early codification of restrictions on the conduct of soldiers, it is not the only one. Other significant unilateral restrictions of their forces' conduct by warring parties include the Tratado de Regularizacion de la Guerra of 1820, during the Colombian war of independence, and the instructions of General Dufour during the Swiss civil war of 1847. See Sandesh Sivakumaran, "Re-Envisaging the International Law of Internal Armed Conflict," *European Journal of International Law* 22 (2011): 260.

4. For a broader discussion on how the concept of military necessity has been interpreted since the Lieber Code, see Gary D. Solis, *The Law of Armed Conflict: International Humanitarian Law in War* (New York: Cambridge University Press, 2011), 258–269.

5. David Bosco, "Moral Principle vs. Military Necessity," *American Scholar* (Winter 2008), http://www.theamericanscholar.org/moral-principle-vs-military-necessity/.

6. Declaration Renouncing the Use, in Time of War, of Explosive Projectiles under 400 Grams Weight, opened for signature November 29, 1968, [1901] ATS 125 [1] (entered into force December 11, 1868).

7. Hague Conference of 1899, Declaration II and III.

8. Ibid. art. 25 ("the attack or bombardment, by whatever means, of towns, villages, dwellings, or buildings which are undefended.").

9. International Committee for the Red Cross, "From the Battle of Solferino to the Eve of the First World War," December 28, 2004, http://www.icrc.org/eng/resources/documents/misc/57jnvp.htm.

10. For more on the history of the ICRC and its involvement in IHL development, see G. Francois Bugnion, "The Role of the Red Cross in the Development of International Humanitarian Law: The International Committee of the Red Cross and the Development of International Humanitarian Law," *Chicago Journal of International Law* 5 (Summer 2004): 191.

11. *The Local*, "Official Report: Dresden Bombing Killed 25,000," March 17, 2010, http://www.thelocal.de/national/20100317-25945.html.

12. Since World War II, civilians have constituted the majority of war casualties. Ruth Leger Sivard, ed., *World Military and Social Expenditures 1996* (Washington, DC: World Priorities, 1996).

13. Chris af Jochnick and Roger Normand, "The Legitimation of Violence: A Critical History of the Laws of War," *Harvard International Law Journal* 35 (Winter 1994): 50.

14. Ryan Goodman and Derek Jinks, "Toward an Institutional Theory of Sovereignty," *Stanford Law Review* 55 (2003): 1749, 1766; Peter M. Haas, "Choosing to Comply: Theorizing from International Relations and Comparative Politics," in *Commitment and Compliance: The Role of Non-Binding Norms in the International Legal System*, ed. Dinah Shelton (New York: Oxford University Press, 2000) 51–52 (noting that according to realist theories, compliance with international law would be lowest for arms control treaties because these issues have the potential to threaten "territorial integrity").

15. Gary D. Solis, *The Law of Armed Conflict: International Humanitarian Law in War* (New York: Cambridge University Press, 2011), 8.

16. Ibid.

Rules of War, Laws of War

*by Gary D. Solis**

[...]

1.1. THE LAW OF WAR: A THUMBNAIL HISTORY

If Cicero (106–43 B.C.) actually said, *"inter arma leges silent"*—in time of war the laws are silent—in a sense, he was correct. If laws were initially absent, however, there were rules attempting to limit armed combat virtually from the time men began to fight in organized groups. Theodor Meron notes that, "Even when followed, ancient humanitarian rules were soft and malleable and offered little if any expectation of compliance."[1] Still, as John Keegan writes, "War may have got worse with the passage of time, but the ethic of restraint has rarely been wholly absent from its practice . . . Even in the age of total warfare when, as in Cicero's day, war was considered a normal condition, and the inherent right of sovereign States presided, there remained taboos, enshrined in law and thankfully widely observed."[2]

When did men begin to fight in groups? Cave art of the New Stone Age, 10,000 years ago, depicts bowmen apparently in conflict.[3] Since that time, there have been few periods in human history when there has not been an armed conflict someplace.[4] Keegan tells us that Mesopotamia developed a military system of defense as early as 3000 B.C. In approximately 2700 B.C. Gilgamesh, who ruled the city of Uruk, apparently undertook one of history's first offensive military campaigns.[5] Thus, warfare came to the world at least 5,000 years ago. Limitations on its conduct were close behind and, we are told, "during the five thousand six hundred years of written history, fourteen thousand six hundred wars have been recorded."[6]

No written early Roman military code survives, although it is known that within the Roman army's ranks, many of today's military criminal offenses were recognized.[7] In the early days of the Empire, few rules applied to combat against non-Romans. "[T]he conduct of [Roman] war was essentially unrestrained. Prisoners could be enslaved or massacred; plunder was general; and no distinction was recognized between combatants and noncombatants."[8]

With time, that changed. Around 1400 B.C., Egypt had agreements with Sumeria and other States regarding the treatment of prisoners.[9] In about 200 B.C., in Asia, a variety of Hindu texts describe numerous rules of war. The *Mahab-*

harata, an epic Sanskrit poem (200 B.C.–200 A.D.) reflected Hindu beliefs. It required that "a King should never do such an injury to his foe as would rankle the latter's heart."[10] It decreed that one should cease fighting when an opponent becomes disabled; that wounded men and persons who surrender should not be killed; noncombatants should not be engaged in combat; and places of public worship should not be molested.[11] The Hindu Code of Manu directs that treacherous weapons, such as barbed or poisoned arrows, are forbidden and that an enemy attempting to surrender, or one badly wounded, should not be killed.[12]

In the sixth century B.C., Sun Tzu counseled limitations on armed conflict as well. "[I]n chariot battles when chariots are captured, then ten-chariot unit commanders will reward the first to capture them and will switch battle standards and flags, their chariots are mixed with ours and driven, their soldiers are treated kindly when given care."[13] Sun Tzu did not suggest that his humanitarian admonitions constituted laws, or even rules of war. They were simply an effective means of waging war.

Roman Emperor Maurice, in the late sixth century A.D., published his *Strategica*. It directed, among other things, that a soldier who injured a civilian should make every effort to repair the injury, or pay twofold damages.[14]

In 621, at Aqaba, Muhammad's followers who committed to a *jihad* for Islam were bound to satisfy a number of conditions in its conduct. "If he has killed he must not mutilate," for example.[15] (Yet, Abyssinian victors often cut off the right hands and left feet of vanquished foes.[16])

Under Innocent II, use of the crossbow was forbidden as "deadly and odious to God" by the Catholic Second Lateran Council in 1139, and the Third Lateran Council prescribed humane treatment of prisoners of war.[17]

During the feudal period, in the twelfth and thirteenth centuries, knights observed rules of chivalry, a major historical basis for the LOAC. "[C]hivalry meant the duty to act honorably, even in war. The humane and noble ideals of chivalry included justice and loyalty, courage, honour and mercy, the obligations not to kill or otherwise take advantage of the vanquished enemy, and to keep one's word. . . . Seldom if ever realized in full . . . while humanizing warfare, chivalry also contributed to the legitimizing of war."[18] To today's war fighter, chivalry may seem an idealistically romantic notion.

> Nevertheless, as a catalogue of virtues and values, it remains an enviable model for honourable conduct in peace and in war. . . . Commands to spare the enemy who asks for mercy, to aid women in distress, to keep one's promise, to act charitably and to be magnanimous transcend any

one particular historical period or sociological con- text. . . . The idea that chivalry requires soldiers to act in a civilized manner is one of its most enduring legacies.[19]

Doubters argue that "chivalric rules actually served to protect the lives and property of privileged knights and nobles, entitling them to plunder and kill peasant soldiers, non-Christian enemies, and civilians . . . ,"[20] but that seems a harsh view. It is true that chivalry's code only applied among Christians and knights. The Scottish nationalist Sir William Wallace—"Braveheart"—was no knight. He was executed in 1305, after being convicted by an English court of atrocities in war, "sparing neither age nor sex, monk nor nun."[21] His conviction followed 1279's Statute of Westminster that authorized the Crown to punish "soldiers" for violations of "the law and customs of the realm."[22] In 1386, Richard II's *Ordinance for the Government of the Army* decreed death for acts of violence against women and priests, the burning of houses, and the desecration of churches.[23] Henry V's ordinances of war, promulgated in 1419, further codified rules protecting women and clergy.

At Agincourt, in 1415, England's Henry V defeated the French in the Hundred Years' War and conquered much of France. Henry's longbow men made obsolete many methods of warring in the age of chivalry. Shakespeare tells us that, at Agincourt, King Harry, believing that the battle was lost and that his French prisoners would soon join with the approaching French soldiers, gave a fateful order:

King Harry: The French have reinforced their scattered men. Then every soldier kill his prisoners. (*The soldiers kill their prisoners.*)[24]

Fluellen: Kill the poys and the luggage! 'Tis expressly against the laws of arms. 'Tis as arrant a piece of knavery, mark you now, as can be offert. In your conscience now, is it not?

Gower: 'Tis certain there's not a boy left alive. And the cowardly rascals that ran from the battle ha' done this slaughter. Besides, they have burned and carried away all that was in the King's tent; wherefore the King most worthily hath caused every soldier to cut his prisoner's throat. O 'tis a gallant king.[25]

Was Henry's order a war crime? Shakespeare's Fluellen and Gower plainly thought so.

1.1.1. The First International War Crime Prosecution?

The trial of Peter von Hagenbach in Breisach, Austria, in 1474 is often cited as the first international war crime prosecution.[26] He was tried by an ad hoc tribunal of twenty-eight judges from Austria and its allied states of the Hanseatic cities for murder, rape, and other crimes. Hagenbach's defense was one still heard today: He was only following orders. His defense met the same response it usually receives today: He was convicted and hanged. Hagenbach's offenses did not actually transpire during a time of war and thus were not war crimes, strictly speaking. It also may be asked whether the prosecuting allied states at von Hagenbach's trial constituted an "international" body.[27] The event is nevertheless significant in representing one of the earliest trials resulting in personal criminal responsibility for the violation of international criminal norms.

1.1.2. The Emergence of Battlefield Codes

Meanwhile, battlefield rules and laws continued to sprout. In Europe, in 1590, the Free Netherlands adopted Articles of War and, in 1621, Sweden's Gustavus Adolphus published his *Articles of Military Lawwes to Be Observed in the Warres*, which were to become the basis for England's later Articles of War. Those English Articles in turn became the basis for the fledgling United States' first Articles of War. The Treaty of Westphalia, in 1648, was the first treaty between warring states to require the return, without ransom, of captured soldiers. Such early European codes, dissimilar and geographically scattered as they were, are significant.[28] They established precedents for other states and raised enforcement models for battlefield offenses—courts-martial, in the case of the British Articles of War. In the second half of the nineteenth century, the previously common battlefield practices and restrictions—customary law of war—began to coalesce into generalized rules, becoming codified and extended by treaties and domestic laws. Manuals on the subject, such as the 1884 British *Manual of Military Law*, were published.

By the mid-nineteenth century, states began writing codes that incorporated humanitarian ideals for their soldiers—the violation of which called for punishments; in other words, military laws. At the same time, there were few multinational treaties that imposed accepted limitations on battlefield conduct, with penalties for their violation. That would have to wait until the Hague Regulation IV of 1907. Even then, battlefield laws would lack norms of personal accountability for crimes in combat.

1.2. WHY REGULATE BATTLEFIELD CONDUCT?

All's fair in love and war? Hardly! Any divorce lawyer will attest that "all" is decidedly not fair in love. Just as surely, all is not fair in war. There are good reasons why warfare needs to be regulated. Simple humanitarian concerns should limit battlefield conduct. War is not a contest to see who can most effectively injure one's opponent. War cannot be simple blood sport. Indeed, modern LOAC has been largely driven by humanitarian concerns.

There are concrete, valid reasons to regulate battlefield conduct. LOAC differentiates war from riot, piracy, and generalized insurrection. It allows a moral acceptance of the sometimes repugnant acts necessarily done on battlefields and it lends dignity, even honor, to the sacrifices of a nation's soldiers. "War is distinguishable from murder and massacre only when restrictions are established on the reach of battle."[29] The idea of war as indiscriminate violence suggests violence as an end in itself, and that is antithetical to the fact that war is a goal-oriented activity directed to attaining political objectives. Even the view that all necessary means to achieving victory are permissible—a short step away from "all's fair in love and war"—implicitly recognizes that hostilities are limited to the means considered "necessary," further implying that violence superfluous to obtaining a military objective is unnecessary and thus may be proscribed.

As it pertains to individuals, LOAC, perhaps more than any other branch of law, is liable to fail. In a sense, its goal is virtually impossible: to introduce moderation and restraint into an activity uniquely contrary to those qualities. At the best of times, LOAC is "never more than imperfectly observed, and at the worst of times is very poorly observed indeed."[30] In fact, one must admit that LOAC really does not "work" well at all. However, Geoffrey Best writes, "we should perhaps not so much complain that the law of war does not work well, as marvel that it works at all."[31]

It may seem paradoxical that war, the ultimate breakdown of law, should be conducted in accordance with laws. But so it is. Why would a state fighting for survival allow itself to be hobbled by legal restrictions? In fact, nations of the eighteenth and nineteenth centuries, when LOAC was in its formative stages, did not regard themselves as fighting for survival. Territory, not ideology, was the usual basis for war. Defeat meant the realignment of national boundaries, not the subjugation of the defeated population nor the dissolution of the vanquished state. "[A]nalysis of war prior to nineteenth-century industrialization and Napoleonic enthusiasm indicates that wars were less violent and less significant and were subject to cultural restraints."[32] War will always constitute suffering and personal tragedy, but rules of warfare are intended to prevent unnecessary suffering that bring little or no military advantage. Critics argue that, in war, states will always put their own interests above all else, and any battlefield law that clashes with those interests will be disregarded. As we shall see, LOAC has been created by states that have their own interests, particularly the interests of their own armed forces, in mind. LOAC is hardly an imposition on states by faceless external authorities.[33]

In modern times, despite Clausewitz's assertion that the laws of war are "almost imperceptible and hardly worth mentioning,"[34] they remain the best answer to the op- posing tensions of the necessities of war and the requirements of civilization. "It is the function of the rules of warfare to impose some limits, however ineffective, to a complete reversion to anarchy by the establishment of minimum standards on the conduct of war."[35] The temporary advantages of breaching LOAC are far outweighed by the ultimate disadvantages.

"Unnecessary killing and devastation should be prohibited if only on military grounds. It merely increases hostility and hampers the willingness to surrender."[36] An example was World War II in the Pacific. After an early series of false surrenders and prisoner atrocities, Pacific island combat was marked by an unwillingness of either side to surrender, and a savagery of the worst kind by both sides resulted.[37] On Iwo Jima, of 21,000–23,000 Japanese combatants, 20,703 were killed. When the island was declared secure only 212 Japanese surrendered[38]—less than 2 percent—because Marines and soldiers fearing that they would be murdered or mistreated if they surrendered simply put surrender out of mind and fought on, thereby increasing casualties to both sides. "Violations . . . can also result in a breakdown of troop discipline, command control and force security; subject troops to reciprocal violations on the battlefield or [in] P.W. camps; and cause the defeat of an entire army in a guerrilla or other war through alignment of neutrals on the side of the enemy and hostile public opinion."[39]

The rapacious conduct of World War II Nazis as they crossed Russia toward Moscow and Stalingrad exacerbated a hatred in the Russian civilian population that led to thousands of German deaths at the hands of partisans. Michael Walzer notes, "The best soldiers, the best fighting men, do not loot and . . . rape, do not wantonly kill civilians."[40] Strategically, battlefield crimes may lessen the prospect of an eventual cease-fire. War, then, must be conducted in the interest of peace.

Does LOAC end, or even lessen, the frequency of battlefield crimes? Was Thucydides correct in noting, "The strong do what they can and the weak suffer what they must"? Can we really expect laws to deter violations of IHL? Idi Amin, who robbed and raped Uganda into misery and poverty, ordered the deaths of

300,000 of his countrymen, and admitted having eaten human flesh, died in palatial comfort in Saudi Arabian exile, never brought to account for the butchery he ordered during his country's internal warfare. Josef Mengele, the World War II Nazi doctor at the Auschwitz extermination camp—the "Angel of Death" who conducted horrific "medical" experiments on prisoners—escaped to a long and comfortable life in Paraguay, and accidentally drowned while enjoying a day at the beach with his family in 1979. He was never tried for his war crimes.

No law will deter the lawless. No criminal code can account for every violator. No municipal or federal law puts an end to civilian criminality. Should we expect more from LOAC? Geoffrey Best writes, "If international law is, in some ways, at the vanishing point of law, the law of war is, perhaps even more conspicuously, at the vanishing point of international law,"[41] but that is no license to surrender to criminality.

Battlefield violations have always occurred, continue to occur, and will occur in the future. Despite training and close discipline, as long as nations give guns to young soldiers, war crimes are going to happen. Recognizing that unpleasant truth is not cynicism so much as an acceptance of reality. Why bother with confining rules in combat, then? The answer: for reasons similar to those that dictate rules in football games—some violence is expected, but not all violence is permitted. Are rules and laws that are frequently violated worthless for their violation? Are speed limits without value because they are commonly exceeded? In the western world, are the Ten Commandments, which are commonly disregarded, therefore, of no worth? There always will be limits on acceptable conduct, including conduct on the battlefield. We obey LOAC because we cannot allow ourselves to become what we are fighting and because we cannot be heard to say that we fight for the right while we are seen to commit wrongs. "Military professionals also have desires for law. For starters, they also turn to law to limit the violence of warfare, to ensure some safety, some decency, among professionals on different sides of the conflict."[42] We obey the law of war if for no other reason than because reciprocity tells us that what goes around comes around; if we abuse our prisoners today, tomorrow we will be the abused prisoners. We obey the law of war because it is the law and because it is the honorable path for a nation that holds itself up as a protector of oppressed peoples. We obey the law of war because it is the right thing to do. "When principle is involved, be deaf to expediency."[43]

In the calm of a college seminar room, it is easy to denounce the actions of others acting in a combat zone—soldiers, Marines, sailors, and airmen who did not have the luxury of discussion, or opportunity to study a treaty, or time for reflection before they acted. However, no armed service member is likely to be prosecuted for a single law of war violation hastily committed without thought in the heat of combat. When the battle is over, when the combatant is seen to have considered his/her actions before acting wrongly, when the action taken was patently contrary to the law of war, or when the violation was of a repeated nature, then it is reasonable to invoke LOAC.

NOTES

1. Theodor Meron, *Bloody Constraint: War and Chivalry in Shakespeare* (New York: Oxford University Press, 1998), 49.

2. John Keegan, *War and Our World* (New York: Vintage Books, 2001), 26.

3. John Keegan, *A History of Warfare* (New York: Knopf, 1993), 119.

4. A brief period from 100 to 200 A.D. is perhaps the only time the world has enjoyed peace. That period resulted from the Roman Empire's military ascendancy over all opposition.

5. Keegan, *War and Our World*, supra, note 2, at 29.

6. James Hillman, *A Terrible Love of War* (New York: Penguin Books, 2004), 17.

7. Col. William Winthrop, *Military Law and Precedents*, 2d ed. (Washington: GPO, 1920), 17.

8. Robert C. Stacey, "The Age of Chivalry," in Michael Howard, George J. Andreopoulos, and Mark R. Shulman, eds., *The Laws of War* (New Haven: Yale University Press, 1994), 27.

9. Jean Pictet, *Development and Principles of International Humanitarian Law* (Leiden: Kluwer, 1985), 7–8.

10. Cited in Leslie C. Green, *The Contemporary Law of Armed Conflict*, 2d ed. (Manchester: Manchester University Press, 2000), 21.

11. Suurya P. Subedi, "The Concept in Hinduism of 'Just War,'" 8–2 *J. of Conflict & Security L.* (Oct. 2003), 339, 355–6.

12. K.P. Jayaswal, *Manu and Yâjñavalkya, A Comparison and A Contrast: A Treatise on the Basic Hindu Law* (Calcutta: Butterworth, 1930), 106.

13. J.H. Huang trans., *Sun Tzu: The New Translation* (New York: Quill, 1933), 46.

14. C.E. Brand, *Roman Military Law* (Austin: University of Texas, 1968), 195–6. Also see: Timothy L.H. McCormack, "From Sun Tzu to the Sixth Committee: The Evolution of an International Criminal Law Regime," in Timothy L.H. McCormack and Gerry J. Simpson, eds., *The Law of War Crimes: National and International Approaches* (The Hague: Kluwer, 1997), 31–63, 35.

15. Majid Khadduri, *War and Peace in the Law of Islam* (Baltimore: Johns Hopkins University Press, 1955), 87.

16. Gerrit W. Gong, *The Standard of "Civilization" in International Society* (Oxford: Clarendon Press, 1984), 122–3.

17. G.I.A.D. Draper, "The Interaction of Christianity and Chivalry in the Historical Development of the Laws of War," 5–3 *Int'l Rev. of Red Cross* (1965). The earliest crossbows date to 400 B.C. and the Chinese army. European crossbows date to about 1200, introduced

from the East during the Crusades. Military effectiveness superceded theological concerns, for crossbows were widely employed until the seventeenth century. Still, Canon 29 of the Second Lateran Council held, "We forbid under penalty of anathema that that deadly and God-detested art of stingers and archers be in the future exercised against Christians and Catholics." Gregory M. Reichberg, Henrik Syse, and Endre Begby, eds., *The Ethics of War* (Malden, MA: Blackwell Publishing, 2006), 97.

18. Meron, *Bloody Constraint*, supra, note 1, at 4–5.

19. Id., at 108, 118.

20. Chris af Jochnick and Roger Normand, "The Legitimation of Violence: A Critical History of the Laws of War," 35–1 *Harvard Int'l L. J.* (1994), 49, 61.

21. Georg Schwarzenberger, "Judgment of Nuremberg," 21 *Tulsa L. Rev.* (1947), 330.

22. Joseph W. Bishop, Jr., *Justice Under Fire: A Study of Military Law* (New York: Charterhouse, 1974), 4.

23. Georg Schwarzenberger, *International Law: As Applied by International Courts and Tribunals*, vol. II (London: Stevens & Sons, 1968), 15–16.

24. William Shakespeare, *Henry V*, IV.vi.35–8.

25. Id., vii.1–10

26. Schwarzenberger, supra note 23, at 462–6.

27. For a lengthier examination of von Hagenbach's case, see "Cases and Materials" at the end of this chapter. Further discussion of the case, and the early development of the law of war generally, are in McCormack, "From Sun Tzu to the Sixth Committee," in McCormack and Simpson, *Law of War Crimes*, supra, note 14, at 37–9.

28. Written European military codes, not necessarily reflecting the law of war, were many. In the fifth century, the Frankish Salians had a military code, as did the Goths, the Lombards, the Burgundians, and the Bavarians. The first French military law code dated from 1378, the first German code from 1487, the first Free Netherlands code from 1590. A Russian military code appeared in 1715. See Winthrop, supra, note 7, 17–8.

29. Michael Walzer, *Just and Unjust Wars*, 3d ed. (New York: Basic Books, 2000), 42.

30. Geoffrey Best, *Humanity in Warfare* (London: Weidenfeld & Nicolson, 1980), 11.

31. Id., 12.

32. Hillman, *A Terrible Love of War*, supra, note 6, 168.

33. Adam Roberts and Richard Guelff, *Documents on the Law of War*, 3d ed. (Oxford: Oxford University Press, 2000), 31.

34. Carl von Clausewitz, *On War*, A. Rapoport, ed. (London: Penguin Books, 1982), 101. However, Clausewitz also wrote, "Therefore, if we find that civilized nations do not put their prisoners to death, do not devastate towns and countries, this is because their intelligence . . . taught them more effectual means of applying force than these rude acts of mere instinct." Id., at 103.

35. Schwarzenberger, supra note 23, at 10.

36. Bert V.A. Roling, "Are Grotius' Ideas Obsolete in an Expanded World?" in Hedley Bull, Benedict Kingsbury, and Adam Roberts, eds., *Hugo Grotius and International Relations* (Oxford: Clarendon Press, 1990), 287.

37. See Eugene Sledge, *With the Old Breed at Peleliu and Okinawa* (Novato, CA: Presidio Press, 1981) for examples of savagery in the Pacific theater. Paul Fussell, *Wartime: Understanding and Behavior in the Second World War* (New York: Oxford University Press, 1989), relates similar accounts from the European theater.

38. Stephen J. Lofgren, ed., "Diary of First Lieutenant Sugihara Kinryu: Iwo Jima, January–February 1945," 59–97. *J. Military History* (Jan. 1995).

39. Jordan J. Paust, letter, 25 *Naval War College Rev.* (Jan–Feb 1973), 105.

40. Michael Walzer, "Two Kinds of Military Responsibility," in Lloyd J. Matthews and Dale E. Brown, eds., *The Parameters of Military Ethics* (VA: Pergamon-Brassey's, 1989), 69.

41. Best, *Humanity in Warfare*, supra, note 30, at 12.

42. David Kennedy, *Of War and Law* (Princeton NJ: Princeton University Press, 2006), 32.

43. Attributed to Cmdr. Matthew Fontaine Maury, USN (1806–73), a groundbreaking oceanographer.

*Gary D. Solis** is an adjunct professor of law at the Georgetown University Law Center. He is an expert on the laws of war.

Gary D. Solis, "Rules of War, Laws of War," in *The Law of Armed Conflict: International Humanitarian Law in War* (New York: Cambridge University Press, 2011), 3–11.

The Legitimation of Violence: A Critical History of the Laws of War

*by Chris af Jochnick and Roger Normand**

I. INTRODUCTION

A. The Gulf War and the Promise of Law

The forty-three-day war waged against Iraq by the United States-led Coalition (the "Coalition") enjoys a reputation as one of the cleanest and most legal wars in history.[1] Despite evidence of disastrous long-term consequences for Iraqi civilians, the image persists of a new kind of war, a modern, high-tech "operation" that decimated the opposing military with minimal damage to the surrounding population. Coalition leaders bolstered this image by repeatedly invoking international law in order to condemn Iraqi conduct and to praise the restraint exhibited by the Coalition forces both in the actual combat and in the events preceding it.[2]

There is a critical unspoken assumption that gives rhetorical power to the idea of a legal war—specifically, that a legal war is more humane than an illegal war. A legal war connotes a war that is proper and just, rather than a war that merely complies with a set of technical guidelines. That the Gulf War is considered to be the most legalistic war ever fought adds to its image as a just and relatively humane war.

This Article challenges the notion that the laws of war serve to restrain or "humanize" war. Examination of the historical development of these laws reveals that despite noble rhetoric to the contrary, the laws of war have been formulated deliberately to privilege military necessity at the cost of humanitarian values. As a result, the laws of war have facilitated rather than restrained wartime violence. Through law, violence has been legitimated.

Viewed from this perspective, the Gulf War does not represent the dawn of a hopeful new age of international law,[3] but rather the continuation and even the intensification of a historical trend to legalize inhumane military methods and their consequences. By obscuring bombing behind the protective veil of justice, the laws of war may have increased the destruction in Iraq. Despite the Coalition's reputation for targeting only military sites, most independent studies have put the civilian death toll at over 100,000.[4]

[…]

The common rationale for the laws of war is the desire to humanize war by balancing military necessity with concerns for humanity. The fundamental principles behind these laws, distinction and proportionality, revolve around the need to maintain this balance.[10] The principle of distinction requires belligerents to distinguish between military and civilian targets, and to attack only the former. The principle of proportionality requires belligerents to refrain from causing damage disproportionate to the military advantage to be gained.

It is important to understand that the development of these legal principles did not introduce restraint or humanity into war. War has long been limited largely by factors independent of the law. For complex military, political, and economic reasons, belligerents tend to use the minimal force necessary to achieve their political objectives.[11] Force beyond that point—gratuitous violence—wastes resources, provokes retaliation, invites moral condemnation, and impedes post-war relations with the enemy nation.[12] These concepts are embodied in the "time honored military concept of 'economy of force'," of which, according to former Chairman of the Joint Chiefs of Staff, General George S. Brown, "the law of 'proportionality' is simply a legal restatement."[13]

The crucial question then becomes whether the laws of war actually limit military conduct beyond the inherent restraints dictated by narrow military self-interest. And if not, what purpose do they serve?

B. The Role of Law in War

To most, law and war occupy mutually exclusive terrain. As Cicero wrote, *"inter arma silent leges"* (in time of war the law is silent).[14] Law implies order and restraint; war epitomizes the absence of both. It is precisely when the legal system fails that conflict turns to violence. Law may act to deter war, but it has no practical role once the fighting has begun.[15]

Yet, attempts to regulate war are as old as war itself. From ancient societies until today, nations have purported to limit the conduct of war with legal codes. Proponents of such efforts assume that bringing war within the bounds of rational rules may somehow "humanize" war and contain its brutalities. The history of war, however, reveals that the development of a more elaborate legal regime has proceeded apace with the increasing savagery and destructiveness of modern war.[16] Nonetheless, succeeding generations continue to call for more laws, without examining, or even understanding, the nature of the legal structure upon which they place their humanitarian hopes.

This apparent paradox may be explained, albeit in simplified form, by the different interests and motives of those who call for laws of war and those who formulate and implement such laws. To the general public, the laws of war should address our humanitarian aspirations and impose some form of restraint, even if minor, on the forms that war may legitimately take. Perhaps the foremost international jurist of his time, Hersch Lauterpacht makes this clear:

> We shall utterly fail to understand the true character of the law of war unless we are to realize that its purpose is almost entirely humanitarian in the literal sense of the word, namely to prevent or mitigate suffering and, in some cases, to rescue life from the savagery of battle and passion. This, and not the regulation and direction of hostilities, is its essential purpose.[17]

Given this motivation, it is not surprising that public agitation for legal regulation tends to be renewed on the heels of war.[18] As Michael Walzer comments, "war is so awful that it makes us cynical about the possibility of restraint, and then it is so much worse that it makes us indignant at the absence of restraint."[19] Thus, the Hague Peace Conferences followed a half century of intensifying conflict among the emerging European nation-states in the nineteenth century; the League of Nations and Kellogg-Briand Pact (which unsuccessfully sought to ban war outright) followed World War I; the Geneva Conventions followed World War II; and the 1977 Protocols to these Conventions followed the Vietnam War.

Yet the noble sentiments that prompted this expansive body of laws have only selectively penetrated the substance of the laws themselves. Notwithstanding public pressure to limit the horrors of war, the diplomats who negotiated the laws and the soldiers who implemented them structured a permissive legal regime. Despite the humanitarian rhetoric, military concerns have dictated the substantive content of the laws of war.

National governments, conceiving their sovereign interests narrowly, have proven unwilling to accept any restrictions, legal or otherwise, on their ability to deploy the level of military power they deem necessary to uphold national security.[20] The structured impotence of the laws of war illustrates a variation of the "prisoners' dilemma": what makes sense for the world, collectively, appears different when viewed through the prism of national self-interest.

C. The Legitimating Role of Law

While the laws of war impose no substantive restraints on pre-existing customary military practices, they nevertheless have an impact on war. The mere belief that law places humane limits on war, even if factually mistaken, has profound consequences for the way people view war, and therefore the way that war is conducted. The credibility of laws of war lends unwarranted legitimacy to customary military practices. Acts sanctioned by law enjoy a humanitarian cover that helps shield them from criticism. As one commentator warned, "precisely because aggression in its crudest form is now so universally condemned, many of the assaults that are made will be dressed up in some more respectable garb. . . . Because public opinion is itself so confused, aggression may secure its fruits without paying the deserved penalty in international goodwill."[21] The "respectable garb" with which belligerents have dressed their assaults is precisely the laws themselves. By legitimating conduct, the laws serve to promote it.

Law legitimates conduct on two levels. Because people generally view compliance with "the law" as an independent good, acts are validated by simply being legal. In particular, sovereign conduct that complies with the law will appear more legitimate than that which violates it.[22] Nations acknowledge the power of this form of legitimation by seeking to explain their actions by reference to law.[23] According to a former Legal Advisor to the U.S. State Department, "legal justification is part of the over-all defence [sic] of a public decision."[24]

[...]

A critical understanding of international law compels a reevaluation of the role of law in deterring wartime atrocities. By endorsing military necessity without substantive limitations, the laws of war ask only that belligerents act in accord with military self-interest.[31] Belligerents who meet this hollow requirement receive in return a powerful rhetorical tool to protect their controversial conduct from humanitarian challenges.[32]

The notion that humanitarian rhetoric can subvert its stated purpose raises several important questions: How does the legal hierarchy of sovereign over individual interests affect the perception of war? How does legal language influence popular attitudes towards wartime violence? How does the law's sanction affect public support for military conduct? Do these effects translate into more or less public pressure on belligerents to adhere to humanitarian standards?

These questions have no clear, empirically based answers.[33] However, the importance of public support for war, coupled with the growing stature of international legal rhetoric, validates the search for a critical understanding of the legitimating effects of law. Moreover, the capacity of the laws of war to subvert their own humane rhetoric carries an implicit warning for future attempts to control wars: the promotion of supposedly humane laws may serve the purposes of unrestrained violence rather than of humanity.

NOTES

1. Colonel Raymond Ruppert, staff judge advocate for U.S. Central Command and General H. Norman Schwarzkopf's personal lawyer during the conflict, declared the Gulf War "the most legalistic war we've ever fought." Steven Keeva, *Lawyers in the War Room*, A.B.A. J., December 1991, at 52.

2. *See* MIDDLE EAST WATCH, NEEDLESS DEATHS IN THE GULF WAR: CIVILIAN CASUALTIES DURING THE AIR CAMPAIGN AND VIOLATIONS OF THE LAWS OF WAR, 75–78 (1991). *See also* DEPARTMENT OF DEFENSE, CONDUCT OF THE PERSIAN GULF WAR: FINAL REPORT TO CONGRESS Appendix O (April 1992) [hereinafter D.O.D. REPORT].

3. Within the political mainstream of the United States, both conservatives and liberals held high hopes that the post-Cold War international cooperation displayed during the Gulf War heralded what former Secretary of State James A. Baker III termed "one of those rare transforming moments in history . . . an era which is full of promise. . . ." James A. Baker III, Address to the Los Angeles World Affairs Council (October 29, 1990), *available in* LEXIS, Nexis Library, Fednew. A representative article in the A.B.A. JOURNAL, exhibiting this optimistic spirit, proclaimed, "There is now a greater worldwide interest in the rule of law than at any time in recent memory." Keeva, *supra* note 1, at 59. Nicholas Rostow, currently Special Assistant to the President for National Security Affairs and Legal Adviser to the National Security Council, commented, "If the Cold War has indeed ended, the international legal disputes that were such an important part of that war may also have come to a close. . . . The profound changes of recent years should permit the world community to test the ideas for world public order set forth in the U.N. Charter and the effectiveness of the United Nations itself." Nicholas Rostow, *The International Use of Force After the Cold War*, 32 HARV. INT'L L.J. 411, 411 (1991).

4. Beth Osborne Daponte, a demographer with the U.S. Census Bureau, estimated that after the war's conclusion, 111,000 Iraqi civilians died from war-related health effects by the end of 1991. Many of these deaths are attributable to "Allied bombing of Iraq's electrical generating capacity, which was needed to fuel Iraq's sewerage and water treatment system." *Study Shows Iraqi Post-War Deaths Greater Than Initially Thought*, PR Newswire, Aug. 17, 1993, *available in* LEXIS, Nexis Library, PR News File. The Census Bureau initially dismissed Ms. Daponte for releasing earlier estimates of Iraqi casualties but later reinstated her. *Agency Reinstates Tabulator of Iraqi War Deaths*, N.Y. TIMES, Apr. 13, 1992, at A14. Ms. Daponte's estimates are supported by a range of other studies. *See, e.g.*, Harvard Study Team, *Public Health in Iraq After the Gulf War* (May 1991) (predicting "170,000 children under five . . . will die in the coming year from delayed effects of the Gulf Crisis.") (relevant pages on file with the *Harvard International Law Journal*); International Study Team, *Health and Welfare in Iraq After the Gulf Crisis: An In-Depth Assessment* (Oct. 1991) (predicting that thousands of Iraqi children would die of malnutrition and disease) (relevant pages on file with the *Harvard International Law Journal*); *Joint WHO/UNICEF Team Report*, A Visit to Iraq, Feb. 16–21, 1991, U.N. SCOR, U.N. Doc. S/22328 (1991); Alberto Ascherio et al., *Special Article: Effect of the Gulf War on Infant and Child Mortality in Iraq*, 327 NEW ENG. J. MED. 931 (1992); I. Lee & A. Haines, *Health Costs of the Gulf War*, 303 BRIT. MED. J. 303 (Aug. 3, 1991).

[...]

10. *See generally* JEAN PICTET, DEVELOPMENT AND PRINCIPLES OF INTERNATIONAL HUMANITARIAN LAW (Nijhoff Publishers ed. & trans., 1985) (1982).

11. This reflects the traditional understanding, articulated by Karl von Clausewitz, that war is the extension of politics by other means. As such, the rules of politics apply in war, albeit in modified form:

The smaller the sacrifice we demand from our adversary, the slighter we may expect his efforts to be to refuse it to us. The slighter, however, his effort, the smaller need our own be. Furthermore, the less important our political object, the less will be the value we attach to it and the readier we shall be to abandon it.

KARL VON CLAUSEWITZ, ON WAR 9 (O.J. Matthijs Jolles trans., 1943). *See also* PICTET, *supra* note 10, at 31.

12. One military commentator has noted, "It is very dubious whether most of the atrocities committed and threatened in recent wars have not been military blunders. Atrocities embitter, and threats frighten the enemy population into prolonged resistance. Decent treatment of prisoners encourages surrender." ERNST H. FEILCHENFELD, PRISONERS OF WAR 97 (1948). This point is borne out by a cursory examination of World War II. German treatment of civilians in occupied territory during World War II spurred active resistance, making these areas harder to control. *See* McDougal & Feliciano, *supra* note 9, at 812. The history of terror bombing and oppressive occupation policies reveals that these policies are frequently counterproductive. *See e.g.*, ALEXANDER DALLIN, GERMAN RULE IN RUSSIA, 1941–1945 70–75 (1957); William V. O'Brien, *Legitimate Military Necessity in Nuclear War*, 2 WORLD POLITY 35, 56–58 (1960). *But see* THE UNITED STATES STRATEGIC BOMBING SURVEY, SUMMARY REPORT (EUROPEAN WAR), at 11–12 *in* THE UNITED STATES STRATEGIC BOMBING SURVEYS (Air University Press ed., 1987) (1945) [hereinafter BOMBING SURVEY] (stating that "studies show that the morale of the German people deteriorated under aerial attack. . . . However, dissatisfied as they were with the war, the German people lacked either the will or the means to make their dissatisfaction evident.")

13. DEPARTMENT OF THE AIR FORCE, JUDGE ADVOCATE GENERAL ACTIVITIES: INTERNATIONAL LAW—THE CONDUCT OF ARMED CONFLICT AND AIR OPERATIONS 1–12 (1976). *See also* McDougal & Feliciano, *supra* note 9, at 811–13; W.T. Mallison, Jr., *The Laws of War and the Juridical Control of Weapons of Mass Destruction in General and Limited Wars*, 36 GEO. WASH. L. REV. 308, 314–315 (1967); JEAN PICTET, HUMANITARIAN LAW AND THE PROTECTION OF WAR VICTIMS 30 (1975).

Robert E. Osgood offers the following definition of the principle of economy of force:

It prescribes that in the use of armed force as an instrument of national policy no greater force should be employed than is necessary to achieve the objectives toward which it is directed; or stated in another way, the dimensions of military force should be proportionate to the value of the objectives at stake.

ROBERT E. OSGOOD, LIMITED WAR: THE CHALLENGE TO AMERICAN STRATEGY 18 (1957). This principle coincides almost exactly with the principle of "military necessity," which has provided the foundation for the laws of war. "Military necessity consists in all measures immediately indispensible and proportionate to a legitimate military end, provided they are not prohibited by the laws of war or by the natural law, when taken on the decision of a responsible commander, subject to judicial review." O'Brien, *Military Necessity*, *supra* note 9, at 138.

14. *Quoted in* QUINCY WRIGHT, A STUDY OF WAR 863 (1965) (citation omitted).

15. General MacArthur was fond of saying, "You can't control war; you can only abolish it." Phillips, *supra* note 7, at 421. Most scholars dispute this simplistic division between law and war. War need not be viewed as distinct from peace, but rather, "it is more realistic in the light of the complex and multifarious nature of international conflict to regard war as the upper extremity of a whole scale of international conflict of ascending intensity and scope." OSGOOD, *supra* note 13, at 20. *See also* Philip C. Jessup, *Should International Law Recognize*

an Intermediate Status Between Peace and War?, 48 AM. J. INT'L L. 98 (1954). Accordingly, it makes little sense to speak of an abstract point beyond which there is no law. *See generally* DAVID KENNEDY, INTERNATIONAL LEGAL STRUCTURES 417–482 (1986).

16. *See, e.g.*, WRIGHT, *supra* note 14 at 370–71 (noting the increasing severity of war); BEST, *supra* note 5, at 57–59.

17. Hersch Lauterpacht, *The Problem of the Revision of the Law of War*, 1952 BRIT. Y.B. INT'L L. 360, 363–64. Similarly, Josef L. Kunz emphasizes that "the whole law of war, including the norms regulating its actual conduct, is humanitarian in character; it is in the truest sense a part of the law for the protection of human rights." Josef L. Kunz, *The Laws of War*, 50 AM. J. INT'L L. 313, 322 (1956).

18. *See* WRIGHT, *supra* note 14 at 1079 (cataloguing the peace movements following conflicts from ancient times through World War I).

19. MICHAEL WALZER, JUST AND UNJUST WARS: A MORAL ARGUMENT WITH HISTORICAL ILLUSTRATIONS 46 (2d ed. 1992).

20. Summarizing this frequently-stated concern, one military historian has noted that "in the simplest terms, nations do not legislate self-denying restrictions on those weapons and techniques that they judge their survival to depend upon." Townsend Hoopes, *Comments, in* LAW AND RESPONSIBILITY IN WARFARE: THE VIETNAM EXPERIENCE 142 (Peter D. Trooboff ed., 1975) [hereinafter LAW AND RESPONSIBILITY].

21. EVAN LUARD, PEACE AND OPINION 53 (1962). *See generally id.* at 51–68.

22. *See generally* ROGER FISHER, INTERNATIONAL CONFLICT (1969); LOUIS HENKIN, HOW NATIONS BEHAVE (1968); Thomas M. Franck, *Legitimacy in the International System*, 82 AM. J. INT'L L. 705 (1988).

23. *See* HENKIN, *supra* note 22, at 31–41.

24. Abram J. Chayes, *The Cuban Missile Crisis, in* INTERNATIONAL LAW: A CONTEMPORARY PERSPECTIVE 340, 344 (Richard A. Falk et al. eds., 1985). Chayes's reflections on this crisis emphasize the importance of legitimating U.S. conduct under international law.

[...]

31. Hays Parks, Special Assistant for Law and War Matters in the Office of the Judge [ext] Advocate General of the U.S. Army, underscores this point:

> Lots of people came out of Vietnam thinking things were illegal when they were not. . . . It has been very important to get commanders to realize that there's a crucial distinction between political discussions and the law. I've given hundreds of lectures on how we could have done in Vietnam everything we did in Iraq, but that policy, not law, restricted us.

Keeva, *supra* note 1, at 56–57. The Department of Defense concluded at the end of the Gulf War: "Adherence to the law of war impeded neither Coalition planning nor execution; Iraqi violations of the law provided Iraq no advantage." D.O.D REPORT, *supra* note 2, at 632.

32. The effectiveness of the law in this respect has not been lost on military lawyers. One journalist, after interviewing many of the Pentagon's top lawyers following the Gulf War, concluded that the commanding officers "have come to realize that, as in the relationship of corporate counsel to CEO, the JAG's [military law officer's] role is not to create obstacles, but to find legal ways to achieve his client's goals—even when those goals are to blow things up and kill people." Keeva, *supra* note 1, at 59.

33. The effects of legitimation are almost impossible to measure. *See* Alan Hyde, *The Concept of Legitimation in the Sociology of Law*, *1983 WIS. L. REV. 379, 426 (1983)* (arguing that "the concept of legitimation . . . has no clear operational meaning, nor agreed[-] upon empirical referent."). *But see* Gordon, *supra* note 26, at 92 n. 85 (recognizing legitimation as a general explanatory tool).

*Chris af Jochnick is director of projects at the Center for Economic and Social Rights.

Roger Normand is director of policy at the Center for Economic and Social Rights.

Chris af Jochnick and Roger Normand, "The Legitimation of Violence: A Critical History of the Laws of War," *Harvard International Law Journal* 35 (Winter 1994): 49–58. Copyright 1994. Reproduced with permission of HARVARD UNIVERSITY/ LAW SCHOOL.

Part 2:
International Humanitarian Law's Relevance for 21st Century Conflict

The previous section discussed the development of modern international humanitarian law (IHL), which regulates conduct in war. Although compliance has been far from perfect, IHL has nonetheless remained the standard by which the conduct of parties in war is judged. But since 2001, a growing chorus of governmental and legal critics have argued that changes in 21st century warfare —and in particular challenges posed by irregular warfare such as global terrorism and insurgency—have made IHL obsolete, if not completely irrelevant. Is 21st century warfare so different that IHL standards are no longer relevant? Should states be bound by IHL even when their terrorist or insurgent opponents disregard it? Are there dynamics in modern warfare that actually improve IHL compliance, or could improve it with stronger clarification and interpretation of certain rules?

IRREGULAR WARFARE CHALLENGES TO INTERNATIONAL HUMANITARIAN LAW

"Irregular warfare" describes warfare in which one or more parties to the conflict do not meet generally accepted standards of regular armed forces—for example, wearing fixed uniforms or insignia, coming under the regular command and control of a state or identifiable armed group, or following the laws of war. In today's legal debates, irregular warfare is used commonly to refer to terrorism and guerrilla warfare or insurgency. Irregular warfare is often "asymmetric" in nature. Asymmetric warfare is when the resources, power, or other war-making capabilities of the warring parties is mismatched and both sides try to take advantage of the others' weaknesses.

Irregular warfare and asymmetric tactics are not new phenomenon. Insurgent tactics are mentioned as early as Chinese commander Sun Tzu's classic military text *The Art of War* (dated between 476 and 221 BCE). They were used in many struggles for independence, from the American Revolution (1775–1783) to the British antiguerilla campaign in the Malay Peninsula (1948–1957) to the French experience in Algeria (1954–1962).[1] Israeli terrorist groups seeking independence from the British in the 1930s and 1940s were the first to use modern terrorist tactics in the Middle East. Later anti-Israeli terrorist acts by Arab groups like the Palestinian Liberation Organization in the 1970s and 1980s came to define modern terrorism.

However, while irregular warfare does not present a *new* challenge to IHL, per se, globalization, and the decline in state-on-state wars has made the threats posed by irregular warfare both more potent and more prominent.[2] Technology is more affordable and accessible to nonstate actors now, giving irregular armed groups greater means to attack states or cause significant harm. While fifty years ago, only a powerful, technologically advanced state could have armed itself with nuclear weapons, many now fear that terrorists could obtain and use a "dirty bomb"—a bomb combining radioactive materials with conventional explosives to give it more destructive power. Even simple, widely available technologies such as mobile phones can be used as weapons. Targets are also more accessible. Advances in global telecommunications and transport have made it harder for states to contain threats or prevent threats from coming to their borders, making far away and diffuse targets—from weapons silos to political offices to civilian commercial centers—more accessible for attack.

IHL is often not well-suited to regulating such modes of conflict. Many of the IHL instruments developed with state-on-state conflict in mind. Many IHL requirements do not apply at all in conflicts involving nonstate actors as one of the parties. Additionally, IHL is more difficult to apply in the more murky battlefields of irregular warfare, as illustrated by U.S. difficulties confronting insurgents in Iraq and Afghanistan. IHL provisions designed for distinct, organized, clearly identifiable warring militaries run aground when insurgent or terrorist combatants are indistinguishable from the population at large.

In 21st century warfare, insurgent or terrorist groups have often tried to offset their military inferiority by using tactics that are not only unconventional but often unlawful under IHL. For example, during U.S. interventions in Iraq and Afghanistan, nonstate actors like Al Qaeda in Iraq or Taliban fighters in Afghanistan repeatedly flouted the Geneva Conventions, directly or indiscriminately targeting civilians and civilian objects, and hiding among the protected civilian population or taking human shields to avoid being attacked. In some cases, they used the U.S. compliance with IHL and sensitivity to civilian casualties as a tactic against them, by creating situations likely to result in civilian casualties and follow-on backlash for U.S. forces.

Such tactics have posed enormous challenges for ensuring IHL compliance in the 21st century, not only because they violate IHL in themselves, but also they may make it harder for opposing parties to comply with provisions like civilian protection. In some cases, it may tempt opposing state parties to relax their own compliance when faced with such asymmetric tactics.[3] In the first article, "Torture and the Terror War," U.S. commentator Patrick J. Buchanan argues that the U.S. should dispense with IHL restrictions when fighting insurgent groups like those in Iraq:

> Can we win a war on terror if we fight by Geneva rules, while our enemy fights by the Maoist rules of people's war, which condone terror and murder, and encourage guerrillas to fight out of uniform and kill the enemy anywhere, any time, any way? . . . Is it possible that our Western standards for fighting a just and moral war, dating to St. Augustine, have so tied our hands in this war in Iraq that we cannot finally defeat the enemy?[4]

LEGAL DEBATES IN THE WAKE OF SEPTEMBER 11

Though these changed dynamics were already in play after the Cold War, it was the terrorist attacks of September 11, 2001, that galvanized legal debate about the changed nature of modern conflict. The sheer level of mass violence and destruction—more than 2,800 people killed and billions of dollars in economic losses—perpetrated by a small number of radical terrorists, launched from a faraway failed state demonstrated how far traditional IHL concepts were from the reality of contemporary threats. In the post–9/11 world, the main threat would stem from disparate, barely identifiable non-state actors or networks that could strike at any time with relatively low-tech and undetectable weaponry. Would IHL—with its focus on mutually bound states; large, industrial-age weaponry; and defined rules of engagement and membership—be capable of dealing with the asymmetric tactics of 21st century conflict?

In response to the September 11 attacks, the Bush administration declared a global war against terror, with a geographic and temporal scope unseen before in warfare. Members of the administration argued that many of the IHL provisions were "obsolete" and did not apply to this new type of warfare.[5] Other (primarily American) academics and analysts also began to call for rethinking international law given the complexities and new dynamics of modern warfare. As one military academic, Glenn M. Sulmasy, argued in a 2005 article (not featured in this volume) "The nature of warfare has changed. International lawyers must not cling to the definitions of the past if history has rendered them obsolete."[6]

In the second excerpt, "The Politics of the Geneva Conventions: Avoiding Formalist Traps," Rosa Brooks identifies some of the ways that traditional interpretations of IHL seem inadequate to dealing with the most prevalent forms of 21st century conflict. She argues that the U.S. conflict with Al Qaeda and other terrorist groups is beyond the reach of traditional law enforcement, and thus might legitimately be engaged under an "armed conflict" rationale. However, she points out that the Geneva Conventions and other IHL provisions offer little guidance on the core dilemmas for states engaged in prolonged counterterrorist fights, including what rights to grant combatants who do not abide by IHL or meet any of the criteria for recognition under IHL, who may not take the form of an entity with whom a peace can be negotiated, or may not strike from or at a discernible "conflict zone," leaving a potential state of war everywhere. She argues for a rethinking of IHL in a way that balances law enforcement and wartime approaches to give states more flexibility to address terrorist threats, but also to guarantee rights protections.

While many scholars and policymakers at the time shared Brooks's concerns about the gaps and ambiguities in IHL—particularly as they relate to internal or "non-international" conflicts—some suggested the solution is not to rethink IHL, but to strengthen and clarify existing provisions. In the third excerpt, the president of the International Committee of the Red Cross, Jakob Kellenberger, suggests that many of the alleged modern problems with the Geneva Conventions are the result of weak compliance, not weak laws. He argues that the basic IHL framework laid out in the Geneva Conventions and surrounding documents is flexible enough to accommodate new modes of warfare, with some further elaboration and clarification.

Others have countered that the problem is not IHL itself, but that it is not the appropriate framework for dealing with terrorism. From the British responses to Irish Republican Army terrorists or Spanish responses to Basque separatists, many countries have dealt with terrorist threats in their past within a domestic law enforcement, rather than through an armed conflict paradigm. When U.S. citizen Timothy McVeigh detonated a truck bomb against a U.S. government building in Oklahoma City on April 19, 1995, killing 168 and injuring over 800, he was arrested as a criminal suspect and tried and sentenced in a regular U.S. court. In the fourth article, Kenneth Roth argues that the "War on Terror" might alternately (and preferably) be dealt with using the same law enforcement tools that were effective in the past. He argues that the disparate (albeit violent) acts of terrorist networks do not clearly meet the threshold for armed conflict. Further, he argues, there are serious policy consequences of dealing with terrorism through a wartime paradigm. Peacetime law enforcement standards are more restrictive of government powers, including requiring more procedures to ensure that the individual is guilty, and limiting the uses of lethal force. If more expansive wartime powers can be used anytime, on an indefinite basis, it has the potential to erode these peace-time standards, and to result in the deprivation of some individuals' rights. Given these consequences, Roth argues, the focus should be on apprehending suspected terrorists through regular law enforcement means unless absolutely unavailable.

In the final article in this section, David P. Fidler, director of the Indiana University Center on American and Global Security, takes a more optimistic view of the future of IHL under modern, irregular warfare. In some forms of irregular warfare, he argues, there may be strategic incentives for stronger IHL compliance and better conduct. He points to some of the central premises of counterinsurgency, or COIN theory, which led the U.S. military and its partners to adopt *more* restrictions on their use of force than were required under IHL in some cases. COIN advocates argue that because insurgents depend on support from the host population, the way to defeat them is often to take measures that decrease their popular support. These can include protecting civilians and strengthening rule of law, which would seem to accord with better compliance with IHL and other wartime regulations, not less.

As you read through these selections, you should ask yourself:
• How different is 21st century warfare from past warfare? Are claims that this is a fundamentally "new" type of conflict that merits new rules inflated?
• Is a terrorist act like the September 11 attack a crime or an act of war? Does it matter if it is an isolated attack or part of a series of attacks? What level of force or organization would be necessary to consider it an act of war?
• One of the concerns with using wartime powers against terrorist networks such as Al Qaeda is that the threat from Al Qaeda might endure for decades without a negotiated end to hostilities. Expansive war powers might be used indefinitely. How do you think this issue should be dealt with? Do such arguments justify not dealing with Al Qaeda through a "wartime" paradigm, and instead relying only or primarily on law enforcement powers (as the Human Rights Watch article suggests)?
• The Buchanan article argues it is unfair and dangerous for the United States to be bound by IHL when its opponents disregard it. Should warring parties only have to abide by the laws of war when their adversaries do? Historically, states have often violated IHL, but this has never been

considered a sufficient excuse for their opponents to do the same. Has the rise in irregular warfare changed things?

• States have often complied with IHL in the past through a mix of humanitarian and strategic rationales. Do you agree with David Fidler that strategies like counterinsurgency theory might offer new strategic incentives for states to comply with IHL, balancing out other disincentives within 21st century conflict?

NOTES

1. See, for example, David Galula, *Counterinsurgency Warfare: Theory and Practice* (New York: Praeger, 1964); Martin van Creveld, *The Changing Face of War: Combat from the Marne to Iraq* (New York: Ballantine Books, 2008); John Nagl, *Learning to Eat Soup with a Knife: Counterinsurgency Lessons from Malaya and Vietnam* (New York: Praeger, 2002).

2. As noted in the introduction to this compendium, state-on-state conflicts have been increasingly rare since the late 1970s, while internal conflict, including civil wars and insurgency, continue to be common and now represent the major sources of conflict. See *supra*, page 12, note 17. See also Jeffrey B. White, "Some Thoughts on Irregular Warfare," Director of Central Intelligence Home Page, https://www.cia.gov/library/center-for-the-study-of-intelligence/csi-publications/csi-studies/studies/96unclass/iregular.htm.

3. Arguments that there should be different standards or application of IHL either for warring parties that repeatedly flout IHL, or in conflicts in which this is the case run against the long-standing principle of equal application of the law. For more on modern debates surround the equal application principle, see Adam Roberts, "The Equal Application of the Laws of War: A Principle Under Pressure," *International Review of the Red Cross* 90 (2008); Gabriella Blum, "On a Differential Law of War," *Harvard International Law Journal* 52 (2011).

4. Patrick J. Buchanan, "Torture and the Terror War," *American Cause*, January 10, 2005, http://www.theamericancause.org/a-pjb-050110-war.htm.

5. Memorandum from Alberto R. Gonzales, White House Counsel, to the President, January 25, 2002 (arguing that the laws of war are "obsolete" to the new "war on terror").

6. Glenn M. Sulmasy, "The Law of Armed Conflict in the Global War on Terror: International Lawyers Fighting the Last War," *Notre Dame Journal of Law, Ethics and Public Policy* 19 (2005): 309.

Torture and the Terror War

by Patrick J. Buchanan*

Are members of al-Qaida entitled to Geneva Convention protections for POWs? Are Taliban fighters and Iraqi insurgents entitled to those protections, by which soldiers are to give name, rank and serial number, but never to be abused to force them to reveal military secrets?

As Alberto Gonzales is discovering, these are not just legal issues. The Geneva Conventions are international law. They are rules for the conduct of war, agreed to by civilized nations, that assumed wars would be fought between armies whose soldiers would respect these rules.

Under the Geneva Conventions, however, soldiers who fight out of uniform or commit atrocities—i.e., murder prisoners or target and kill noncombatants—may be sent before firing squads.

Wehrmacht soldiers who penetrated American lines in the Battle of the Bulge by wearing U.S. Army uniforms hastily shed them to fight in German uniforms—or else they could have been shot when captured. OSS agents, dropped behind enemy lines to kill German pilots and Nazi collaborators, knew they were not entitled to the same protections as 82nd Airborne troops dropped behind German lines on D-Day.

Here we come to America's dilemma. While the Afghan and Iraqi soldiers who fought the U.S. invasions are surely entitled to Geneva Convention protections for POWs, what of al-Qaida? What of the jihadis and foreign fighters who kidnap and behead aid workers?

What of Iraqis who plant roadside explosives or enlist in security forces to plant bombs in U.S. Army mess halls? Are they also entitled to the Geneva Convention protections of wartime soldiers?

In America, serial murderers Ted Bundy and John Wayne Gacy were accorded constitutional protections, not only against abuse, but against self-incrimination. Both received trial by jury. Both were guaranteed a taxpayer-subsidized legal defense.

Should we—because it is the American way of justice—extend such constitutional protections to al-Qaida terrorists caught on U.S. soil?

Should we extend Geneva Convention protections to all captured insurgents? Can we win a war on terror if we fight by Geneva rules, while our enemy fights by the Maoist rules of people's war, which condone terror and murder, and encourage guerrillas to fight out of uniform and kill the enemy anywhere, any time, any way?

In World War II, FDR did not hesitate to execute, after secret trials, six German saboteurs caught on U.S. soil, though they had not killed a single American or exploded a single bomb. They were saboteurs, out of uniform behind American lines, and under the rules of warfare, we had every right to execute them. And we did.

Have we the same right to execute terrorists who come here to massacre civilians as we did those Nazi saboteurs?

Apparently, while the Geneva Conventions permit us to execute captured al-Qaida, we may not inflict pain on them to force them to reveal secrets that might prevent another 9-11?

Because we find torture abhorrent and degrading, and do not want it used on our soldiers, we adhere to proscriptions against it in international law. But if we are to win this war on terror, we must at least tell al-Qaida this: If you are caught on U.S. soil, bent on slaughtering innocent Americans, you have no more rights than those German saboteurs, and we will execute you, speedily, after military trials.

With Iraqi insurgents, we face the problem the British Army faced in Ireland from 1919 to 1921 and the French faced in Algeria from 1954 to 1962. In Ireland's war of independence, IRA "flying squads" of gunmen attacked British troops, then melted away into a supportive population. British veterans of the Western Front, not knowing how to find and fight such an enemy, engaged in reprisals against Irish civilians. Thus, Britain lost the Irish people, and Ireland, forever.

In Algeria, terror attacks on French soldiers and civilians brought in Gen. Massu's "paras," who tortured terror suspects for information to eradicate the FLN. Thus was the Battle of Algiers won—and Algeria lost.

Whatever we may think of their tactics, the IRA of yesteryear, the FLN, the Afghan mujahideen of the 1980s and Hezbollah in the 1990s succeeded in expelling those they saw as occupiers. The Iraqi insurgents are using these same tactics, plus the now-familiar car bomb and suicide bomber made famous by Hamas.

It may be that Americans, revolted as we are by the methods and means necessary to crush such an insurgency, are incapable of winning a long war against an enemy who rejects Geneva rules. Is it possible that our Western standards for fighting a just and moral war, dating to St. Augustine, have so tied our hands in this war in Iraq that we cannot finally defeat the enemy?

If so, let us find out soon.

*Patrick J. Buchanan is an American conservative political commentator and author.

Patrick J. Buchanan, "Torture and the Terror War," *American Cause*, January 10, 2005, available at http://www.theamericancause.org/a-pjb-050110-war.htm.

Used by permission.

The Politics of the Geneva Conventions: Avoiding Formalist Traps

*by Rosa Brooks**

It always feels good to do what you're good at, and, as Sam Estreicher observed during an earlier session, lawyers are good at formalism. When we talk about the Geneva Conventions, it's particularly tempting to retreat into formalism, because emotions so easily start running high: after all, if we leave the tidy formalist world, we're into a messy argument about good and evil, right and wrong, terror and torture, cruelty and necessity. Few lawyers are good at that sort of conversation.

Nonetheless, I am not making news when I say that formalism has limits, as well as virtues, and these limits are quite quickly reached when the subject is the Geneva Conventions. Let me say a bit about what those limits are—and what it would take to somehow move beyond them.

The Geneva Conventions were drafted in 1949, in another world. The world of the Geneva Conventions' "framers" is still familiar to all of us, though increasingly it is familiar from movies and books rather from the evening news or, still less, our own lived experience. The world in which the Conventions were drafted was a world of states: powerful states, weak states, predatory states, law-abiding states, but states all the same. Soldiers wore uniforms designed by their states, carried weapons issued by their states, obeyed orders given by their commanders, and fought against the armies of other states.

Well—most of the time, anyway. It's true that even then, there were actors and conflicts that didn't fit the mold. There were partisans who wore no uniforms and answered to no recognized authority, and guerillas and resistance fighters who straddled the line between civilian and combatant. But although it is sometimes hard to make students see this, lawmaking is an imaginative enterprise: lawmakers look at the existing world, project onto it an image of a better, tidier world, and then try to develop contingency plans for dealing with various imaginable forms of untidiness. In this sense lawmaking is inevitably backward looking, because none of us is very good at correctly predicting future changes.

So the diplomats who negotiated the Geneva Conventions took the raw materials already at hand, from the Hague Conventions and from international custom, and coupled these with their own searing sense of what had gone wrong in the world war just ended. In a sense, the Geneva Conventions read like an attempt to revisit the Second World War, without the mess, confusion, cruelty, and slaughter of civilians. This is not surprising.

Inevitably, the Geneva Conventions were "out of date" from the moment they entered into force; they laid out rules for a world more orderly than the world they had inherited, and hoped that by doing so, they would encourage life to imitate art.

Up to a point, it worked. The Conventions have been normatively important. They have led powerful states to integrate Convention rules into their own domestic law, and they have provided an important tool for shaming parties to conflicts into behaving better than they might otherwise.

But the Conventions were always aspirational, and since their entry into force, human ingenuity has devised new and different ways to fight and kill. We now fear the terrorist's bomb, anthrax in the mail system, sabotage of critical infrastructure, or a lethal virus released deliberately as much as we fear an invasion by a powerful state.

The threats we face today are not necessarily "worse" than the threats we used to face. It is important to emphasize this. There is no satisfying way to quantify the risks we face today and compare them to the risks we faced three or four decades ago. Yes, a "dirty bomb" in New York could be catastrophic, potentially killing thousands and making a major city uninhabitable. Is this "worse," though, than the Cold War risk of nuclear war? Worse than the risk of ethnic slaughter, exemplified by the Holocaust?

Still, the increased threat of terrorism, though perhaps not a "worse" threat than any prior threat, is certainly a "different" threat in crucial ways. Guerillas and terrorists have always existed, and never fit neatly into the Geneva Conventions framework, but they operated on the margins until globalization scattered the tools of mass destruction around the world. The hijacked airplane, the simple materials to make a hundred or a million IEDs, the cell-phone detonators, the viruses in test-tubes: these are new. Globalization has turned the marginal, nuisance threat of terrorism into a threat that even powerful states must take seriously.

Even in powerful states, intelligence services, militaries and laws all evolved to handle "traditional" conflicts and traditional threats from belligerent foreign states. Yet terrorists—like other non-state actors—are, by definition, not party to the Geneva Convention. They play by a different set of rules—if indeed there is any set of rules they follow.

As a result, the formal framework of the Geneva Conventions does not fit the struggle against terrorism well. Too many of its threshold distinctions are premised on the continued existence of a rapidly vanishing world.

The Geneva Conventions take it for granted, for instance, that we can draw meaningful spatial distinctions between zones of conflict and zones of peace, but this breaks down when the enemy is a geographically diffuse terrorist network, neither confined to one state nor interested in controlling territory. If al Qaeda has a secret cell in Yemen—or in Germany, or in the United States—from which it plans and trains for terrorist attacks, is Yemen (or Germany, or the United States) in a conflict zone? The Geneva Conventions offer no way to answer this question.

Temporal boundaries between war and peace, as well as spatial boundaries, are challenged by the rise of non-state actors. The Geneva Conventions assume a world in which diplomacy and negotiations can bring an end to a conflict, but with loosely organized terrorist organizations, there is often no one with whom one could negotiate, and no one with the authority to bring about a peace. Attacks may be constant, or intermittent, and the Geneva Conventions don't offer helpful standards for determining when a conflict begins or ends in the absence of agreements between parties to the conflict.

Most troubling, given recent events, the Geneva Conventions don't offer satisfying answers to the question of which people are entitled to benefit from its protections. On the one hand, the text is clear that the Conventions apply only to "High Contracting Parties," which, by definition, are states.[1] On the other hand, we have Common Article 3,[2] which may—or may not—be taken to apply to all parties to all conflicts not otherwise covered, regardless of nationality and state allegiance. And even when we're confident that the Conventions apply to a conflict within a territory, what do we do about combatants who wear no uniforms, or don't appear to work within a traditional military command structure? A strict reading of the Geneva Conventions suggests that the Bush Administration is not unjustified in its claim that neither al Qaeda nor Taliban detainees captured in Afghanistan are entitled to prisoner of war status.

I have written extensively about these issues elsewhere, so I won't run through additional examples here.[3] The point is that an entirely formalist read of the Geneva Conventions leads to the conclusion that the Conventions just aren't applicable, for the most part, to the "war on terror."

To human rights advocates (of whom I am one), this is an unpalatable conclusion, for it appears to suggest that there are virtually no rules of international law governing how the war on terror is waged. It suggests that the United States is legally entitled to offer few or no protections—procedural or substantive—to those it suspects of being terrorists, and in fact can treat suspected terrorists in a manner that would be clearly illegal in both a domestic criminal context and in a traditional armed conflict context.

Most rights advocates adopt one of two strategies in reaction to this dilemma. The first strategy consists of agreeing that a formalist read of the Geneva Conventions makes them hard to apply to terrorism, but shrugging this off on the grounds that terrorism is not a form of armed conflict at all, and is merely criminal activity. Obviously, if terrorism is simply a form of crime, and not a form of armed conflict, it is subject not to the Geneva Conventions but to domestic criminal and constitutional law, which offer relatively robust protections for suspects.

The second strategy employed by many rights advocates consists of what one could call "modified formalism": it consists of accepting that terrorism is a form of armed conflict, but arguing that the Geneva Conventions should be interpreted less like a statute than a constitution. That is, a treaty should be interpreted according to its "spirit" and according to the "intent" of its framers, which in this case was to protect fundamental human rights during armed conflicts. A modified version of this argument is that some of the substantive aspects of the Geneva Conventions are customary law, and that customary law imposes additional obligations on detaining powers beyond those outlined in the Conventions. Both variants of this theory can then be used to justify demanding POW-like protections even for those detainees who most clearly lack any entitlement to them on a strict formalist reading of the Conventions.

Neither approach overcomes the problems I have discussed. The first has a head-in-the-sand quality, since international terrorism is different from ordinary crime in significant and obvious ways, and it seems clear that traditional criminal investigations and trials are not an adequate means of combating terrorists who seek to cause mass death and who operate in many different countries. For the most part, serious rights advocates have abandoned this line of argument, and acknowledged that at least some of the time, if not all of the time, the activities of terrorist groups look more like armed conflict than crime.

The second approach is better, but it is also problematic. First, it raises unresolved questions about treaty interpretation. There is no clear legal basis for insisting that the Geneva Conventions be read according to their "spirit" rather than their letter, and in any case it is far from clear that the framers of the Convention would have chosen to accord terrorists most of the rights given to POWs, had they foreseen international terrorism of the sort we now face. There is also little consensus about which aspects of the Geneva Conventions reflect (or have become) binding customary international law. Certainly core provisions, such as those that prohibit the intentional targeting of civilians, reflect customary international law—but more subtle questions of due process are less easily resolved by reference to custom.

This means, among other things, that Attorney General Alberto Gonzales was not wrong when, during his days as White House Counsel, he advised President Bush that some provisions of the Geneva Conventions seem "quaint" or even "obsolete" when applied to terrorists.[4]

It is difficult—almost impossible—to advance this proposition without generating enormous opposition from most rights advocates, but I think that the opposition is knee-jerk and misplaced. Acknowledging that the Bush Administration's read of the Geneva Conventions is not implausible does not require agreement with the Administration's policies. It is entirely possible to accept that the Geneva Conventions don't apply to terrorist suspects, but still consider the Administration's detention and interrogation policies both morally bankrupt and strategically foolish.

The Geneva Conventions should not be sacralized. They are important, relevant, and often useful. But if we resist Bush Administration policies by treating the Geneva Conventions as sacred cows, we do the long-term cause of promoting human rights a disservice. The Conventions are not perfect—how could they be? They are the product of a time and a place, of divisive negotiations between human beings who sought to represent the interests of their states.

Indeed, before the "war on terror" rallied rights advocates around the Conventions, some in the human rights community were themselves attacking the Convention framework for its inadequacies, arguing that the Geneva Conventions actually legitimize (and—by implication—can worsen) the violence of states. These are important critiques, and we need to clear enough intellectual space to have them.

The only way to do that is to stop treating the Geneva Conventions as our sole or most crucial point of reference. To be sure, the Geneva Conventions are the law we've got, so it is useful to ask what the Geneva Conventions require, what they permit, and what issues they just don't address; it's also useful to identify areas of consensus and discord about how and when they are applicable. But if we value the rule of law, this needs to be done in an honest and disinterested way. This means facing up to it when the Conventions are silent or seem archaic, and acknowledging it when the questions we face are primarily policy questions, not legal questions.

In practice, this does not happen much. In the debate about post-9/11 U.S. practices, few of the participants are willing to move beyond formalism or faux formalism of one sort or another. As I suggested at the beginning, perhaps this is because we find the policy discussions too difficult and emotional. But it is dangerous to avoid them.

When we refuse to admit the limits of formalism, we inevitably have to start stretching rules and ordinary meanings. And if rights advocates adopt a rigid formalism, it becomes difficult to focus clearly on important differences between various Administration arguments, which in turn makes it hard to develop effective rejoinders.

Take three different examples.

First, consider the Bush Administration's decision to deny POW status to Taliban detainees. As noted above, a strict formalist read of the Geneva Conventions makes the Administration's decision seem perfectly plausible, though hardly inevitable. It would be possible to argue that the Administration was just wrong, however, either on the facts or on the law; one could argue, for instance, that most Taliban soldiers wore distinctive emblems and otherwise met Geneva requirements, or that at any rate some did, and therefore individualized status hearings were required.

Second, consider the Administration's arguments relating to torture, contained in the Bybee Memo of August 1, 2002, which concluded that under federal law, "torture" must involve only the sort of pain associated with organ failure and death.[5] The response here would be that Administration lawyers were not simply mistaken about the conclusions warranted by statute, treaty, and case law, but that they were engaging in illegitimate and arguably unethical forms of legal argumentation, ignoring and selectively misreading various relevant texts in order to reach a predetermined conclusion.

Third, consider the arguments, also in the Bybee memo, claiming that the President has the inherent constitutional power to override conflicting federal law when he deems it necessary.[6] These arguments are legal in their form—they rely on the President's commander in chief powers—but their implications go beyond law, insofar as they assert, in some fundamental sense, that political power is simply beyond law's reach.

In each of these three cases, Administration arguments are couched in the language of formalism. Everyone wants the law on their side, so this is understandable. But the kinds of arguments are fundamentally different.

Think of law—of the enterprise of legal interpretation—as a game, like basketball or tennis. The game of legal interpretation has rules, some written, some customary, some bright-line, some ambiguous. But although it is difficult to say just what elements make tennis, we all know that there is a difference between playing tennis in a way that pushes the envelope between the permissible and the impermissible, cheating, and leaving the game. Thus: calling a ball "in" when it just touches the outside of the baseline is skirting the edge of the permissible, but it is clearly within the rule. Calling a ball "in" when one knows it to have landed outside the baseline is cheating, but it is still playing tennis: it is just cheating at tennis. Pausing to beat up one's opponent when he objects to cheating is no longer tennis, however; the resort to force destroys the game entirely.

Map this onto the three different Administration arguments I mentioned above. The Bush administration claim that Taliban detainees are not entitled to POW status or individualized hearings on the question may be wrongheaded in a strategic or moral sense. But if we think of law as a game, the Administration is clearly playing by the rules here, though perhaps pushing boundaries a bit.

The claim about torture relies on cheating, insofar as it depends on selective and misleading citation and odd logical leaps. Nonetheless, cheating, however reprehensible, is a way to play the game; by definition, if you are cheating at a game you are still accepting most aspects of the game itself.

But the claim about inherent executive powers is of a different order. Though couched in formalist terms, it's a game-ending move, the rough equivalent of a threat: "Play by my rules or I'll crush you."

Although law is "gamelike" in many respects, it is, of course, crucially different from tennis. The "rules" of law and legal interpretation are not there for the entertainment of the players; they're not merely self-referential. Law is supposed to bear some relation to facts on the ground, and law enables coercive action to be taken in ways that alter the facts on the ground. If we create a legal system in which cheating is widespread—or, worse, if we overlook game-ending moves and treat them as legitimate modifications of the game—then it isn't merely rules that get bent, but the rule of law altogether.

This is what makes it so important to move beyond the sacralization of the Geneva Conventions to a more particularized discussion of just what morality and strategy require. As long as we insist that the Geneva Conventions and related law and custom set the terms of the debate about post-9/11 U.S. actions, we create strong incentives for players to push the envelope, cheat, and even go outside the law altogether in one way or another. This dangerously weakens the rule of law.

The Geneva Conventions—what they permit, what they require, and what they do not reach—should thus be the beginning of the discussion, not the end. If we're serious about both rights and security, we should make an effort to get back to basics: what sort of world do we want to live in? Knowing that terrorism will persist, and that technological development will continue to give tools of mass destruction to non-state actors, what principles ought to govern how terrorist suspects are treated, and how states respond to real or perceived threats from terrorists?

This requires thinking both about morality and about strategy. And the process, if taken seriously, might help break through impasses and allow us to identify areas of agreement that are obscured when the Geneva Conventions dictate the terms of debate.

Imagine, for instance, that we live in the "all security, all the time" world, in which collective physical security always outweighs individual rights. There is no free expression, no freedom of movement, no right to due process. None of us would want to inhabit so totalitarian a state—and most of us would wonder, in any case, if "perfect" security is even a realistic goal. We do not strive for "perfect" road safety, because we value convenience, speed, and a relatively low level of state monitoring, and because we probably could not achieve perfect safety in any case. Security from terrorist threats is not inherently different; at some point one realizes diminishing returns on further rights restrictions.

Of course, few of us would want to inhabit an "all rights, all the time" state either, one in which state authorities entirely lacked the power to adapt law and policy to meet new kinds of threats if doing so meant longer detentions or more limited due process rights.

Imagining an "all security, all the time" world versus an "all rights, all the time" world helps get us past the tendency to assume that security must trump rights or rights must trump security, and recasts the questions as one about precisely which tradeoffs are worthwhile. But even this is still a bit misleading, since conceptualizing the debate in terms of a tradeoff between rights and security obscures the possibility—indeed, the strong likelihood—that "security" and "rights" are causally linked.

That is: it is quite possible that some rights-restricting U.S. actions in the war on terror have actually increased the terrorist threat against the United States. Our policy of open-ended detentions at Guantanamo, for instance, justified by the Bush Administration on security grounds, has alienated even many of our allies. Accept, for the sake of the argument, that at least most, if not all, of the Guantanamo detainees are dangerous terrorists who, if released, will continue their efforts to attack the United States in some way. A level-headed policy maker needs to take this prospect seriously, and critics of Guantanamo Bay should not assume that all detainees are innocent or harmless. But a level-headed policy maker should also take into account the externalities of Guantanamo. These are difficult to measure, but might include some or all of the following: greater difficulties in persuading "friendly" states to share intelligence information, greater difficulties in persuading ordinary people in Iraq, Afghanistan and elsewhere to trust U.S. forces and share information; and greater difficulty discouraging some from actively supporting al Qaeda and other anti-U.S. organizations.

All these externalities create new security risks that must be evaluated alongside the risks of releasing potentially dangerous terrorists. Note, too, that the "moral" and "strategic" arguments prove to be intertwined. Regardless of how U.S. policy makers view the morality of open-ended detentions, they may have serious costs to the United States as long as many others view them as immoral.

Of course, one can, and should, turn this around as well. High levels of physical insecurity make the enjoyment of other human rights difficult or impossible, and terrorism is itself a human rights violation of enormous magnitude. If a rigid insistence on procedural due process rights for terror suspects led to a massive increase in catastrophic terrorist attacks, we would not be better off. The often-repeated claim that it is our very openness that makes us vulnerable is not entirely frivolous.

All this implies, I think, that we need to evaluate the various kinds of threats and potential responses with some specificity. Certain restrictions on rights—limited in duration—might well be justifiable in the face of an imminent catastrophic threat (nuclear weapons, for instance). But the phrase "the war on terrorism" lumps together, by implication, a wide range of different threats, most of which would not justify serious restrictions on rights. The captured Taliban soldier, for instance, however resolutely anti-American, will probably do the United States no great harm if released—even if he promptly rejoins the Taliban. Osama bin Laden, if captured, would present a different story. Similarly, if we are concerned about biological attacks on the United States, it may be that massive investments in our dysfunctional public health system are a more effective response to this threat than weakening norms against torture through the use of various "coercive" interrogation techniques.

It's beyond the scope of this short essay to discuss concrete means of dealing with the variety of security threats we now face. My point is that we need to walk back from the panicky, post-9/11 sense that anything goes in the name of fighting terrorism. We need to develop responses to terrorism that are nuanced and proportionate, and acknowledge both that the varying forms of terrorism do not pose equal threats and that every response has costs of its own.

That will be a monumental undertaking, but not a hopeless undertaking. The work of several of the participants in this conference makes valuable contributions to the project I have outlined. To some extent, we're facing empirical questions: how severe are the various threats, and what can be done about each? Lawyers may be good at formalism, but increasingly, many of us are also good at making cost-benefit analyses, and a bit more of this would be useful here. So too would be looking to the experience of other nations that have addressed terrorist threats through domestic legislation. While other nations have at times restricted certain rights to combat terrorism, none have found it necessary to turn to torture or indefinite detention. It seems likely that we could learn from a careful study of the effectiveness of different domestic legal regimes.

Paul Stephan opened this conference by asking, "Who owns the Geneva Conventions? Who gets to say what is in them, and should be in them?" My answer, on some level, is: why not us? Why not begin the process of imaging a new law of armed conflict, and new domestic laws, right here and right now?

It's easy to respond that this is too hard, and will take too long, and opens up too many cans of worms. But this is a cop-out. It may be a hard, long, and divisive process, but we certainly won't be able to develop a new consensus if we don't try.

NOTES

1. E.g., Geneva Convention Relative to the Treatment of Prisoners of War, Aug. 12, 1949, art. 1, 6 U.S.T. 3316, 3318, 75 U.N.T.S. 135, 136 [hereinafter GPW].

2. E.g., id. art. 2, 6 U.S.T. at 3318-20, 75 U.N.T.S. at 136–38.

3. Rosa Ehrenreich Brooks, War Everywhere: Rights, National Security Law, and the Law of Armed Conflict in the Age of Terror, 153 U. Pa. L. Rev. 675 (2004).

4. Memorandum from Alberto R. Gonzales, White House Counsel, to the President (Jan. 25, 2002).

5. Memorandum from Jay S. Bybee, Assistant Attorney General, to Alberto Gonzales, Counsel to the President (Aug. 1, 2002).

6. Id.

*Rosa Brooks is a law professor at Georgetown University Law Center. She has served as counselor to the undersecretary of defense and deputy assistant secretary of defense and special coordinator for rule of law and humanitarian policy.

Rosa Brooks, "The Politics of the Geneva Conventions: Avoiding Formalist Traps," *Virginia Journal of International Law* 46 (Fall 2005): 1–7; available at http://rosabrooks.squarespace.com/the-politics-of-the-geneva-con/. Copyright 2005.

Sixty Years of the Geneva Conventions: Learning from the Past to Better Face the Future

by Jakob Kellenberger*

We gather here to mark a significant coming of age. Sixty years ago today, the Geneva Conventions were adopted. This defining event played a central role in expanding the protection provided to victims of armed conflicts. It also expanded the ICRC's humanitarian mandate, and facilitated our access as well as our dialogue with States.

It would be natural, on this date, to reflect with a certain pride and satisfaction on the achievements and successes over the decades, and to allow at least a modest degree of self-congratulation. It cannot be denied that much more attention is paid to situations where the rules are violated than to the many situations where their respect is ensured.

At the same time, this anniversary is an opportunity to anticipate the next decade and beyond, ensuring that the Geneva Conventions are well-prepared for the increasing challenges and risks that still lie ahead.

Without a doubt, the journey so far has not always been plain sailing. The extent to which armed conflict has evolved over the past 60 years cannot be underestimated. It almost goes without saying that contemporary warfare rarely consists of two well-structured armies facing each other on a geographically defined battlefield. As lines have become increasingly blurred between various armed groups and between combatants and civilians, it is civilian men, women and children who have increasingly become the main victims. International humanitarian law, IHL, has necessarily adapted to this changing reality. The adoption of the first two Additional Protocols to the Geneva Conventions in 1977, with the rules they established on the conduct of hostilities and on the protection of persons affected by non-international armed conflict, is just one example. Specific rules prohibiting or regulating weapons such as anti-personnel mines and, more recently, cluster munitions are another example of the adaptability of IHL to the realities on the ground.

The traumatic events of 9/11 and its aftermath set a new test for IHL. The polarisation of international relations and the humanitarian consequences of what has been referred to as the "global war on terror" have posed a huge challenge. The proliferation and fragmentation of non-state armed groups, and the fact that some of them reject the premises of IHL, have posed another. These challenges effectively exposed IHL to some rigorous cross-examination by a wide range of actors, including the ICRC, to see if it really does still stand as an adequate legal framework for the protection of victims of armed conflict.

In short, the result of this sometimes arduous process was a resounding reaffirmation of the relevance and adequacy of IHL in preserving human life and dignity in armed conflict. However, as I made clear at the outset, this is no time to rest on our laurels. The nature of armed conflict, and of the causes and consequences of such conflict, is continuing to evolve. IHL must evolve too.

The priority for the ICRC now is to anticipate and prepare for the main challenges to IHL in the years ahead. While these challenges have a legal and often a political dimension, I must stress that our ultimate concern is purely humanitarian; our only motivation is to contribute to achieving better protection for the victims of armed conflict.

I shall refer to some of these challenges and consider some ways in which they might be addressed, including what and how the ICRC, for its part, stands ready to contribute in terms of guidance and advice. It almost goes without saying however that the effort required to address these challenges is the responsibility—be it legal or moral—not just of the ICRC, but of a wide range of actors including States and non-state actors, military forces and legislators.

I shall focus firstly on certain challenges related to armed conflict in general and secondly on those related specifically to non-international armed conflicts.

So what are some of the ongoing challenges to IHL? The first relates to the conduct of hostilities. I referred earlier to the changing nature of armed conflict and the increasingly blurred lines between combatants and civilians. Civilians have progressively become more involved in activities closely related to actual combat. At the same time, combatants do not always clearly distinguish themselves from civilians, neither wearing uniforms nor openly carrying arms. They mingle with the civilian population. Civilians are also used as human shields. To add to the confusion, in some conflicts, traditional military functions have been outsourced to private contractors or other civilians working for State armed forces or for organised armed groups. These trends are, if anything, likely to increase in the years ahead.

The result of this, in a nutshell, is that civilians are more likely to be targeted—either mistakenly or arbitrarily. Military personnel are also at increased risk: since they cannot properly identify their adversary, they are vulnerable to attack by individuals who to all appearances are civilians.

IHL stipulates that those involved in fighting must make a basic distinction between combatants on the one hand, who may lawfully be attacked, and civilians on the other hand, who are protected against attack unless and for such time as they directly participate in hostilities. The problem is that neither the Geneva Conventions nor their Additional Protocols spell out what precisely constitutes "direct participation in hostilities".

To put it bluntly, this lack of clarity has been costing lives. This is simply unjustifiable. In an effort to help remedy this situation, the ICRC worked for six years with a group of more than 50 international legal experts from military, academic, governmental and non-governmental backgrounds. The end result of this long and intense process, published just two months ago, was a substantial guidance document. This document serves to shed light firstly on who is considered a civilian for the purpose of conducting hostilities, what conduct amounts to direct participation in hostilities, and which particular rules and principles govern the loss of civilian protection against direct attack.

Without changing existing law, the ICRC's Interpretative Guidance document provides our recommendations on how IHL relating to the notion of direct participation in hostilities should be interpreted in contemporary armed conflict. It constitutes much more than an academic exercise. The aim is that these recommendations will enjoy practical application where it matters, in the midst of armed conflict, and better protect the victims of those conflicts.

Direct participation in hostilities is not the only concept relating to the conduct of hostilities that could benefit from further clarification. Differences exist over the interpretation of other key notions such as "military objective", the "principle of proportionality" and "precaution".

The debate has been prompted in part by the growing number of military operations conducted in densely populated urban areas, often using heavy or highly explosive weapons, which have devastating humanitarian consequences for civilian populations. The media images of death, injury and destruction—of terrible suffering—in such situations of conflict in different parts of the world are surely all too familiar to everyone here today.

Another key issue here is the increasingly asymmetric nature of modern armed conflicts. Differences between belligerents, especially in terms of technological and military capacities have become ever more pronounced. Compliance with the rules of IHL may be perceived as beneficial to one side of the conflict only, while detrimental to the other. At worst, a militarily weak party—faced with a much more powerful opponent—will contravene fundamental rules of IHL in an attempt to even out the imbalance. If one side repeatedly breaks the rules, there is a risk that the situation quickly deteriorates into a free-for-all. Such a downward spiral would defy the fundamental purpose of IHL—to alleviate suffering in times of war. We must explore every avenue to prevent this from happening.

I would also like to briefly address the humanitarian and legal challenges related to the protection of internally displaced people. In terms of numbers, this is perhaps one of the most daunting humanitarian challenges arising in armed conflicts around the world today, from Colombia to Sri Lanka and from Pakistan to Sudan. This problem not only affects the many millions of IDPs, but also countless host families and resident communities.

Violations of IHL are the most common causes of internal displacement in armed conflict. Preventing violations is therefore, logically, the best means of preventing displacement from occurring in the first place.

On the other hand, people are sometimes forcibly prevented from fleeing when they wish to do so. During displacement, IDPs are often exposed to further abuses and have wide-ranging subsistence needs. Even when IDPs want to return to their place of origin, or settle elsewhere, they are often faced with obstacles. Their property may have been destroyed or taken by others, the land might be occupied or unusable after the hostilities, or returnees may fear reprisals if they return.

As part of the civilian population, IDPs are protected as civilians in armed conflicts.

If parties to conflicts respected the basic rules of IHL, much of the displacement and suffering caused to IDPs could be prevented. Nevertheless, there are some aspects of IHL concerning displacement that could be clarified or improved. These include in particular questions of freedom of movement, the need to preserve family unity, the prohibition of forced return or forced resettlement, and the right to voluntary return.

These various humanitarian and legal challenges exist in all types of armed conflict, whether international or non-international. However, I would now like to highlight some specific challenges concerning the law regulating non-international armed conflicts.

Non-international armed conflicts are by far the most prevalent type of armed conflict today, causing the greatest suffering. Yet there is no clear, universally-accepted legal definition of what such a conflict actually is. Both Article 3 common to the four Geneva Conventions and the second Additional Protocol give rise to certain questions on this. How can a non-international armed conflict be more precisely distinguished from other forms of violence, in particular organized crime and terrorist activities? And what if a non-international armed conflict spills over a State border, for example?

The lack of clear answers to such questions may effectively allow parties to circumvent their legal obligations. The existence of an armed conflict may be refuted so as to evade the application of IHL altogether. Conversely, other situations may inaccurately or prematurely be described as an armed conflict, precisely to trigger the applicability of IHL and its more permissive standards regarding the use of force, for example.

Even where the applicability of IHL in a non-international armed conflict is not in dispute, the fact that treaty-based law applying to these situations is at best limited has led to further uncertainties.

Let us remember however that non-international armed conflicts are not only governed by treaty law. The substantial number of rules identified in the ICRC's 2005 Study on Customary International Humanitarian Law provides additional legally binding norms in these situations.

But while customary IHL can fill some gaps, there are still humanitarian problems arising in these types of conflicts that are not fully addressed under the current applicable legal regime.

IHL applicable in non-international armed conflict contains general principles but remains insufficiently elaborate as regards material conditions of detention and detainees' right of contact with the outside world, for example. Lack of precise rules on various aspects of treatment and conditions of detention and the lack of clarity surrounding detention centres may have immediate and grave humanitarian consequences on the health and well-being of detainees. Therefore, even if the primary humanitarian challenge lies in the lack of resources by detaining authorities and in the lack of implementation of existing general principles, more precise regulation of conditions of detention in non-international armed conflict could usefully complement some of IHL's fundamental requirements.

Other areas that suffer from a lack of legal clarity include procedural safeguards for people interned for security reasons. In an effort to clarify minimum procedural rights, in 2005 the ICRC issued a set of procedural principles and safeguards applicable to any situation of internment, based on law and policy.

The ICRC has been relying on this position in its operational dialogue with detaining authorities in a number of contexts around the world. Adequate protection could nevertheless be better ensured if procedural safeguards were put on a more solid legal footing by States.

Humanitarian issues arise in other areas as well, in part because of a lack of rules, or because the rules are too broad or vague, leaving much to subjective interpretation. These areas include access to populations in need of humanitarian assistance, the fate of missing persons and protection of the natural environment. And this list is not exhaustive.

To address these humanitarian and legal challenges, the ICRC has been intensively engaged for the past two years in a comprehensive internal research study. The study aims firstly to explain in simple terms the scope of application of the law to the whole range of aforementioned humanitarian concerns arising in non-international armed conflicts, including the challenge of improving compliance with the law by all parties to such conflicts. On the basis of this, its second aim is to evaluate the legal responses provided in existing law to these humanitarian concerns. Based on a comprehensive assessment of the conclusions of this research, which is still underway, a case will be made for the clarification or further development of specific aspects of the law. The research will be followed by proposals on how to move forward, both substantively and procedurally.

Within the scope of this study, the ICRC is also looking at aspects of Article 3 common to the Geneva Conventions that need to be further clarified. Article 3 is widely regarded as a mini Convention in itself, binding States and non-state armed groups; a baseline from which no departure, under any circumstances, is allowed. It applies minimum legal standards to the treatment of all persons in enemy hands, regardless of how they may be legally or politically classified or in whose custody they may be. We are preparing a consolidated reading of the protective legal and policy framework applicable in non-international armed conflicts that meet the threshold of common Article 3.

The ICRC has a responsibility in ensuring that the Conventions will continue to stand the test of time. Of course it is the political and legal responsibility primarily of States, which have universally ratified the Conventions, to ensure that they are implemented and enforced.

Ideally of course, all parties to an armed conflict, whatever they call themselves or each other, would appreciate that it is in their own best interest to apply the legal restraints provided by IHL. After all, combatants on both sides have obligations as well as rights. On the other hand, failure to prevent abuse against others ultimately removes the safeguard against similar abuse in return. The result, simply put, is spiralling human suffering.

However, the lack of respect for existing rules remains, as ever, the main challenge. I hardly need to remind you of the catalogue of flagrant violations of IHL frequently witnessed in armed conflicts around the world today. This situation—sadly—is compounded by a prevailing culture of impunity. True, there have been significant positive developments towards strengthening accountability for war crimes through various international tribunals and the International Criminal Court. National legislators and courts are also finally starting to live up to their respective responsibilities of ensuring that domestic legislation recognises the criminal responsibility of those who violate IHL, and of actually enforcing such legislation.

Public pressure and international scrutiny of conduct in an armed conflict are also significant factors in improving compliance with IHL. This presupposes adequate knowledge and training in IHL not just by lawyers and military commanders, but by wider sectors of the public at large. After all it was public pressure—and the collective shame of governments in failing to stop the atrocities in the former Yugoslavia and Rwanda—that led to the establishment of the ad-hoc tribunals for those countries in the mid-1990s.

Ignorance of the law is no excuse. At least the guidance, clarification and proposals coming out of the various ICRC initiatives I mentioned will make recourse to this excuse by parties to a conflict even less credible.

The ICRC can only contribute one part of what must be a concerted international effort to improve compliance with IHL. On the 60th anniversary of the Geneva Conventions, I make a heartfelt plea to States and non-state armed groups who are also bound by their provisions, to show the requisite political will to turn legal provisions into a meaningful reality. I urge them to show good faith in protecting the victims of armed conflicts - conflicts that in view of the challenges I have mentioned today are likely to become ever-more pernicious in the years to come.

Sixty years ago, the Geneva Conventions were born out of the horrors experienced by millions of people during the Second World War and its aftermath. The essential spirit of the Geneva Conventions—to uphold human life and dignity even in the midst of armed conflict—is as important now as it was 60 years ago. Thank you for doing all you can to keep that spirit alive.

*Jakob Kellenberger is president of the International Committee of the Red Cross.

Jakob Kellenberger, "Sixty Years of the Geneva Conventions: Learning from the Past to Better Face the Future," address at the ceremony to celebrate the sixtieth anniversary of the Geneva Conventions, Geneva, August 12, 2009.

The Law of War in the War on Terror

*by Kenneth Roth**

The Bush administration has literalized its "war" on terrorism, dissolving the legal boundaries between what a government can do in peacetime and what's allowed in war. This move may have made it easier for Washington to detain or kill suspects, but it has also threatened basic due process rights, thereby endangering us all.

This language stretches the meaning of the word "war." If Washington means "war" metaphorically, as when it speaks about a "war" on drugs, the rhetoric would be uncontroversial, a mere hortatory device intended to rally support for an important cause. Bush, however, seems to think of the war on terrorism quite literally—as a real war—and this concept has worrisome implications. The rules that bind governments are much looser during wartime than in times of peace. The Bush administration has used war rhetoric precisely to give itself the extraordinary powers enjoyed by a wartime government to detain or even kill suspects without trial. In the process, the administration may have made it easier for itself to detain or eliminate suspects. But it has also threatened the most basic due process rights.

LAW AT PEACE, LAW AT WAR

By literalizing its "war" on terror, the Bush administration has broken down the distinction between what is permissible in times of peace and what can be condoned during a war. In peacetime, governments are bound by strict rules of law enforcement. Police can use lethal force only if necessary to meet an imminent threat of death or serious bodily injury. Once a suspect is detained, he or she must be charged and tried. These requirements—what one can call "law-enforcement rules"—are codified in international human rights law.

In times of war, law-enforcement rules are supplemented by a more permissive set of rules: namely, international humanitarian law, which governs conduct during armed conflict. Under such "war rules," unlike during peacetime, an enemy combatant can be shot without warning (unless he or she is incapacitated, in custody, or trying to surrender), regardless of any imminent threat. If a combatant is captured, he or she can be held in custody until the end of the conflict, without any trial.

These two sets of rules have been well developed over the years, both by tradition and by detailed international conventions. There is little law, however, to explain exactly when one set of rules should apply instead of the other. For example, the Geneva Conventions—the principal codification of war rules—apply to "armed conflict," but the treaties do not define the term. Fortunately, in its commentary on them, the International Committee of the Red Cross (ICRC), the conventions' official custodian, has provided some guidance. One test that the ICRC suggests can help determine whether wartime or peacetime rules apply is to examine the intensity of hostilities in a given situation. The Bush administration, for example, has claimed that al Qaeda is at "war" with the United States because of the magnitude of its attacks on September 11, 2001, its bombings of the U.S. embassies in Kenya and Tanzania, its attack on the U.S.S. Cole in Yemen, and the bombing of residential compounds in Saudi Arabia. Each of these attacks was certainly a serious crime warranting prosecution. But technically speaking, was the administration right to claim that they add up to a war? The ICRC's commentary does not provide a clear answer.

In addition to the intensity of hostilities, the ICRC suggests considering factors such as the regularity of armed clashes and the degree to which opposing forces are organized. Whether a conflict is politically motivated also seems to play an unacknowledged role in deciding whether it is a "war" or not. Thus organized crime or drug trafficking, although methodical and bloody, are generally understood to fall under law-enforcement rules, whereas armed rebellions, once sufficiently organized and violent, are usually seen as "wars." The problem with these guidelines, however, is that they were written to address political conflicts rather than global terrorism. Thus they do not make it clear whether al Qaeda should be considered an organized criminal operation (which would not trigger the application of war rules) or a rebellion (which would).

Even in the case of war, another factor in deciding whether law-enforcement or war rules should be applied is the nature of a given suspect's involvement. Such an approach can be useful because war rules treat as combatants only those who are taking an active part in hostilities. Typically, this category includes members of a military who have not laid down their arms as well as others who are fighting or approaching a battle, directing an attack, or defending a position. Under this rule, even civilians who pick up arms and start fighting can be considered combatants and treated accordingly. But this definition is difficult to apply to terrorism, where roles and activities are clandestine and a person's relationship to specific violent acts is often unclear.

HARD CASES

Given that so much confusion exists about whether to apply wartime or law-enforcement rules to a given situation, a better approach would be to make the decision based on its public policy implications. Unfortunately, the Bush administration seems to have ignored such concerns. Consider, for example, the cases of Jose Padilla and Ali Saleh Kahlah al-Marri. Federal officials arrested Padilla, a U.S. citizen, in May 2002 when he arrived from Pakistan at Chicago's O'Hare Airport, allegedly to scout out targets for a radiological ("dirty") bomb. As for al-Marri, a student from Qatar, he was arrested in December 2001 at his home in Peoria, Illinois, for allegedly being a "sleeper" agent: an inactive terrorist who, once activated, would help others launch attacks. President Bush, invoking war rules, has declared both men to be "enemy combatants," allowing the U.S. government to hold them without charge or trial until the end of the war against terrorism—whenever that is.

But should Padilla and al-Marri, even if they have actually done what the government claims, really be considered warriors? Aren't they more like ordinary criminals? A simple thought experiment shows how dangerous are the implications of treating them as combatants. The Bush administration has asserted that the two men planned to wage war against the United States and therefore can be considered de facto soldiers. But if that is the case, then under war rules, the two men could have been shot on sight, regardless of whether they posed any immediate danger to the United States (although they might have been spared under what is known as the doctrine of "military necessity," which holds that lethal force should not be used if an enemy combatant can be neutralized through lesser means). Under the administration's logic, then, Padilla could have been gunned down as he stepped off his plane at O'Hare, and al-Marri as he left his home in Peoria. That, after all, is what it means to be a combatant in time of war.

But the Bush administration has not claimed that either suspect was anywhere near to carrying out his alleged terrorist plan. Neither man, therefore, posed the kind of imminent threat that would justify the use of lethal force under law-enforcement rules. Given this fact, it would have been deeply disturbing if they were shot as enemy soldiers. Of course, the White House has not proposed killing them; instead, it plans to detain the two men indefinitely. But if Padilla and al-Marri should not be considered enemy combatants for the purpose of killing them, they should not be considered enemy combatants for the purpose of detaining them, either.

A similar classification problem, although with a possibly different result, arose in the case of Qaed Salim Sinan al-Harethi. Al-Harethi, who Washington alleges was a senior al Qaeda official, was killed by a drone-fired missile in November 2002 while driving in a remote tribal area of Yemen. Five of his companions, including a U.S. citizen, also died in the attack, which was carried out by the CIA. The Bush administration apparently considered al-Harethi to be an enemy combatant for his alleged involvement in the October 2000 U.S.S. Cole bombing. In this instance, the case for applying war rules was stronger than with Padilla or al-Marri (although the Bush administration never bothered to spell it out). Al-Harethi's mere participation in the 2000 attack on the Cole would not have made him a combatant in 2002, since he could have subsequently withdrawn from al Qaeda; war rules permit attacking only current combatants, not past ones. And if al-Harethi were a civilian, he could not have legally been attacked unless he was actively engaged in hostilities at the time. But the administration alleged that al-Harethi was a "top bin Laden operative in Yemen," implying that he was in the process of preparing future attacks. If true, this would have made the use of war rules against him more appropriate. And unlike in the cases of Padilla and al-Marri, arresting al-Harethi may not have been an option. The Yemeni government has little control over the tribal area where he was killed; indeed, 18 Yemeni soldiers had reportedly died in an earlier attempt to arrest him.

Although there may have been a reasonable case for applying war rules to al-Harethi, the Bush administration has applied these rules with far less justification in other episodes outside the United States. For example, in October 2001, Washington sought the surrender of six Algerian men in Bosnia. At first, the U.S. government followed law-enforcement rules and secured the men's arrest. But then, after a three-month investigation, Bosnia's Supreme Court ordered the suspects released for lack of evidence. Instead of providing additional evidence, however, Washington simply switched to war rules. It pressured the Bosnian government to hand the men over anyway and whisked them out of the country—not to trial, but to indefinite detention at the U.S. naval base at Guantánamo Bay.

The administration followed a similar pattern in June 2003, when five al Qaeda suspects were detained in Malawi. Malawi's high court ordered local authorities to follow the law and either charge or release the five men, all of whom were foreigners. Ignoring local law, the Bush administration then insisted that the men be handed over to U.S. security forces instead. The five were spirited out of the country to an undisclosed location—not for trial, but for interrogation. The move sparked riots in Malawi. The men were released a month later in Sudan, after questioning by Americans failed to turn up any incriminating evidence.

A Bad Example

These cases are not anomalies. In the last two and a half years, the U.S. government has taken custody of a series of al Qaeda suspects in countries such as Indonesia, Pakistan, and Thailand. In many of these cases, the suspects were not captured on a traditional battlefield. Yet instead of allowing the men to be charged with a crime under local law-enforcement rules, Washington had them treated as combatants and delivered to a U.S. detention facility.

There is something troubling about such a policy. Put simply, using war rules when law-enforcement rules could reasonably be followed is dangerous. Errors, common enough in ordinary criminal investigations, are all the more likely when a government relies on the kind of murky intelligence that drives many terrorist investigations. If law-enforcement rules are used, a mistaken arrest can be rectified at trial. But if war rules apply, the government is never obliged to prove a suspect's guilt. Instead, a supposed terrorist can be held for however long it takes to win the "war" against terrorism. And the consequences of error are even graver if the supposed combatant is killed, as was al-Harethi. Such mistakes are an inevitable hazard of the battlefield, where quick life-and-death decisions must be made. But when there is no such urgency, prudence and humanity dictate applying law-enforcement standards.

Washington must also remember that its conduct sets an example for governments around the world. After all, many other states would be all too eager to find an excuse to eliminate their enemies through war rules. Israel, to name one, has used this rationale to justify its assassination of terrorist suspects in Gaza and the West Bank. It is not hard to imagine Russia doing the same to Chechen leaders in Europe, Turkey using a similar pretext against Kurds in Iraq, China against Uighurs in Central Asia, or Egypt against Islamists at home.

Moreover, the Bush administration should recognize that international human rights law is not indifferent to the needs of a government facing a security crisis. Criminal trials risk disclosure of sensitive information, as the administration has discovered in prosecuting Zacarias Moussaoui. But under a concept known as "derogation," governments are permitted to suspend certain rights temporarily when they can show that it is necessary to meet a "public emergency threatening the life of the nation." The International Covenant on Civil and Political Rights, which the United States has ratified, requires governments seeking derogation to file a declaration justifying the move with the UN secretary-general. Among the many governments to have done so are Algeria, Argentina, Chile, Colombia, Peru, Poland, Russia, Sri Lanka, and the United Kingdom. Yet the United States, determined to avoid the formal scrutiny involved, has not bothered.

The Justice Department has defended the administration's use of war rules by citing a U.S. Supreme Court decision from World War II, Ex Parte Quirin. In that case, the Court ruled that German army saboteurs who landed in the United States could be tried as enemy combatants before military commissions. The Court distinguished its ruling from an earlier Civil War-era case, Ex Parte Milligan, which held that a civilian resident of Indiana could not be tried in military court because local civil courts remained open and operational. Noting that the German saboteurs had entered the United States wearing at least parts of their uniforms, the Court in Quirin held that the Milligan protections applied only to people who are not members of an enemy's armed forces.

There are several reasons, however, why Quirin does not justify the Bush administration's broad use of war rules. First, the saboteurs in Quirin were agents of a government—Germany's—with which the United States was obviously at war. Whether the United States is actually at "war" with al Qaeda, however, remains uncertain under the law. Second, although the Court in Quirin defined a combatant as anyone operating with hostile intent behind military lines, the case has arguably been superseded by the 1949 Geneva Conventions (ratified by the United States), which, as noted above, rule that people are combatants only if they either are members of an enemy's armed force or are taking active part in hostilities. Quirin thus does not help determine whether, under current law, people such as Padilla and al-Marri should be considered civilians (who, under Milligan, must be brought before civil courts) or combatants (who can face military treatment). Moreover, Quirin only establishes who can be tried before a military tribunal. The Bush administration, however, has asserted that it has the right to hold Padilla, al-Marri, and other detained "combatants" without a trial of any kind—in effect, precluding serious independent assessment of the grounds for potentially lifelong detention. Finally, whereas the government in Quirin was operating under a specific grant of authority from Congress, the Bush administration has acted on its own in taking the difficult decision to treat Padilla and al-Marri as combatants, without allowing the popular input that a legislative debate would provide.

Stay Safe

The United States should not lightly suspend due process rights, as the Bush administration has done with its "enemy combatants"—particularly when a mistake could result in death or lengthy detention without charge or trial. Law-enforcement rules should presumptively apply to all suspects in the "war" on terror, and the burden should fall on those who want to invoke war rules to demonstrate that they are necessary and appropriate.

The best way to determine if war rules should apply would be through a three-part test. To invoke war rules, Washington should have to prove, first, that an organized group is directing repeated acts of violence against the United States, its citizens, or its interests with sufficient intensity that it can be fairly recognized as an armed conflict; second, that the suspect is an active member of an opposing armed force or is an active participant in the violence; and, third, that law enforcement means are unavailable.

Within the United States, the third requirement would be nearly impossible to satisfy—as it should be. Given the ambiguities of terrorism, we should be guided more by Milligan's affirmation of the rule of law than by Quirin's exception to it. Outside the United States, Washington should never resort to war rules away from a traditional battlefield if local authorities can and are willing to arrest and deliver a suspect to an independent tribunal—regardless of how the tribunal then rules. War rules should be used in such cases only when no law-enforcement system exists (and the other conditions of war are present), not when the rule of law happens to produce inconvenient results. Even if military forces are used to make an arrest in such cases, law-enforcement rules can still apply; only when attempting an arrest is too dangerous should war rules be countenanced.

This approach would recognize that war rules have their place—but that, given the way they inherently compromise fundamental rights, they should be used sparingly. Away from a traditional battlefield, they should be used, even against a warlike enemy, as a tool of last resort—when there is no reasonable alternative, not when a functioning criminal justice system is available. Until there are better guidelines on when to apply war and law-enforcement rules, this three-part test, drawn from the policy consequences of the decision, offers the best way to balance security and civil rights. In the meantime, the Bush administration should abandon its excessive use of war rules. In attempting to make Americans safer, it has made all Americans, and everyone else, less free.

*Kenneth Roth, the executive director of Human Rights Watch, is one of the world's leading independent organizations dedicated to defending and protecting human rights.

Kenneth Roth, "The Law of War in the War on Terror," December 22, 2003, http://www.hrw.org/news/2003/12/22/law-war-war-terror.

Used by Permission.

Counterinsurgency, Rule of Law Operations, and International Law

by David P. Fidler*

In the second week of September 2007, leading U.S. military and diplomatic officials provided long-awaited reports to Congress and the President on U.S. political and military activities in Iraq. These hearings focused attention on how much progress U.S. counterinsurgency (COIN) efforts have made in Iraq. Although debate surrounding these events centered on the question of the withdrawal of U.S. troops, the testimony and hearings connect the ongoing attempts by the U.S. government to adjust to the challenges presented by waging COIN campaigns. In the wake of perceived failings of the United States in fighting insurgencies in Afghanistan and Iraq, leaders in the U.S. military have led efforts to develop doctrine and guidance for future COIN operations, including a new COIN field manual for the U.S. Army and Marines[1] and a "rule of law handbook" for military lawyers.[2] Interestingly, this new doctrine and guidance frequently emphasize the importance of international law to waging effective COIN campaigns and undertaking rule of law activities in COIN and post-conflict contexts. This Insight considers how these new strategies involve international law.

DEVELOPMENT OF DOCTRINE FOR COUNTERINSURGENCY OPERATIONS

Basic Features of the New COIN Doctrine

The difficulties the United States has experienced fighting insurgencies in Afghanistan and Iraq stimulated a renaissance of interest in COIN theory, policy, and practice. Experts agreed that, after Vietnam, U.S. political and military thinking marginalized or ignored COIN capabilities, leaving civilian agencies and military forces badly unprepared for the insurgencies they faced after U.S. interventions into Afghanistan and Iraq.[3] This painful realization provided the impetus for the development by the U.S. Army and Marine Corps of new joint doctrine for COIN, which was finalized in December 2006 in the form of the Counterinsurgency Field Manual. The U.S. military's new COIN doctrine has been called "paradigm shattering"[4] and has received an enormous amount of attention from experts, politicians, the media, potentially affected groups, and the general public.

The complexity of the new COIN doctrine challenges any attempt to summarize it, but identifying a few themes provides a glimpse at what the doctrine seeks to achieve. Insurgents and counterinsurgents compete for legitimacy and power, with the objective in that struggle being "the acceptance by the people of the state or region of the legitimacy of one side's claim to political power."[5] The new doctrine stresses that COIN forces cannot prevail in this competition through military means alone. COIN is predominantly a political not a military challenge that requires unity of purpose and effort from both civilian and military assets and the application of all elements of national power.

COIN forces must also apply their political, economic, diplomatic, military, and legal capabilities in a manner that comprehensively understands the society and culture in which COIN activities take place.[6] Winning the hearts and minds of the target population requires counterinsurgents to engage in a synchronized manner in a number of actions, including combat operations, civil security measures, training host-nation security forces, providing essential services, engaging in economic development, building governance structures, and conducting information operations.[7] These actions are also interdependent, meaning that COIN campaigns cannot ignore some to concentrate resources on a select few.[8] The doctrine describes the end state of successful COIN operations as the creation of a legitimate host-nation government capable of providing sustainable security, governance, and economic opportunities within the framework of the rule of law.[9]

International Law and the New COIN Doctrine

Unlike controversies about the relevance of international law in the global war on terror, the new COIN doctrine incorporates international law as an important tool for COIN forces to understand and utilize. In terms of international law, three themes emerge from the doctrine.

First, the doctrine makes international law immediately relevant by stressing the COIN objectives of legitimacy and the rule of law. The doctrine acknowledges that COIN actions will be measured against applicable rules and standards found in international law, even when insurgents show no respect for any legal rules.[10] In this sense, dismissing or marginalizing international law proves harmful to COIN efforts to compete for legitimacy and power and to convince the target population that the rule of law informs not only the ultimate objective but the way in which legitimate government will be created.[11]

Second, the doctrine focuses on international law as an important component of specific COIN operations. For example, the doctrine argues that COIN detention and interrogation activities must comply with international legal obligations, such as those found in Common Article 3 of the Geneva Conventions.[12] The doctrine takes the same approach to training host-nation security forces, emphasizing that such training must seek to equip host-nation military and police forces with the ability to provide security in compliance with relevant norms of international law.[13]

Third, international law becomes important as a potentially mediating source of rules in situations where U.S. understandings of good governance and the rule of law create tensions with cultural assumptions and political traditions of the host nation. The doctrine recognizes the need for COIN forces to work within the existing cultural and societal context of the host nation, but it also argues that local practices should not prevail when they damage the COIN effort. For example, the chapter on developing host-nation security forces states: "U.S. forces must make clear that they do not intend to undermine or change the local religion or traditions. However, Soldiers and Marines have a mission to reduce the effects of dysfunctional social practices that affect the ability to conduct effective security operations."[14]

International legal rules and standards, particularly those found in treaties and other instruments adopted by the host nation, provide one way to change host nation behavior without imposing, or being perceived to impose, the "American way" on the host nation. Seeing international law as communicating "international best governance practices" also resonates with multinational and non-governmental organizations that often play significant roles in COIN campaigns and the cooperation of which is important in establishing legitimacy.

In sum, the new COIN doctrine incorporates international law as a strategically and tactically important instrument for counterinsurgents in their struggle with insurgency movements for legitimacy and power. This approach contrasts with the often polarized and polemical debate over the role of international law in the global war on terror.

Practical Guidance for Military Lawyers Conducting Rule of Law Operations

The emphasis in COIN efforts on producing legitimate governments that can provide security and economic opportunity under the rule of law has directly affected military and civilian lawyers operating in the COIN contexts of Afghanistan and Iraq. Lessons learned from such lawyers revealed a need to provide more guidance for undertaking complex rule of law operations. Reflecting on the expanding nature of rule of law tasks for military lawyers, the Center for Law and Military Operations at the Judge Advocate General's Legal Center and School and the Joint Force Judge Advocate at U.S. Joint Forces Command collaborated to produce the Rule of Law Handbook: A Practitioner's Guide for Judge Advocates, which was finalized in July 2007.[15]

Unlike the Field Manual, the Handbook does not contain doctrine for rule of law operations but instead seeks to provide pragmatic guidance for Judge Advocates practicing law during military operations in COIN or post-conflict environments.[16] The Handbook is not specific to COIN, but the rule of law challenges found in the COIN contexts of Afghanistan and Iraq produced this new guidance for military lawyers. Predictions that the United States will continue to face COIN challenges in the next decade and beyond make the Handbook particularly relevant for the implementation of the new COIN doctrine.

Unlike the Field Manual, the Handbook grapples with the meaning of the "rule of law" concept and provides a working definition of the rule of law for deployed Judge Advocates.[17] The Handbook classifies rule of law operations as part of stability operations undertaken by civilian agencies and military forces in COIN and post-conflict situations. The practical guidance provided to deployed Judge Advocates for conducting rule of law operations pays significant attention to U.S. law, host nation law, and international law.

In terms of international law, the Handbook argues that, above all, the reader should take away one central lesson from its contents: "joint, inter-agency and multinational coordination is the basic foundation upon which all rule of law efforts must be built."[18] Put another way, "coordination and synchronization is to the rule of law what fires and maneuver is to the high intensity conflict."[19] The emphasis on multinational coordination and synchronization brings international law into the spotlight of rule of law operations because international law will be critical to how such multinational collaboration will unfold in terms of both process and substance. The Handbook discusses, for example, problems that can arise in rule of law operations when coalition partners share different international legal obligations or diverse interpretations of shared duties.[20]

The Handbook further recognizes the importance of international law in rule of law operations by dedicating an entire chapter to the international legal framework for rule of law operations.[21] The Handbook observes that "deployed Judge Advocates working on rule of law operations need to be mindful of the universe of international legal rules applicable to rule of law operations, and especially how those rules vary from those applicable to more traditional military operations."[22] In terms of the framework for the rule of law, treaty law and customary international law on armed conflict, occupation, and human rights receive particular emphasis.[23]

Like the Field Manual, the Handbook adopts a pragmatic approach to the use of international law. For example, in terms of international human rights law, the Handbook asserts that, "[e]ven if one were to ignore legal obligations, in post-conflict settings, rule of law operations should be guided and informed by human rights law purely as a matter of efficacy."[24] Echoing the new COIN doctrine, the Handbook argues that "detention procedures adopted by US forces during the post-conflict phase may serve as a model for the administrative detention procedures that the host nation adopts for domestic use, and should consequently comply with international human rights norms."[25] The Handbook further parallels the new COIN doctrine in asserting that, "in light of the need to establish legitimacy of the rule of law among the host nation's populace, conduct by US forces that would be questionable under any mainstream interpretation of international human rights law is unlikely to have a place in rule of law operations."[26]

In short, just as international law is a critical resource under the new COIN doctrine, the Handbook makes clear the significance of international law to the process and substance of rule of law operations undertaken by civilian and military lawyers in COIN and post-conflict environments.

Conclusion

Experts predict that waging COIN campaigns and engaging in rule of law operations will be important challenges for the United States and other countries in the next phase of 21st century international politics. The Field Manual and the Handbook do not pretend that international law provides an easy solution to defeating ruthless insurgencies and crafting the rule of law in COIN and post-conflict situations. These documents avoid the drama surrounding international law's place in the global war on terror and focus on pragmatic and principled strategies for defeating insurgency violence and building sustainable, rule-of-law governance in countries traumatized by war. The COIN doctrine and the guidance for rule of law operations seem uninterested in the question whether international law is relevant and are more concerned with developing capabilities, in the United States and abroad, for implementing policies and practices comprehensively informed by international law.

Notes

1. U.S. Army and Marine Corps, *Counterinsurgency Field Manual* (U.S. Army Field Manual No. 3-24; Marine Corps Warfighting Publication No. 3-33.5) (Chicago: University of Chicago Press, 2007) [hereinafter *Counterinsurgency Field Manual*].

2. *Rule of Law Handbook: A Practitioner's Guide for Judge Advocates* (V. Tasikas, T. B. Nachbar, and C. R. Oleszycki, eds.) (Charlottesville, VA: Center for Law and Military Operations, 2007) [hereinafter *Rule of Law Handbook*].

3. John A. Nagl, "Foreword to the University of Chicago Press Edition: The Evolution and Importance of Army/Marine Corps Field Manual 3–24, *Counterinsurgency*," *in Counterinsurgency Field Manual, supra* note 1, at xiii (arguing that "the sad fact is that when an insurgency began in Iraq in the late summer of 2003, the Army was unprepared to fight it. . . . It was . . . unprepared for an enemy who understood that it could not hope to defeat the U.S. Army on a conventional battlefield, and who therefore chose to wage war against America from the shadows.").

4. Sarah Sewall, "Introduction to the University of Chicago Press Edition: A Radical Field Manual," in *Counterinsurgency Field Manual, supra* note 1, at xxxv.

5. Counterinsurgency Field Manual, supra note 1, at 137.

6. Id. at 27 ("Cultural knowledge is essential to waging a successful counterinsurgency.") and 40–41 (stating that "[s]uccessful conduct of COIN operations depends on thoroughly understanding the society and culture within which they are being conducted.").

7. Id. at 154–173 (describing the logical lines of operations in COIN).

8. Id. at 157.

9. Id. at 37–39 (discussing primary COIN objective of fostering development of effective governance by a legitimate government that can provide security, acceptable governance, and economic development within the rule of law).

10. Id. at 52 (observing that insurgents "are constrained by neither the law of war nor the bounds of human decency as Western nations understand them.").

11. For an extended discussion of legal issues in COIN, see id. at 347–361 (Appendix D. Legal Considerations).

12. Id. at 251, 352.

13. Id. at 214.

14. Id. at 219.

15. *Rule of Law Handbook, supra* note 2.

16. Id. at ii–iii (discussing what the *Rule of Handbook* is and is not).

17. Id. at 6.

18. Id. at ii.

19. Id.

20. Id. at 47–50.

21. Id. at 57–67 (Chapter IV).

22. Id. at 57.

23. Id. at 61–67.

24. Id. at 66.

25. Id.

26. Id. at 67.

*David P. Fidler is the James Louis Calamaras Professor of Law at Indiana University School of Law, Bloomington, and is the director of the Indiana University Center on American and Global Security.

David P. Fidler, "Counterinsurgency, Rule of Law Operations, and International Law," *ASIL Insights* 11, no. 24 (September 19, 2007), available at http://www.asil.org/insights070919.cfm.

Used by Permission.

Part 3:
International Humanitarian Law and Civilian Protection

The previous section explored arguments that changes due to globalization and technological advancement, the greater prevalence of global terrorism and asymmetric tactics, and to the decline in conventional state-on-state wars, are producing an era of "new warfare," meriting new or dramatically revised rules for armed conflict. The authors in this section consider some of the same questions but from the viewpoint of ground commanders and soldiers trying to apply international humanitarian law (IHL) in the often muddled world of today's contemporary conflicts. In particular, the authors focus on the application of one of the most critical areas of IHL: protection of civilians. Do modern dynamics of conflict place civilians at a greater risk than was the case in the past? Have changes in the way war is fought made complying with civilian protection principles virtually impossible in practice? The authors in this part consider these questions in light of two of the biggest factors affecting the protection of civilians in contemporary conflicts: irregular warfare and technological advancement.

CIVILIAN PROTECTION UNDER INTERNATIONAL HUMANITARIAN LAW

Efforts to uphold basic tenets of "humanity" and minimize unnecessary suffering have long been a part of modern IHL. But it was the devastation wrought by World War II that led to some of the strongest protections for noncombatants in warfare. Civilian casualties, mass displacement, forced labor, and property destruction were widespread. Millions were killed in concentration camps. Entire cities were destroyed by the new advances in air power and nuclear power. Conditions for prisoners of war were abysmal.

The four 1949 Geneva Conventions negotiated in the wake of the war put the protection of civilians and others not taking part in hostilities (sick, wounded, shipwrecked, or captured combatants) at the core of modern IHL. State parties negotiated two Additional Protocols to the Geneva Conventions in 1977 ("API" and "APII") to better articulate and codify the key requirements and prohibitions related to international conflicts (those between two or more states) and noninternational conflicts (those between a state[s] and a nonstate group[s]), respectively. API provided some of the most explicit standards of civilian protection in IHL. These apply both to civilian persons and to civilian "objects," or property, ranging from industrial factories to farmlands to mosques to individual homes and possessions inside of them.[1]

Though civilian protection is central to IHL, not all civilian casualties are unlawful. IHL accepts that "collateral damage" may result from a lawful attack. However, IHL attempts to minimize the harm to civilians by creating principles that force warring parties to take into account the human cost of war, and by prohibiting certain tactics or types of attack that have been most likely to result in unnecessary suffering or harm. The most commonly cited principles guiding warring parties' activities in this regard are: distinction, prohibition on indiscriminate attacks, proportionality, and feasible precautions.

The bedrock protection for civilians lies in the principle of *distinction*. Warring parties are required to distinguish between civilian and military targets and make all efforts to spare civilian persons and objects, such as homes, businesses, or schools.[2] Only military persons or objects may be deliberately targeted. Many of the other principles related to civilian protection, including the following three, flow from this principle.

Warring parties are prohibited from conducting *indiscriminate* attacks, which are methods or means of attack that are incapable of distinguishing between civilians and military targets. For example, many types of landmines or unexploded ordnance—which can be anything from a roadside bomb in Afghanistan[3] to unexploded cluster munitions in Lebanon[4]—are considered "indiscriminate" because they harm whoever happens upon them, civilian or combatant, without distinction.[5]

The rule of *proportionality* is a balancing test that requires warring parties to weigh the likely risk to civilians against the military benefits of an attack. Attacks in which the expected civilian harm outweighs the anticipated military advantage are *disproportionate* and unlawful. For example, a suicide attack on an Iraqi military recruiting station in 2007 killed 59 people and injured more than 100.[6] Though a few soldiers were reported killed and the station itself may have been a valid military target, the vast majority of those casualties were civilians standing outside—a seemingly disproportionate level of collateral damage to the military advantage gained.

In both offensive and defensive operations, warring parties must take all *feasible precautions* for the protection of noncombatants. Complying with this rule could mean planning an aerial attack at a time when civilians are known to be absent. Another way to satisfy the obligation would be to warn the civilian population of an oncoming attack and advise them of measures to ensure their safety. For example, in 2006, during the conflict between Israel and Hezbollah, the Israeli Defense Forces warned Lebanese civilians prior to some attacks. In addition to traditional broadcast methods, such as dropped leaflets and radio broadcasts, the Defense Forces disseminated the message through Web sites, and text messages and phone calls to cell phones.[7]

Although some principles of IHL may be binding only for parties to the treaty containing them, the principles of distinction, prohibition on indiscriminate attacks, proportionality, and feasible precautions are generally accepted as limitations on all warring party actions in warfare. They have become what is known as "customary international law"[8] for both international and noninternational conflicts,[9] and are binding on all state parties and on nonstate actors.[10]

CIVILIAN PROTECTION AND NEW WARFARE

Principles like distinction and proportionality are among the most widely accepted principles in IHL, but it has been challenging to apply them in twenty-first-century conflict because of the tactics common to irregular warfare. Distinguishing between civilians and combatants is much easier if the civilians are geographically separate from the battlefield locations; in today's warfare they are not. Weaker nonstate armed groups hide among urban or semi-urban populations—towns, villages, and cities—as a means of defense. The battlefield has been moved right into the heart of the civilian population, making IHL more difficult to apply and conflict more dangerous for civilians.

Another key difficulty in applying the principle of distinction is that nonstate combatants rarely wear distinctive signs or uniforms or carry arms openly, thus blending into the local population. Some insurgent or terrorist fighters have deliberately donned civilian dress to give them an advantage in attacking (actions that would violate IHL provisions against "perfidy")[11] or deliberately used civilians as "human shields" to defend themselves, also a war crime.[12]

The first excerpt from an article by Laurie Blank and Amos Guiora, "Teaching an Old Dog New Tricks: Operationalizing the Law of Armed Conflict in New Warfare," argues that the difficulty of applying principles such as distinction to modern conflict situations suggests that we are in an era of "new warfare," and that IHL must keep pace. Blank and Guiora suggest that the solution to better IHL compliance and protection of civilians in modern warfare lies in making the rules more practical for commanders on the ground. In particular, they argue, IHL theorists should work to operationalize and clarify ambiguous concepts like distinction and proportionality in ways that resonate with the asymmetric tactics of contemporary conflicts. Binary distinctions like combatant and noncombatant do not give commanders clear enough guidance in the murky situations of today's conflict, in which an individual may act as a fighter one day and a civilian the next, or offer varying degrees of support. The authors call for a more nuanced classification system that allows varying degrees of targeting (distinguishing those who could be killed from those who could only be detained) depending on individual levels of direct or indirect support, and on a continuous or part-time basis.

In "Fighting the Laws of War: Protecting Civilians in Asymmetric Conflict," a book review of two recent books challenging the validity and adequacy of IHL, Charli Carpenter agrees that additional clarification of IHL may be necessary to help warring parties distinguish legitimate targets from civilians, but pushes against any weakening of civilian protection provisions. In one of the two books Carpenter reviews, *Moral Dilemmas of Modern War*, political ethicist Michael Gross argues that IHL prohibitions against civilian harm unfairly handicap state parties in irregular warfare against insurgents, often because of the same distinction issues that Blank and Guiora raise. IHL restricts targeting of those who give indirect support to warring parties, and is ambiguous, at best, about when those who do not continuously participate may be targeted. Gross argues that this puts states in the position of bending or breaking IHL if they want to win against insurgents who directly manipulate such rules. Carpenter counters that Gross overstates the case. While insurgent tactics may force state militaries to take on more risk than would be involved in dropping precision bombs on well-marked and separated military targets, that does not mean that IHL is inadequate or unfair, she argues. "[T]his sacrifice is precisely what the logic of just war requires: that civilians not become more expendable than a country's armed forces."[13] She suggests instead that IHL provisions aimed at protecting civilians be strengthened, including clarifying when an individual may be targeted, and reviewing what military necessity means in modern warfare.

TECHNOLOGY, CIVILIAN PROTECTION, AND "UNINTENDED" HARM

The Carpenter review equally addresses a second important factor in the protection of civilians in contemporary conflict: the role of technology. Advanced weaponry has in some ways made it easier for warring parties to avoid civilian casualties. For example, advances in intelligence gathering and communication have enabled new ways of taking feasible precautions to avoid civilian harm. As weapons systems—for example, precision-guided munitions—have become more accurate, they may allow warring parties to distinguish between civilians and combatants with greater accuracy and potentially limit collateral damage.

However, not all take such a sanguine view of the role of technology and the progress of advanced militaries in limiting the costs of war, as illustrated by the second book reviewed by Carpenter, *Inventing Collateral Damage* by Stephen Rockel and Rick Halpern. Rockel and Halpern argue that far from making war safer, technological developments like precision weapons have put civilians at greater risk: the illusion of precision lulls warring parties (and their populaces) into thinking that war is costless, and they take less care to limit civilian harm.[14]

In addition to concerns that technology has created a false sense of costless war, Rockel and Halpern argue that IHL itself has helped rationalize and obscure the costs of war. As Carpenter paraphrases their arguments: "The notion that civilian deaths are permissible if unintended, the authors argue, has allowed militaries to whitewash the destructiveness of their operations. In other words, the existing laws of war, which prohibit intentional civilian targeting but permit 'accidental' civilian deaths, are part of the problem."[15]

While Rockel and Halpern critique state parties for not doing enough, but military analyst Max Boot argues, in "Sparing Civilians, Buildings and Even the Enemy," that the standards for advanced militaries have gotten too high. IHL judges warring parties in part on their ability to anticipate and prevent civilian harm not just on whether they actually succeed (after all, "unintended" harm may be lawful in many cases). Thus, those warring parties who are more capable of predicting and avoiding harm due to assets like precision technology or more advanced intelligence and surveillance systems may be judged more harshly when civilian casualties result. Boot contends that the U.S. military has become so good at accurate targeting that it is now held to unfairly high standards: to an expectation of no civilian collateral damage.[16] Describing mistakes that have occurred during recent conflicts—such as the NATO bombing of the Chinese embassy in Belgrade or a U.S. bombing of a wedding party in Afghanistan—Boot noted, "Such accidents once would have been unremarkable; today they are a scandal, because 100 percent accuracy is assumed to be the norm."[17]

Carpenter's defense of IHL takes issue with both Boot and Rockel and Halpern's positions. She suggests that states can and should do more to reduce civilian deaths, and could start by working within the IHL framework to reconsider the discriminate or indiscriminate nature of some new weapons of war and to introduce stronger measures of redress and amends when civilians have been unintentionally harmed. However, she disagrees with Rockel and Halpern's larger point that IHL has blinded us to the costs of war and sanitized civilian deaths.

However extensive the collateral damage in Afghanistan, for example, there is a world of difference between accidentally hitting civilians in Kandahar with not-so-smart bombs and firebombing Dresden to break the population's morale. The distinction between accidental and intentional killing—and the firm rule that military necessity does not excuse the intentional targeting of civilians—has saved countless civilian lives in the past half century.[18]

Though each of the authors in this section offer potential approaches or amendments to IHL that they argue would result in better civilian protection, or a more just framework for regulating war, in the end, protection of civilians will always be controversial. The harsh reality of war is that innocent civilian deaths are inevitable. No matter what rules IHL imposes, the death of innocents will never seem fair or be easily justifiable, and for good reason.

As you read these selections, consider some of these perspectives:
• Some authors have suggested that rules like distinction and proportionality are so mismatched to modern asymmetric conflicts that warring parties should not be bound by them until they are amended and updated. Do you think states should be able to default from the rules when they no longer fit modern situations? Should states have to abide by the same rules when facing insurgent or terrorist groups who not only do not?
• In response to the argument that IHL is unfairly tying the hands of state militaries like that of the United States against insurgent groups, Carpenter responds that the solution is not to relax IHL rules but for state militaries to work harder on developing different tactics and approaches to counter insurgent tactics. She admits that some of these countertactics may be more risky for troops, but that troop lives should not be privileged over civilian lives. How would you argue for or against this position? Carpenter also argues that IHL has always anticipated that saving civilian lives may be more costly to troops. Do you agree with this position? Is there anything in the nature of modern warfare that might change this calculus?
• Both the Rockel and Halpern book discussed in Carpenter's piece and the Jochnick and Normand article from Part 1 argued that the laws of war may be doing more harm than good by rationalizing killing and blinding the international community to the costs of war. Do you agree or disagree?

- Do you agree with Max Boot that critiques of advanced militaries are unfair? International monitors, states, and nongovernmental organizations regularly criticize nonstate armed groups for violating IHL protections of civilians, often in harsher terms. Is there a higher standard for states with higher technology and capacity to avoid civilian harm than for the low-tech suicide bomber, or is this just the way debates are reflected in the media? Should there be?

NOTES

1. Protocol Additional to the Geneva Conventions of August 12, 1949, and Relating to the Protection of Victims of International Armed Conflicts (Protocol I), June 8, 1977, 1125 U.N.T.S. 3 [hereinafter Additional Protocol I], at art. 52.

2. Additional Protocol I, art. 52(1).

3. Human Rights Watch, "The Human Cost: Civilian Accounts," April 15, 2007, http://www.hrw.org/en/node/10984/section/5.

4. See, for example, Human Rights Watch, "Israeli Cluster Munitions Hit Civilians in Lebanon Israel Must Not Use Indiscriminate Weapons," Press Release, July 24, 2006, http://www.hrw.org/en/news/2006/07/24/israeli-cluster-munitions-hit-civilians-lebanon.

5. Certain types of mines might not be per se "indiscriminate" if they were capable of being used in ways that only targeted combatants—for example, a mine detonated by a control device. These weapons might still be used indiscriminately however.

6. Hugh Sykes, "Suicide Attack Kills Iraqi Army Recruits in Baghdad," BBC News, August 17, 2010.

7. Peter Feuilherade, "Israel Steps Up 'Psy-Ops' in Lebanon," BBC Monitoring, July 26, 2006, http://news.bbc.co.uk/2/hi/5217484.stm.

8. A general principle of international law is that the provisions of a treaty are binding only on those states that are party to them. Exceptions to this are principles or rules that have risen to the level of "customary international law," which are binding on all states unless they have been a persistent objector to that principle. Although a full discussion of these issues is beyond the scope of the book, a study of the provisions of customary international law by the International Committee of the Red Cross (ICRC) is a helpful starting point for exploring customary IHL rules. Jean-Marie Henckaerts and Louise Doswald-Beck, eds., Customary International Humanitarian Law (New York: ICRC and Cambridge University Press, 2005) (hereinafter, ICRC Study on Customary IHL).

9. A rule may rise to the level of being customary international law for either international or noninternational conflicts, or both. The ICRC study of customary IHL noted earlier denotes which customary rules apply for international and noninternational conflicts separately.

10. Generally, nonstate armed groups may also be subject to IHL norms that have risen to the level of customary international law, although there is some disagreement about whether all provisions of customary international law might be equally binding on state and nonstate warring parties. See, for example, International Criminal Tribunal for the former Yugoslavia, Prosecutor v. Haradinaj, Case no. IT-04-84-84-T, Judgment (Trial Chamber), April 3, 2008,

¶60; *Prosecutor v. Sam Hinga Norman*, Case No. SCSL-2004-14-AR72(E), Decision on Preliminary Motion Based on Lack of Jurisdiction (Child Recruitment), May 31, 2004, ¶22. For a discussion of which rules apply to nonstate actors see Annyssa Bellal, Gilles Giacca, and Stuart Casey-Maslen, "International Law and Armed Non-state Actors in Afghanistan," *International Review of the Red Cross* 93, no. 881 (March 2011): 62.

11. When a warring party deceptively takes advantage of the protections of IHL in order to trick the opposing party and gain an advantage, this is called "perfidy," and it is one of the longest standing prohibitions under IHL. Examples of this would include feigning civilian disguise (to prevent being attacked by the targeted party), feigning surrender, or feigning any other "protected status" under IHL that would prevent the opposing party from attacking. See, for example, Additional Protocol I, art. 37(1); ICRC Study on Customary IHL, "Rule 65."

12. The prohibition on taking human shields is a long-standing provision of IHL, and prohibits warring parties from deliberately intermingling military persons or objects within civilian ones in order to avoid being targeted. See, for example, art. 28; Additional Protocol I, art. 51(7), ICRC Study on Customary IHL, "Rule 97."

13. Charli Carpenter, "Fighting the Laws of War: Protecting Civilians in Asymmetric Conflict," *Foreign Affairs* (March/April 2011), http://www.foreignaffairs.com/print/67448/.

14. A concrete example of this was documented in a 2003 report by Human Rights Watch exploring the use of cluster munitions by international forces in Iraq. Technical improvements that made cluster munitions less likely to result in duds—unexploded munitions that can act like mini-mines and indiscriminately harm civilians who come upon them—led British forces to be less careful about where they used them, according to the report. As noted in the report: "Ironically the promise of a lower dud rate may have made the British less careful about where they used the L20A1. 'There was less of a reluctance to use them because of the increased reliability,' Colonel Baldwin said." Bonnie Docherty, "Off Target: The Conduct of the War and Civilian Casualties in Iraq," *Human Rights Watch* (2003): 112–13.

15. Carpenter, "Fighting the Laws of War."

16. Max Boot, "Sparing Civilians, Buildings and Even the Enemy," *New York Times*, March 30, 2003, http://www.nytimes.com/2003/03/30/weekinreview/the-nation-sparing-civilians-buildings-and-even-the-enemy.html.

17. Ibid.

18. Carpenter, "Fighting the Laws of War."

Teaching an Old Dog New Tricks: Operationalizing the Law of Armed Conflict in New Warfare

*by Laurie Blank and Amos Guiora**

Gone are the days of soldiers facing each other across large battlefields, tanks shelling tanks, and fighter jets engaging in dogfights. War, or armed conflict, to use a more precise legal term, now takes place *everywhere*—in cities, refugee camps and other historically non-military areas—and involves or affects nearly everyone in the area. These changes have a powerful impact on the conduct of hostilities. The law of armed conflict ("LOAC"), also known as the laws of war or international humanitarian law ("IHL"),[1] was developed and codified in times of more traditional state-state conflicts. It must now adapt to these new and more complicated conflicts, which we call new warfare. More important, re-categorizing or re-defining the ever-expanding variety of individuals who participate in and are affected by hostilities in new warfare is a critical next step. These multiple categories of participants pose great challenges to the implementation of LOAC on the ground.

The law of armed conflict governs the conduct of both states and individuals during armed conflict and seeks to minimize suffering in war by protecting persons not participating in hostilities and by restricting the means and methods of warfare.[2] New warfare poses extraordinary dilemmas for the application of two key humanitarian law principles: the principle of distinction and the principle of proportionality. The principle of distinction requires soldiers to differentiate between people they can target and people they are obligated to protect from harm. The principle of proportionality requires soldiers to not attack a target if the expected innocent casualties are excessive in relation to the anticipated military advantage gained. Applying these two principles in new warfare brings us to the fundamental question: who can be lawfully targeted, when, and how often?[3]

The essence of new warfare is that states are engaged with non-state actors.[4] In traditional conflicts between states, which pit soldier against soldier, the categories were clear; in what we define as "new warfare", the categories are, at best, blurred. Simply put: the clear-cut traditional military paradigm is largely a relic of the past. As we write these lines, the following is a sample of contemporary conflicts demanding this issue be addressed candidly, if not resolved:

- United States, British, and other NATO soldiers are engaged with the Taliban and other insurgent groups in Afghanistan;
- United States Predator drones are regularly attacking Taliban and al-Qaeda targets in Pakistan; and
- United States forces are under attack in Iraq outside the major cities.

In each of these three conflicts, military forces face a disturbing lack of clarity[5] regarding *both* the operational mission and the identification of the enemy.

Some argue that LOAC is inapplicable or simply cannot work in new warfare;[6] others contend that, while still relevant, LOAC needs new treaties or protocols to be effective.[7] Indeed, one of us has recently advocated for a re-articulation of international law,[8] while still reinforcing that until principles are replaced or re-articulated, commanders must comply with pre-existing conventions and obligations.[9] However, present application of LOAC does not provide sufficient guidance for commanders facing extraordinarily complex *new* operational dilemmas.

When those who are fighting (insurgents, guerrillas, terrorists or comparable terms) melt into the civilian population and persons who appear to be civilians periodically engage in hostilities, determining who is a legitimate target becomes nearly impossible. Commanders on the ground face a growing tension as they seek simultaneously to fulfill their operational mission and to uphold LOAC, particularly because doing so requires them to apply traditional legal concepts to complex and ever-changing circumstances. At the most basic level, commanders need to train troops under their command to make a critical set of determinations, day after day: (1) who and when can they shoot, (2) who and when can they detain, and (3) who do they have to protect?

To find answers to these questions, commanders need more relevant and specific categories of individuals than the ones LOAC currently uses. For LOAC to have continued merit and effectiveness, those responsible for its "on the ground" application must both respect it and find it relevant. The two are not the same—even if commanders respect the law, they will be hard-pressed to apply it in new warfare if doing so exacerbates their challenges instead of facilitating solutions. To ensure LOAC's continued relevance, we must examine the role of multiple participants in state versus non-state conflict: commanders, innocent civilians, and the many types of legitimate targets.

First, we re-frame the traditional combatant-civilian paradigm to reflect the realities of new warfare and meet the operational realities of commanders on the ground more effectively. Commanders view the zone of combat in terms of friend or foe, innocent civilians or legitimate targets. An *innocent civilian* is a person who takes no part in hostilities[10] and is therefore immune from attack. A *legitimate target* is a person or object that can be lawfully targeted. In new warfare, the range of persons who fall into the latter category is expanding rapidly. This expansion requires two critical adjustments in how we approach "open fire" determinations: greater sensitivity among both policy-makers and commanders to *new* and more carefully defined sub-categories of hostile persons; and development of a more conduct-specific checklist of factors for commanders to determine if an individual can be targeted. We define and analyze each of the following key sub-categories in the body of this article:

- *Legitimate subjects of detention* provide some assistance to those who are fighting but do not participate directly in hostilities. They cannot be targeted.
- *Transitory targets* participate in hostilities one or two times or with no regularity. They can only be targeted when directly participating in hostilities.
- *Recurring targets* follow a pattern of participation in hostilities on a recurring and frequent basis, returning to civilian pursuits in between their hostile acts. They can only be targeted when directly participating in hostilities, unless the frequency and regularity of their participation rises to the level of more continuous participation.
- *Permanent targets* participate in hostilities on a continuous basis. They can be targeted at all times.

We approach this subject from different perspectives but with a similar focus. Our purpose is to operationalize the law of armed conflict to give military commanders the tools to meet twin goals: fulfilling their operational missions while protecting their soldiers and innocent civilians alike. This two-fold objective is extraordinarily complicated; it is also an absolute necessity.

[...]

4. Operationalize

Operationalizing international law requires that LOAC be adapted to the realities of new warfare; otherwise, the commander will be in the "twilight zone", which poses extraordinary dangers to soldiers, innocent civilians, and others alike. From the commander's perspective, operationalizing LOAC requires both new training regimes and different operational guidelines.

In the classic military paradigm, the conflict was easily explained to those who were fighting because the enemy was obvious and the role of civilians as passive victims of war was generally clear.[34] The objective—to defeat a clearly identified enemy—was easily articulated; the means—military hardware—were obvious; and the outcome, from a military perspective, was black and white— one side surrendered. Opposing soldiers openly carrying weapons posed dangers that led to concise and precise "open fire" orders. The rules of engagement ("ROE") in the traditional context were uncontroversial and simple to interpret: soldiers killed soldiers[35] and protected innocent civilians and others *hors de combat*. In that sense, the rules of yesterday's battles were obvious.

In the contemporary and future paradigm, the overwhelming majority of armed conflicts will involve soldiers operationally engaged with non-state actors.[36] The commander is required by law to distinguish between an innocent civilian and an individual who, although dressed in civilian attire, may pose an immediate threat and is therefore a legitimate target. In addition, the commander must assess whether and when to target manifestly hostile persons deliberately hiding among the civilian population. Respect for LOAC is the essence of command; therefore, what we call operationalizing LOAC focuses on providing guidelines for how to distinguish among persons. When neither hostile persons nor members of armed groups wear uniforms or carry their arms openly, commanders face a tension between respect for IHL and protecting the unit—the fundamental challenge in new warfare. In a word, both sets of persons appear to be innocent civilians, but the rules are a source of controversy and uncertainty. Operationalizing LOAC gives commanders the tools to determine when civilians are not innocent, knowledge that is key to protecting soldiers and civilians.

B. The Commander's Perspective

In early 2006, the Multi-National Corps—Iraq ("MNCI") began compiling statistics about the number of escalation of force incidents in Iraq.[37] Escalation of force incidents are primarily situations in which civilians "unwittingly drove too close to convoys or checkpoints and triggered a reaction in gunners who considered them a threat."[38] During the first two months of 2006, MNCI recorded an average of ten escalation of force incidents per day; of those incidents, "about 5 percent resulted in an Iraqi civilian's death [and e]leven percent resulted in an Iraqi injury."[39] Some estimates concluded that over 1000 Iraqi civilians were killed in escalation of force incidents between 2003 and early 2006.[40] The British Army's statistics showed that forty-nine Iraqi civilians died in similar incidents with British forces between May 2003 and March 2004.[41] Preplanned attacks can also result in large numbers of civilian deaths when the lines between legitimate target and innocent civilian are blurred. In Pakistan, where U.S. drones attack al Qaeda and Taliban leaders, rough estimates claim that "more than 600 civilians are likely to have died from the attacks", approximately ten civilians for every militant killed.[42] These statistics illustrate the fundamental question a commander confronts in combat: whether and when an "open fire" order can be given. To meet standard ROE requirements, the commander must be satisfied both that he has identified a legitimate target presenting an immediate threat *and* that opening fire is the only way to neutralize the threat.

The fact that hostile persons are indistinguishable from innocent persons in new warfare requires both new training methods and new understandings of operational dilemmas. Military training for new warfare is extraordinarily complex: militaries train soldiers to shoot (and if necessary, to kill) but at the same time require them to wait an additional second precisely to verify that the individual they face poses an immediate threat and is therefore a legitimate target. In the "zone of combat"—which has replaced the traditional battlefield—an extra second can literally be the difference between life and death. If the soldier waits that extra second and the individual was not an "innocent", then in all probability, the soldier will be killed. Conversely, if the soldier does not wait and, failing to evaluate the threat presented thoroughly, fires at an innocent individual, the resulting death or injury of a person who was not a legitimate target may escalate the never-ending cycle of violence and human tragedy.

[…]

III. FUTURE RECOMMENDATIONS AND ANALYSIS

Our new framework and guidelines for commanders operationalize the law of armed conflict to address the challenges of new warfare. But these guidelines cannot necessarily tackle unforeseen challenges from unknown new types of future conflicts. To do so, LOAC needs to be more agile. Agility means that the law can adapt to changing circumstances and meet the needs of policymakers and commanders on the ground alike. It means that the law must allow room for new ways of thinking that uphold the law's goals and principles precisely when they are under fire. Agility means that when old approaches are not working, the law helps us find the answers.

As new warfare became a prevalent, and now predominant, form of conflict, the law did not adapt appropriately to the complicated scenarios new warfare presented. The international community continued to focus on traditional visions of combatants and civilians, notwithstanding the disconnect between that framework and the reality on the ground in new warfare. Most criticisms of the law argued that the law could no longer apply, when, in fact, such critiques simply did not examine how it could apply in a more agile way.

We focus on maximizing that agility to enable LOAC to meet the demands of new warfare while still preserving the principles and goals that form the law's foundation. The steps we take here are precisely the steps that must be taken in future situations that pose existential challenges to LOAC:

First, we analyze why new warfare creates grave difficulties for LOAC as traditionally applied. LOAC requires that commanders distinguish between those who are fighting and those who are not, but the traditional legal framework offers few clues for how to do so in new warfare. As an example, future conflicts are almost certain to involve significantly greater use of cyber-warfare and technological capabilities we cannot predict. In these situations, delineating between military and civilian objectives may prove to be almost impossible without new understandings of these legal terms that are relevant to future conflicts.

Second, we identify the key legal principles at risk in new warfare: distinction and proportionality. When new warfare makes distinguishing between persons extraordinarily complicated, fulfilling the obligations of distinction and proportionality becomes equally difficult. Future conflicts may pose unforeseen challenges for other legal obligations and principles whose application seems straightforward today; only by zeroing in on the specific principles can we maximize LOAC's adaptability in the future.

Third, we use the basic goals of the legal principles at issue to create a new, more workable framework. Distinction and proportionality rely on the ability to classify and distinguish among persons in conflict, so we created new subcategories to sharpen commanders' ability to distinguish and to respond accordingly. This third step is critical to making LOAC agile—if we cannot find ways to adapt how we apply the law, we will be left only with the claims that the law can no longer work, an unacceptable result.

Fourth, we turn the new framework into operational, on-the-ground guidelines that make LOAC relevant and useful for commanders and policymakers. The conduct-specific checklist and the Commander's Top Ten above give commanders concrete steps to use the law effectively in training their troops, preparing for missions, and fulfilling these missions. With these new tools, commanders can distinguish between innocent civilians and legitimate targets and, just as important, distinguish among the various types of legitimate targets to find the best and most appropriate operational response for each situation.

NOTES

1. We will generally use the term law of armed conflict because that is the term favored by militaries—the key players we focus on here—and when referring to IHL, will do so interchangeably with LOAC.

2. *See* International Committee of the Red Cross ("ICRC"), *International Humanitarian Law in Brief*, http://www.icrc.org/web/eng/siteeng0.nsf/htmlall/section_ihl_in_brief. The law of armed conflict is set forth primarily in the four Geneva Conventions of August 12, 1949, and their Additional Protocols. Geneva Convention for the Amelioration of the Condition of the Wounded and Sick in Armed Forces in the Field, Aug. 12, 1949, 6 U.S.T. 3114, 75 U.N.T.S. 31 [hereinafter GC I]; Geneva Convention for the Amelioration of the Condition of Wounded, Sick and Shipwrecked Members of Armed Forces at Sea, Aug. 12, 1949, 6 U.S.T. 3217, 75 U.N.T.S. 85 [hereinafter GC II]; Geneva Convention Relative to the Treatment of Prisoners of War, Aug. 12, 1949, 6 U.S.T. 3316, 75 U.N.T.S. 135 [hereinafter GC III]; Geneva Convention Relative to the Protection of Civilian Persons in Time of War, Aug. 12, 1949, 6 U.S.T. 3516, 75 U.N.T.S. 287 [hereinafter GC IV]; Protocol Additional to the Geneva Conventions of 12 August 1949, and Relating to the Protection of Victims of International Armed Conflicts (Protocol I), *adopted by Conference* June 8, 1977, 1125 U.N.T.S. 3 [hereinafter AP I]; Protocol Additional to the Geneva Conventions of 12 August 1949, and Relating to the Protection of Victims of Non-International Armed Conflicts (Protocol II), *adopted by Conference* June 8, 1977, 1125 U.N.T.S. 609 [hereinafter AP II].

3. *See* Nils Melzer, *Interpretive Guidance on the Notion of Direct Participation in Hostilities under International Humanitarian Law*, 90 INTL. REV. RED CROSS 991 (2008) (adopted by ICRC Assembly Feb. 26, 2009), *available at* http://www.cicr.org/web/eng/siteeng0.nsf/html/review-872–p991 [hereinafter *Interpretive Guidance*].

4. New warfare also includes conflicts between and among non-state actors, but in this article we will focus solely on conflicts in which states are engaged with non-state actors.

5. This lack of clarity can contribute to an increase in civilian casualties. In Afghanistan, for example, the United Nations reports as follows: "As the conflict intensifies and spreads, it is taking an increasingly heavy toll on civilians, as the growing civilian death toll registered by UNAMA (United Nations Assistance Mission to Afghanistan) Human Rights each year since 2007 indicates. In the first six months of 2009, UNAMA recorded 1013 civilian deaths, compared with 818 for the same period in 2008, and 684 in 2007. . . . This represents an increase of 24% of civilian casualties in the first six months of 2009 as compared to the same period in 2008. Both anti-government elements and pro-government forces are responsible for the increase in civilian casualties. UNAMA Human Rights figures indicate that more civilians are being killed by [Anti-Government Elements ("AGEs")] than by [Pro-Government Forces ("PGF")]. In the first six months of 2009, 59% of civilians were killed by AGEs and 30.5% by PGF. This represents a significant shift from 2007 when PGF were responsible for 41% and AGEs for 46% of civilian deaths." UNITED NATIONS ASSISTANCE MISSION TO AFGHANISTAN, HUMAN RIGHTS UNIT MID YEAR BULLETIN ON PROTECTION OF CIVILIANS IN ARMED CONFLICT 1 (2009), http://unama.unmissions.org/portals/unama/human%20rights/09july31-unama-human-rights-civilian-casualties-mid-year-2009-bulletin.pdf [hereinafter UNAMA Report].

6. *See, e.g.*, Dan Belz, *Is International Humanitarian Law Lapsing into Irrelevance in the War on International Terror?*, 7 THEORETICAL INQ. L. 97 (2006); Rosa E. Brooks, *War Everywhere: Rights, National Security Law, and the Law of Armed Conflict in the Age of Terror*, 153 U. PA. L. REV. 675, 706 (2004); *cf.* Gabor Rona, *International Law Under Fire: Interesting Times For International Humanitarian Law: Challenges from the "War on Terror"*, 27 FLETCHER F.

WORLD AFF. 55 (2003) (explaining that to the extent the "war on terror" constitutes an armed conflict, humanitarian law applies); Andrew Buncombe, *Change Obsolete Rules of Warfare, Says Bush Envoy; Geneva Conventions, Legal Foundation for the Red Cross, Has Helped Maintain Humanity and Dignity in Combat for 140 Years*, THE INDEPENDENT, Feb. 22, 2002, at 2; Robert J. Delahunty & John C. Yoo, Op-Ed., *Rewriting the Laws of War for a New Enemy*, L.A. TIMES, Feb. 1, 2005, at B11; Thomas Harding, *Reid Urges Review of Geneva Convention*, DAILY TELEGRAPH, Apr. 4, 2006, at 2; Avril McDonald, *The Challenges to International Humanitarian Law and the Principles of Distinction and Protection from the Increased Participation in Hostilities* 1 (Univ. of Teheran & Harvard Univ. Humanitarian Law Research Initiative on the Interplay Between Int'l Humanitarian Law & Int'l Human Rights Law, Working Paper, 2004), http://www.asser.nl/Default.aspx?site_id=9&level1=13337&level2=13379&text id=34447.

7. Marshall J. Breger & Marc D. Stern, *Symposium on Reexamining the Law of War: Introduction to the Symposium on Reexamining the Law of War*, 56 CATH. U. L. REV. 745 (2007); Peter Wallstein, *Geneva Convention Overhaul Considered*, L.A. TIMES, JAN. 7, 2005, AT A24.

8. *See* Amos N. Guiora, Anniversary Contributions, *Use of Force: International Law: Where Have We Been; Where Are We Going?* 30 U. PA. J. INT'L L. 1323 (2009).

9. For further discussion, *see* Amos N. Guiora & David Luban, *An Exchange on Law and Israel's Gaza Campaign*, 31 ABA Nat'l Sec. L. Rep. 1, 12 (2009).

10. For the purposes of this article, we define direct participation in hostilities as acts intended to harm the enemy or the civilian population in a direct or immediate manner. *See infra* Section II.B.

[...]

34. Traditional wars do, however, offer well-documented examples of civilians picking up arms, such as Yugoslav partisans under Tito's control in World War II and the French resistance under Nazi occupation in the same war.

35. Tennyson's famous line: "Theirs not to reason why/ Theirs but to do & die" is a tragically apt description of the life of an infantryman locked in battle with another infantryman. LORD ALFRED TENNYSON, THE CHARGE OF THE LIGHT BRIGADE (1854), *available at* http://etext.lib.virginia.edu/images/modeng/public/TenChar/TenChar1.jpg. For a description of traditional warfare, *see* MICHAEL HOWARD, WAR IN EUROPEAN HISTORY (Oxford University Press, 2009) (1976).

36. *See generally*, THOMAS X. HAMMES, THE SLING AND THE STONE: ON WAR IN THE 21ST CENTURY (2004).

37. Nancy Montgomery, *U.S. Seeks to Reduce Civilian Deaths at Iraq Checkpoints*, STARS & STRIPES, Mar. 18, 2006, *available at* http://www.stripes.com/article.asp?section=104&article=35816.

38. *Id.*

39. *Id.*

40. *Id.*

41. Al Skeini v. Sec'y of State for Def., [2004] EWHC 2911, ¶ 46 (Eng).

42. Daniel Byman, *Do Targeted Killings Work?*, FOREIGN POLICY ONLINE, June 14, 2009, http://www.foreignpolicy.com/articles/2009/07/14/do_targeted_killings_work.

***Laurie Blank** is director of the International Humanitarian Law Clinic at Emory University School of Law.

Amos Guiora is professor of law at S.J. Quinney College of Law, The University of Utah.

Laurie Blank and Amos Guiora, "Teaching an Old Dog New Tricks: Operationalizing the Law of Armed Conflict in New Warfare," *Harvard National Security Journal* 1 (2010): 45–50, 83–85.

Fighting the Laws of War: Protecting Civilians in Asymmetric Conflict

by Charli Carpenter*

In December 2008 and January 2009, Hamas and Israel waged a fierce three-week battle in the Gaza Strip. The Israel Defense Forces targeted urban infrastructure in Gaza, devastating populated areas as they attempted to end the barrage of Qassam rockets fired indiscriminately by Hamas toward southern Israeli cities. The war ended inconclusively in January, when Israel declared a unilateral cease-fire amid concerns about mounting civilian casualties. But the conflict shifted from Gaza to Geneva in April, when the UN Human Rights Council appointed former South African judge Richard Goldstone—chief UN prosecutor in Yugoslavia and Rwanda during the 1990s—to lead a fact-finding mission to Gaza. In September, Goldstone's team announced its conclusion: both Hamas and Israel had violated the laws of war, and both had possibly committed crimes against humanity.

Many have interpreted the Goldstone report, as it has become known, as yet another battle in the Israeli-Palestinian conflict, waged by other means. But the report addressed a more far-reaching issue—namely, the difficulty of distinguishing civilians from combatants in modern urban warfare.

Two recent books explore that dilemma by examining the relationship between the laws of war and civilian protection during battle. In *Moral Dilemmas of Modern War*, Michael Gross contends that the current safeguards against civilian casualties are too stringent to address the complexities of today's wars, barring states from adequately combating irregular forces. Meanwhile, Stephen Rockel and Rick Halpern argue in *Inventing Collateral Damage* that the current international regulations are too weak, permitting and even enabling states to harm civilians during combat.

From two widely different perspectives, the books cast doubt on the value of the existing international regulations presumably designed to mitigate war's impact on civilians. But a closer look suggests that these authors overstate the tensions between the laws of war and the modern battlefield and underestimate just how well the existing statutes are working. Although the laws of war require strengthening, they constitute a firm foundation on which to better protect civilians.

Too Much or Too Little?

The current laws of war regarding civilian protection resulted from a process of treaty development that included nineteenth-century agreements to safeguard the sick and wounded, which were gradually extended in the twentieth century to prisoners of war and then to civilians caught in conflict. A cardinal rule of the existing framework insists that civilians may not be deliberately targeted, unless they participate directly in hostilities. The laws stipulate that military forces must direct their operations toward combatants and military objectives only and must conduct themselves in a manner that allows their adversaries to distinguish them from civilians—by wearing uniforms, for example, or carrying arms openly. The drafters of the Geneva Conventions carefully delineated combatants and civilians to assist militaries in distinguishing between them. In addition, the conventions state that when in doubt, military forces should assume the targets are civilians and that some number of combatants among a civilian population does not render that civilian population a legitimate target.

Gross argues that this legal structure unfairly favors insurgents on the modern battlefield. Many of today's wars are fought in dense urban environments, largely between uniformed state militaries and guerrillas in civilian clothing. The problem, he believes, is not that the rules inadequately protect civilians but that they provide too much protection for nonstate armed groups in this new type of war, on the mistaken assumption that civilians are always innocent bystanders. This hobbles Western militaries in their attempts to protect those considered by Gross to be "truly innocent" civilians—those who reside in democracies and are subject to guerrilla violence and terrorism.

Many civilians in modern wars are agents and not just bystanders, as Gross correctly points out: they aid and abet insurgents by storing their weapons, producing their propaganda, providing them with food and shelter, and even agreeing to act as civilian shields. It is no surprise to him, then, that powerful states such as Israel and the United States would expand the circle of "legitimate targets" to include civilians who assist insurgents, because it is otherwise difficult to see how they could successfully wage war at all. Gross justifies this expansion by arguing that it is vital for democracies to prevail in asymmetric conflicts. In such conflicts, he argues, democratic states are protecting their own civilians, and in some cases the citizens of other nations, from terrorist attacks.

By contrast, Rockel, Halpern, and other contributors to their volume are far more critical of powerful governments' records in war. Whereas Gross emphasizes moral asymmetry in modern war—highlighting the distinction between democratic armies defending their citizens and guerrillas who attack civilians using the cover of their own countries' populations—Rockel and Halpern focus on the asymmetry of force between powerful state militaries and their weaker guerrilla adversaries. They claim that the West's callous indifference to "unintended" civilian casualties in the developing world today is analogous to its historical record of atrocities in imperial wars, which often involved depredations against civilians. Just as colonial states in those wars used dehumanizing euphemisms, such as calling natives "savages," to legitimize their actions, modern Western militaries unacceptably justify and sanitize civilian casualties by invoking the concept of "collateral damage"—a military term used to describe regrettable but unintended, and therefore lawful, casualties of war. The notion that civilian deaths are permissible if unintended, the authors argue, has allowed militaries to whitewash the destructiveness of their operations. In other words, the existing laws of war, which prohibit intentional civilian targeting but permit "accidental" civilian deaths, are part of the problem.

Marc Herold's chapter in *Inventing Collateral Damage* lends credence to the notion that modern technologies and legal statutes meant to protect civilians may in fact be used in ways that place them in greater danger. His data suggest that the ratio of civilian deaths to tons of ordnance dropped has actually increased in the past 20 years, as precision weapons have been introduced in greater numbers. Herold argues that Western militaries have become overconfident in their ability to safely deploy weapons such as smart bombs and drones in dense urban neighborhoods and at night. This may explain the high number of estimated civilian casualties from drone strikes in Pakistan; the New America Foundation calculates that approximately a third of drone-strike casualties are civilians. It troubles Rockel and Halpern that the laws of war permit such high levels of civilian casualties. In their view, the rules are designed to legitimize violence rather than restrain it.

Both books are thus skeptical about the ability of the existing laws of war to balance national security and the protection of civilians. As interpreted by the Goldstone report, international law appears to handicap states' ability to target insurgents who purposefully operate in civilian areas—revealing, according to Gross, the inability of the current system to adapt to new modes of war. Meanwhile, in their book, Rockel, Halpern, and the other contributors argue that the existing body of laws protecting civilians during wartime actually sanctions their deaths at the hands of states operating behind the shield of "collateral damage." Do the laws of war, then, need to be adapted to the current era, and if so, how?

STRIKING A BALANCE

In outlining the limitations presented by the laws of war in addressing modern conflicts, Gross argues that the current legal framework for civilian protection must change to meet state interests. He is sympathetic to the new tendency among Western states to broaden the scope of acceptable military targets to include civilians who assist insurgents. Yet this is a deviation from the existing norm by states seeking to pursue their interests outside the bounds of the law. Were this trend adopted as a new legal standard, it would be nothing less than an abandonment of the current rules, weakening civilian protection rather than strengthening it.

Moreover, underlying Gross' belief that the laws of war must change to meet states' needs is the historically flawed notion that modern combat presents unique challenges. The kinds of asymmetries in the warfare he writes about are hardly unprecedented. The laws of war have in fact already adapted to many of the questions that, according to Gross, have been raised for the first time by recent wars. The current framework distinguishes, for example, between civilians who support warring factions by providing food and shelter, who are not automatically rendered legitimate targets, and civilians who take up arms themselves, who do lose their immunity. Gross points out that these rules place critical restraints on the actions of state militaries. But he overstates the case when he suggests that the laws of war tie their hands completely. To Gross, there seem to be only two options for state forces engaged in asymmetric wars: bend the rules by fighting guerrillas with an expanded notion of legitimate targets, or prepare to lose.

Yet a third option exists: militaries can choose to place their uniformed men and women in harm's way rather than cede the moral high ground by placing civilians in greater danger. When Gross describes the fundamental dilemma of asymmetric war as "who do we bomb when there are no more accessible military targets?" he assumes that states must deploy aerial firepower to defeat their unconventional enemies. But this is not the only tool in the arsenals of Western states. To combat insurgents and protect civilians simultaneously, governments could choose to use ground troops, which are arguably better equipped to discriminate between innocent bystanders and insurgents and their accomplices. Although militaries risk significantly higher casualties by deploying their troops rather than dropping precision bombs, this sacrifice is precisely what the logic of just war requires: that civilians not become more expendable than a country's armed forces.

Gross is not alone in his undue cynicism about the existing principles. Rockel and Halpern argue that the very idea of "collateral damage," a tenet of the existing laws of war, increases military leaders' apathy toward the consequences of their operations and encourages crimes against civilians. But in making this claim, the authors conflate "collateral damage," which describes regrettable yet lawful casualties of war, and "war crimes," which result when governments deliberately target civilians. For example, many of their book's chapters detail atrocities to which the concept of "unintended casualties" does not apply, such as sexual violence. Moreover, nothing in the case studies shows even a correlation, much less a causal relationship, between the invention of the euphemism "collateral damage" during the Cold War and a purported rise in unintended civilian casualties. In fact, U.S. government documents disclosed by the whistle-blower Web site WikiLeaks last October suggest the opposite: in those papers, U.S. troops appeared to invoke the risk of collateral damage to justify their failure to fire at legitimate military targets.

Inventing Collateral Damage does successfully document the brutalities of warfare before the 1949 Geneva Conventions. If anything, however, this suggests that the treaties' norms may have reduced such horrors since World War II. In fact, according to Simon Fraser University's *Human Security Report 2005*, the overall plight of civilians in recent hostilities appears to have vastly improved relative to earlier times. However extensive the collateral damage in Afghanistan, for example, there is a world of difference between accidentally hitting civilians in Kandahar with not-so-smart bombs and firebombing Dresden to break the population's morale. The distinction between accidental and intentional killing—and the firm rule that military necessity does not excuse the intentional targeting of civilians—has saved countless civilian lives in the past half century.

But Rockel and Halpern are right to note that although the international community has worked to reduce intentional civilian targeting, it has been too complacent about reducing unintended civilian casualties. Protection for civilians against the effects of lawful military operations remains scant, and international discussion about increasing those safeguards has been minimal. Many of the contributors to Inventing Collateral Damage suggest that such complacency renders the entire effort to regulate war an exercise in hypocrisy. Yet as in the case of Gross' concerns, a more pragmatic approach would be to explore options for strengthening, expanding, and clarifying the existing rules.

STRENGTHENING CIVILIAN PROTECTION

Although *Moral Dilemmas of Modern War* and *Inventing Collateral Damage* suggest otherwise, the laws of war have never been static and have often improved to reflect changing times. Points of confusion in the law regarding civilians can be clarified today through the same process that has been used to ban land mines or protect displaced persons in recent years. Specific rules will need to be worked out by states, but nongovernmental organizations and legal experts are proposing many ideas about what these rules could look like.

First, any international effort to reduce and respond to the civilian costs of war will need a mechanism for measuring and categorizing casualties of war. The Geneva regime currently provides no formal means of tracking who dies and how in military operations worldwide, leaving states' humanitarian policies to be guided by wildly conflicting and ad hoc measures. The Oxford Research Group, a London-based nongovernmental organization dedicated to sustainable security, recently created the Recording Casualties of Armed Conflict project and, with several humanitarian organizations, has issued a memorandum calling on governments to establish rules standardizing this process. Such data, as Gross and Rockel and Halpern argue, are crucial in resolving moral debates over the proportionality of various methods of combat.

Governments should additionally reconsider whether certain weapons, such as high-yield explosives, can really be considered discriminate when deployed in urban areas. A 2010 report by Landmine Action demonstrates that civilian casualties caused by these devices—artillery shells, bombs, and mortars among them—are exceedingly high in populated areas, and especially so among children. The damage is even greater when the secondary impacts of urban warfare are considered, including disease, malnutrition, and economic ruin. If the goal is to better protect civilians from the incidental effects of war, limits on the use of such weapons, at least in urban areas, may be required.

Yet even new regulations governing the deployment of explosives in populated areas would still likely leave some civilians in the crossfire. And in such cases, the Campaign for Innocent Victims in Conflict, a Washington-based nongovernmental organization, argues that governments should provide compensation to civilians accidentally harmed during legitimate combat operations, just as they sometimes pay reparations to victims of war crimes. The U.S. government has actually taken the lead on this issue, initiating a system of condolence payments for the families of civilian casualties of the wars in Afghanistan and Iraq. Several other countries, including Georgia, Germany, and Pakistan, are beginning to follow suit, and Israel has paid reparations in several limited cases. If widely adopted, this practice would not only provide some solace to civilians when disaster strikes but also, perhaps, incentivize militaries to take greater care to avoid causing such casualties in the first place.

Even if no new laws are developed in the near future, military planners, government officials, and lawyers could reduce civilian casualties by simply modifying their interpretations of the existing legal doctrines. To begin, clarifying the notion of what constitutes direct civilian participation in hostilities would help states more accurately judge when civilians remain protected and when they have lost their immunity. The International Committee of the Red Cross has already drafted language defining "direct participation" as acts that cause direct harm either to enemy forces or to the enemy's military operations and capacity, but states should develop a consensus around a definition so that they and others can be better held accountable for their actions.

Additional questions in need of resolution include how to determine whether, in the words of international treaties, a government has taken "all feasible precautions" to prevent civilian harm and whether it has inflicted "excessive" civilian casualties in relation to its military gains. The current laws of war leave these issues to states' discretion, but governments could collaborate to limit the gray area between civilian deaths considered unfortunate and those deemed unlawful. New or clarified rules will need to balance humanitarian principles in war with the human security costs of doing too little in cases in which insurgents or terrorists prey intentionally on the innocent. Many militaries are already grappling not just with how to weigh civilian casualties against military necessity but also with how to balance the risk of civilian casualties during a given strike against the benefits that such a strike could provide to those civilians by neutralizing predatory militias.

Some might argue that further innovations in the laws of war are unlikely. But the international rules that are now taken for granted—say, the right of wounded soldiers to receive aid from neutral humanitarians on the battlefield—once seemed just as far-fetched. And reconsiderations of humanitarian law have often occurred in times of systemic crisis such as these, when the human costs of the mismatch between existing laws and changing times become clear. One such transformation took place in the 1970s, when the Additional Protocols to the Geneva Conventions were established. States recognized that the most recent Geneva regulations, passed in 1949 and designed to address the conditions of World War II, required updating to respond to the unconventional wars associated with decolonization. The Additional Protocols extended the definition of "lawful combatants" to nonstate parties fighting wars of national liberation and codified the existing rules against targeting civilians, whose protection had previously been instituted only in relation to civilian conditions in occupied territories. Similarly, the 1998 Rome Statute, which created the International Criminal Court, represented an effort to bolster the Geneva regime. The court was created in response to the atrocities in Bosnia and Herzegovina and Rwanda in the 1990s—horrors that underscored the need for an international judicial body to prosecute and punish war criminals. According to the *Human Security Report 2005*, the number of war crimes and genocides committed by government forces is dropping. This may well be in part because the original rules were augmented and are now influencing military doctrine worldwide.

Collateral damage in modern warfare, too, can be minimized by more clear-cut regulations. Governments should work to reduce both long-term and short-term civilian harm in war, atone for lawful as well as unlawful deaths, and cooperate to bring nonstate actors that target civilians to justice. But to achieve this, states must work together to strengthen the rules themselves. And assessments of the existing laws of war should be balanced and forward-looking rather than cynically pessimistic. It is well within the power of the international community to strengthen civilian protection in the twenty-first century.

***Charli Carpenter** is associate professor of international affairs at the University of Massachusetts-Amherst.

Charli Carpenter, "Fighting the Laws of War: Protecting Civilians in Asymmetric Conflict," *Foreign Affairs* (March/April 2011), http://www.foreignaffairs.com/print/67448.

Sparing Civilians, Buildings and Even the Enemy

*by Max Boot**

Watching images of the bombing of Baghdad brought to mind another American bombing campaign 58 years ago. On March 9, 1945, more than 300 B-29 Superfortresses attacked Tokyo. Their napalm bombs and magnesium incendiaries turned 16 densely packed square miles into an inferno. An estimated 84,000 people, mostly civilians, were killed, making this one of the deadliest days of warfare ever.

The enormity of the destruction is almost impossible to comprehend today, because the American armed forces fight so differently now. The new way of war emphasizes precision and aims for minimal casualties on both sides. This approach represents a considerable advance, but it also brings its own set of problems.

Although air strikes on Baghdad have intensified, leading to what Iraqi officials claim are more than 70 civilian casualties, the city is hardly being pounded into rubble. Electricity and other services remain. In the war's early days, Baghdad residents even stood on their balconies to watch bombs and missiles pummel their city—secure in the knowledge that only a handful of government buildings would be hit.

This is a bit reminiscent of the first Battle of Bull Run in 1861, which drew as spectators the crème de la crème of Washington society. It is almost as if the United States has left behind the total war of the 20th century and returned to an earlier time of more limited combat, when columns of professional soldiers marched toward each other across open fields and civilians were hurt only by accident.

Actually, in some ways the United States has gone beyond the chivalrous warfare of the 18th and 19th centuries. Nowadays the military tries to spare not only civilians, but enemy combatants as well. During the 1991 Persian Gulf war, images of the devastation along the road leading from Kuwait to Basra—the so-called Highway of Death—helped persuade the first Bush administration to stop the ground war after just 100 hours, even though it later turned out that few Iraqi soldiers had been killed.

Today, American forces are still not bombing some Iraqi regular army formations in the hope that they will defect en masse and spare themselves a beating, which the administration fears would make America unpopular.

What accounts for the change? Is it that the United States has grown more moral in the last 50 years—or, depending on your point of view, more squeamish? Perhaps. But, more likely, moral standards have changed because technology has changed.

John Warden, a retired Air Force colonel who helped plan the air campaign for the first gulf war, explained: "During World War II, an average B-17 bomb during a bombing run missed its target by some 2,300 feet. Therefore, if you wanted a 90 percent probability of having hit a particular target, you had to drop some 9,000 bombs." Most of those 9,000 bombs, of course, would have ended up landing on a nearby civilian neighborhood, not on the target of the raid.

The inaccuracy of such campaigns led World War II generals to make what they saw as a virtue out of necessity: They would engage in "area" bombing, like the 1945 raids on Tokyo or Dresden, ostensibly intended to cripple enemy industry but really aimed at breaking enemy morale. This was accepted with hardly a peep of protest from both the British and the American public.

Luckily, the military no longer has to employ such blunt tactics. Precision-guided weapons make it possible to obliterate a target with one carefully aimed bomb. But even "smart" bombs miss their target 7 percent to 10 percent of the time. And costly mistakes inevitably occur. During the first gulf war, United States planners bombed a shelter that housed Iraqi commanders; unknown to them, it also housed hundreds of civilians, who died. During the Kosovo war the United States flattened the Chinese Embassy in Belgrade. During the Afghanistan war, the military blew up a wedding party and a group of Canadian soldiers. Just last week, a missile hit a Syrian bus near the Iraqi border, and Iraqi officials claim air strikes hit two crowded Baghdad markets.

Such accidents once would have been unremarkable; today they are a scandal, because 100 percent accuracy is assumed to be the norm. Some human-rights campaigners want to charge American airmen with war crimes because their bombs killed Serb civilians during the Kosovo campaign. Nothing has happened so far, but the two pilots who killed four Canadian soldiers in Afghanistan were arraigned before a military tribunal on manslaughter charges. The hearing officer recommended against court-martial; no final decision has been made.

To avoid such accidents, American planners are extraordinarily careful. Almost all decisions on targets are vetted by lawyers, who decide if the expected benefits outweigh the risks of civilian casualties. Such careful consideration can get in the way of swift action. In the early days of the Afghan war, a Predator drone armed with Hellfire missiles spotted a convoy believed to contain Mullah Muhammad Omar. But the military took so long to process this information that a possible opportunity to kill the Taliban leader was lost.

During the current war, dozens of important targets were placed off limits because of fears of "high collateral damage." Pentagon planners hoped instead to rely on a "shock and awe" bombing campaign to topple the regime, but that bloodless victory did not materialize.

Iraq is well aware of the United States' sensitivity to civilian casualties and tries to exploit it. When not showing pictures of dead American soldiers, Iraqi television broadcasts images of wounded or dead civilians. Saddam Hussein has tried to increase the chances of civilian casualties by placing military installations near hospitals, mosques and schools. In addition, the Saddam Fedayeen, a militia commanded by Saddam's son Uday, have attacked coalition soldiers while hiding behind "human shields." In all these cases, an inhumane regime is using our humanity against us.

This problem could become more severe when allied troops enter Baghdad. Because commanders will probably not be willing to flatten whole blocks, they may expose their soldiers to the extreme perils of close-quarters combat.

The military must struggle with the deadly calculus of how many casualties it is willing to incur among its own forces to save civilian lives. In this regard, the words of Gen. Curtis LeMay, who led the American bombing campaign against Japan in 1945, are worth remembering: "Actually I think it's more immoral to use less force than necessary, than it is to use more. If you use less force, you kill off more of humanity in the long run because you are merely protracting the struggle."

*Max Boot is Olin Senior Fellow at the Council on Foreign Relations and author of *The Savage Wars of Peace: Small Wars and the Rise of American Power* (Basic Books, 2002).

Max Boot, "Sparing Civilians, Buildings and Even the Enemy," *New York Times*, March 30, 2003.

Part 4:
Participation in Hostilities

Part 3 discussed some of the challenges 21st century warfare poses for civilian protection provisions of international humanitarian law (IHL). The seemingly simple task of identifying who is a civilian and who is a combatant is difficult when irregular armed groups blend in with the civilian population—often intentionally. The picture is made even more complex by the increasing role civilians are playing in conflicts. This section explores who may be targeted and who may not be when the lines are muddy. Given all the ways that civilians contribute to war—from providing food and shelter, to supporting planning and operations—where does IHL draw the line between a civilian and a combatant? Is a civilian bodyguard who accompanies a military force a combatant? What about a civilian who uses a drone to kill a combatant from half a world away? Although the general rule of IHL is that civilians may not be targeted in conflict, civilians who are "directly participating in hostilities" may be targeted for the time they are participating. When does this exception kick in, for what activities, and for how long would it apply?

THE FADING LINE BETWEEN CIVILIANS AND COMBATANTS

Under IHL, the central mechanism for regulating conduct during war has been to distinguish between civilians and combatants and to accord separate protections and privileges for each of these categories. Of course, this dichotomy works only if warring parties can tell the difference between civilians and combatants, a distinction that modern modes of warfare have severely tested. As a technical legal matter, many of today's warriors do not meet the IHL standards for recognizing a combatant, for example, wearing a uniform or other sign, carrying arms openly, or having significant command and control.[1] Nor do civilians fit traditional conceptions of "noncombatants," as civilians have increasingly been integrated into the war-fighting apparatus of both state and nonstate armed groups.

State Actors

In the first article in this section, Andreas Wenger and Simon J. A. Mason argue the "civilianization" of conflict is the most significant source of legal ambiguity in modern conflict. They argue that high-end military technological development simultaneously accelerated the integration of civilians into state war-making structures and made them more likely to be targets. In World War I and World War II, industrialization brought civilians more directly into war-making activities, including weapons production, maintenance, and transportation of war materials.[2] Civilian roles in war have expanded further as complex and sophisticated technology has become even more central to modern warfare. Civilians dominate the development and maintenance of high-tech weapons systems in advanced militaries.

Technology has not been the only driver of this civilianization of conflict; states have also increasingly delegated military tasks to civilians. In contemporary warfare, civilians participate in the planning and operational phases of combat activities, and even direct targeting. U.S. drone strikes in Pakistan against alleged Taliban, Al Qaeda, and other terrorist groups are reportedly operated remotely by civilian intelligence agents in the United States.[3] Recent trends toward counterinsurgency strategy—which argues that civilian development and governance advances can be as important to defeating an insurgency as tactical military victories—have made civilian aid and diplomatic activities more prominent in military campaigns.

Another important factor that Wenger and Mason point to has been the increasing role of private military and security companies in state military operations. In 2010, private military contractors made up 52 percent of the U.S. Department of Defense's workforce in Afghanistan and Iraq.[4] Though the majority of these contractors perform maintenance and support roles, some wear uniforms and use weapons—seemingly taking on the appearance and duties of a soldier.

The dependence on civilian sectors and infrastructure, such as mobile phones, power grids, television, and the Internet, for fighting a war may tempt opposing parties to consider dual-use civilian facilities—ones serving both civilian and military functions—as legitimate military targets. The case study included in the Amnesty International report in this section analyzes 1999 NATO bombing of a Serbian television station during the Kosovo air campaign. Amnesty International concludes that NATO violated international law in targeting the station because its propaganda activities contributed to the Serbian military campaign.[5]

> Amnesty International recognizes that disrupting government propaganda may help to undermine the morale of the population and the armed forces, but believes that justifying an attack on a civilian facility on such

grounds stretches the meaning of "effective contribution to military action" and "definite military advantage" beyond the acceptable bounds of interpretation.[6]

Nonstate Armed Groups

Civilians have also become central to the war-making activities of nonstate armed groups. Civilians in conflicts from Gaza to the Philippines may support nonstate insurgent groups by producing propaganda, supplying militant groups with intelligence, acting as lookouts, or by supplying food, shelter, or other logistical support. Nonstate armed groups in asymmetric conflicts depend on this civilian support to hide from and survive against a more powerful adversary—a strategy that often results in these civilians being mistakenly targeted.

Nonstate armed groups may also deliberately organize civilians into direct participation in hostilities. As Wenger and Mason note, in many noninternational armed conflicts "civilians are victims, but they are also perpetrators."[7] The 1994 Rwandan genocide, in which more than 800,000 minority Tutsis were killed over the course of about 100 days, was perpetrated almost exclusively by ordinary civilians, not members of organized armed forces or groups.[8]

Finally, in irregular conflicts, individuals may go back and forth, acting as fighters one day, civilians the next. The following excerpt from a 2009 BBC article illustrates the difficulty of identifying combatants in the context of ongoing fighting between Israeli Defense Forces (IDF) and Hamas fighters, or affiliates, in the Gaza Strip:

> The bloodied children are clearly civilians; men killed as they launch rockets are undisputedly not. But what about the 40 or so young Hamas police recruits on parade who died in the first wave of Israel's bombing campaign in Gaza? . . . the Israeli human rights group B'Tselem, which has raised the issue in a letter to Israel's attorney general, says it appears those killed were being trained in first aid, human rights and maintaining public order.

> The IDF says it has intelligence that members of the police force often "moonlight" with rocket squads, but has given no details about the specific sites or individuals targeted.

> However, campaign group Human Rights Watch (HRW) argues that even if police members do double as Hamas fighters, they can only be legally attacked when actually participating in military activities.[9]

This so-called revolving door problem—when individuals act like fighters one day, civilians the next—blurs the lines even further because it raises the level of suspicion over all civilians, increasing the risk that civilians will be wrongfully targeted.

Participation in Hostilities

As a result of this blurring of lines, international legal scholars and some domestic courts have struggled to develop clear rules for distinguishing combatants from civilians in modern warfare. Article 51(3) of Additional Protocol I—governing international armed conflicts—provides that "Civilians shall enjoy the protection afforded by this Section unless and for such time as they take a direct part in hostilities."[10] Article 13(3) of Additional Protocol II—governing non-international armed conflicts—includes the same provision.[11] If an individual fires on an enemy combatant, plants a bomb, or perpetrates some other form of hostile act, he loses his civilian status while doing so. In short, even though they are not members of armed forces or combatants, if civilians directly participate in fighting, they can be targeted. This begs two questions:

1. What acts constitute "direct participation"?

2. When does direct participation begin and end?

Acts That Constitute Direct Participation

Given the range of ways that civilians might support fighting in modern conflicts, what constitutes direct participation such that an individual might be killed or captured freely? Are kinetic activities alone—firing a gun or detonating a bomb—sufficient or do some of the more indirect support roles—gathering intelligence, assembling weapons, or providing transportation—also count as participation in hostilities?

Civilians have long played an important role in supporting military efforts, many of which have been relatively uncontroversial. But views on these types of activities have changed as civilian activities have become more important in warfare, and as civilians have become more geographically mixed in the conflict. For example, transporting weapons, supplies, and other materials to troops is critical to any wartime effort. However, many would argue that a commercial railway employee performing an overall civilian function (working on a railway line) far from the battlefield is not participating in hostilities just because the military benefits from his work (although the rail lines themselves might be justifiably targeted and the railroad worker collaterally harmed). But others have drawn a distinction between the railroad worker and those performing analogous transport functions closer to the battlefield. Take the example of a Pakistani truck driver who knowingly transported weapons and fuel to NATO troops in Afghanistan, versus a truck driver who transported suicide bomb materials, or other munitions, to the point of attack. Would you consider either of those activities to be direct participation?

In practice, warring parties often target individuals engaged in such transport activities when they are close to an active battlefield, but legal experts remain split on whether this is lawful. In its often-cited decision, *The Public Committee Against Torture in Israel v. The Government of Israel* (2005), the Supreme Court of Israel argued that if a civilian truck driver is taking ammunition "to the place from which it will be used for the purposes of hostilities, he should be seen as taking a direct part in the hostilities."[12] The International Committee of the Red Cross (ICRC)—which, as discussed in previous sections, has often led the development and clarification of IHL—organized a six-year consultative process among experts on direct participation issues. The resulting ICRC report, "Interpretive Guidance on the Notion of Direct Participation in Hostilities under International Humanitarian Law," defined participation narrowly, demanding a "direct causal link between the act and the harm likely to result from that act,"[13] which would not include "the production and shipment of weapons," it argued.[14]

There has been broader consensus that indirect support activities—providing food, shelter, or medical support—do not constitute "direct participation" in hostilities. These were the findings of both the Supreme Court of Israel in the *Public Committee Against Torture* case, and the ICRC's "Interpretive Guidance." Nonetheless, in practice, warring parties have frequently targeted civilians giving food, shelter, medical, or financial support to opposing groups. In early 2009, the Sri Lankan military reportedly deliberately targeted civilian individuals and facilities alleged to be supporting Tamil Tiger rebels, including directly targeting civilians and hospitals.[15] Taliban fighters in Afghanistan have continuously threatened and killed civilians working for the Afghan government or international forces or organizations in Afghanistan since 2002.[16]

Finally, one of the most controversial issues has been whether other indirect support activities might constitute direct participation. The ICRC "Interpretive Guidance" argues that "financial, administrative and political support" does not constitute direct participation.[17] However, since the Al Qaeda attacks on September 11, 2001, the United States has alleged that some types of financial support to terrorist groups may be targetable under the laws of war.[18] In the third article Dapo Akande, co-director of the Oxford Institute for Ethics, Law and Armed Conflict, questions a 2009 U.S. mandate that allowed U.S. forces to "kill or capture drug traffickers in Afghanistan who have links to the Taliban" as combatants.[19] Not only is drug trafficking an illegal activity in Afghanistan, but it has also provided critical financial support for the Taliban and other militant groups, with many drug traffickers directly allied with the insurgency. Despite the tight connections to insurgent activity, Akande argues that putting drug traffickers on a kill or capture list, the same as combatants, violates international law:[20]

> The reason they are now being subject to targeting is not the illegality of their activity but the consequences of their conduct—that it funds the adverse party. From that perspective, their activity is no different to that of an executive in any industry (say, oil or manufacturing) which provides the bulk of the income of a belligerent State.[21]

The destruction of the civilian property connected to the drug trade— poppy farms and drug labs—is a tougher question, he argues. While it might be conceivable under international forces' dual law enforcement mandate in Afghanistan, it would not be allowed under international humanitarian law alone, Akande argues, because there is not a direct enough connection here between the drug-related property and military activities: "The fact that an object provides the finances for military action is not sufficient. Otherwise, all facilities/ industries that generate taxes for a State would be liable to attack in time of armed conflict."[22] This, he argues, would be a return to a policy of total war, which IHL (at least since World War II) is designed to prevent.

Temporal Questions

The more broadly direct participation is defined, the more concerns there are with how long a civilian might be targeted. IHL states that if a civilian does do something that constitutes direct participation, making him eligible to be killed or captured, he can be targeted only for such time as he participates. While it is clear that he could be fired on when he was planting a bomb, could he be killed on his way home from planting the bomb? Could he be fired on in his civilian home weeks or months later, assuming he took no further part in hostilities?

These temporal questions are even more difficult to grapple with because of the ambiguity of membership in irregular warfare. Traditionally, a member of a warring party can be targeted at any time—whether on the front lines or having dinner in his bunker far from the fighting. In irregular warfare, membership is not always clear. An individual may act like a civilian by day, a fighter by night, or engage in hostilities for a period of time, but then stop. This makes it more difficult to determine whether the individual is a combatant who can be targeted at any time, even when performing relatively innocuous, civilian-like activities, or a civilian who is not directly participating in hostilities at the time (and thus cannot be targeted).

The final article by the Program on Humanitarian Policy and Conflict Research (PHPCR) discusses how international legal scholars, courts, and states have tried to grapple with direct participation in hostilities issues, including these temporal questions. Some experts have tried to deal with this question by arguing that a civilian participating in hostilities may be targeted based on *specific acts* they have engaged in, by assuming they are targetable unless they *affirmatively disengage* (stop being a combatant), or based on analogizing their *membership* in an armed group to membership in a regular armed force. The ICRC has suggested that those who are performing a "continuous combat function" would be targetable at any time like regular combatants. However, even this approach begets concerns: it is unclear how to assess whether participation is continuous, or how an individual would signal disengagement from "continuous combat."[23]

What participation in hostilities means in contemporary warfare is one of the most difficult issues in modern IHL debates. There has never been a clear consensus on what actions constitute direct participation, what would cause a civilian to lose his or her protections, and for how long. The complexities of modern warfare have made these questions even more difficult. Despite guidance from a range of sources—including those discussed above—there is no consensus. As you read through the PHPCR and other articles, think about where you would draw the line.

- How would you treat an individual in an irregular conflict who has supported some war activities, but largely lives and acts like a civilian—a "part-time" combatant?
- Akande argues that those supplying direct financial support should not be targeted, that doing so would be akin to considering all who pay taxes to be "combatants" and would return us to a state of "total war." Do you agree? Do you see any distinction in fundraising for nonstate versus state actors?
- When trying to identify whether a particular job or action would signify "directly participating in hostilities," how would you weigh the

following: the nature of the act (kinetic versus supporting), proximity to the battlefield, importance of the act to the military strategy?

• In the case of the Serbian television station, NATO argued that the propaganda and communication activities of the television station significantly contributed to military effectiveness. Do you agree that civilians making propaganda are combatants, given the importance of such "soft power" weapons in contemporary warfare?

• In the examples above about those engaged in transport activities, where would you draw the line? Is the World War II railroad worker far from the battlefield engaged in hostilities? What about the truck driver transporting materials and supplies to U.S. troops in Afghanistan? Or transporting a suicide bomber to the scene of an attack?

• The ICRC "Interpretive Guidance" suggests that the production of weapons is too indirect for individuals engaged in those activities to lose civilian status. Should a worker in a munitions factory far from the battlefield be a legitimate target? What about a suicide bomb maker near to the battlefield? What about those individuals or companies who sell weapons directly to a warring party during ongoing fighting?

• In October 2011, the United States killed Anwar Al-Awlaki, a U.S. citizen living in and operating out of Yemen, using an armed drone. Al-Awlaki was alleged to be a recruiter for Al Qaeda and to have motivated specific attacks against U.S. citizens and targets. Do you think recruiting and motivating attacks should count as direct participation? Can you think of civilian individuals in the United States who could be argued to motivate attacks against Al Qaeda? Should they also be justifiably targetable as combatants?

NOTES

1. IHL defines combatants as those who are under some form of command and control, wearing a "fixed distinctive sign recognizable at a distance," carrying arms openly, and conducting operations according to IHL. See, e.g., Geneva Convention Relative to the Treatment of Prisoners of War, August 12, 1949, 6 U.S.T. 3316, 75 U.N.T.S. 135, at art. 4, 2 (a-d).

2. During World War II, international lawyers argued whether a munitions factory, or the workers within it, were valid military targets given their central significance for war-fighting. E. Camins, "The Past as Prologue: The Development of the 'Direct Participation' Exception to Civilian Immunity," *International Review of the Red Cross* 90, no. 872 (December 2008): 868–70.

3. Salman Masood, "Pakistani General, in Twist, Credits Drone Strikes," *New York Times*, March 9, 2011, http://www.nytimes.com/2011/03/10/world/asia/10drones.html.

4. Moshe Schwartz and Joyprada Swain, "Summary," *Department of Defense Contractors in Iraq and Afghanistan: Background and Analysis* (Washington, DC: Congressional Research Service), July 2, 2010, http://www.fas.org/sgp/crs/natsec/R40764.pdf.

5. For more on the other rationales for targeting the station, including that some of the television station's relay equipment and towers were integrated into the broader military communication systems, see International Criminal Tribunal to the former Yugoslavia, *Final Report to the Prosecutor by the Committee Established to Review the NATO Bombing Campaign Against the Federal Republic of Yugoslavia*, ¶¶ 71 – 79, http://www.icty.org/sid/10052#IVB3.

6. Amnesty International, "NATO/Federal Republic of Yugoslavia 'Collateral Damage' or Unlawful Killings? Violations of the Laws of War by NATO during Operation Allied Force," *AI Index: EUR 70/18/00* (June 2000): 41, http://www.amnesty.org/en/library/asset/EUR70/018/2000/en/e7037dbb-df56-11dd-89a6-e712e728ac9e/eur700182000en.pdf.

7. Andreas Wenger and Simon J. A. Mason, "The Civilianization of Armed Conflict: Trends and Implications," *International Review of the Red Cross* 90, no. 872 (2008): 843.

8. BBC News, "Rwanda: How the Genocide Happened," December 18, 2008, http://news.bbc.co.uk/2/hi/1288230.stm.

9. Heather Sharp, "Gaza Conflict: Who Is a Civilian?" *BBC News*, January 5, 2009, http://news.bbc.co.uk/2/hi/7811386.stm.

10. Protocol Additional to the Geneva Conventions of August 12, 1949, and Relating to the Protection of Victims of International Armed Conflicts, June 8, 1977, 1125 U.N.T.S. 4, art. 51(3).

11. Protocol Additional to the Geneva Conventions of August 12, 1949, and Relating to the Protection of Victims of Non-International Armed Conflicts, June 8, 1977, 1125 U.N.T.S. 609, art. 13(3).

12. *The Public Committee Against Torture in Israel v. The Government of Israel*, HCJ 769/02. The Supreme Court Sitting as the High Court of Justice, December 11, 2005, http://elyon1.court.gov.il/Files_ENG/02/690/007/a34/02007690.a34.htm, at ¶35.

13. International Committee of the Red Cross, "Interpretive Guidance on the Notion of Direct Participation in Hostilities Under International Humanitarian Law," *International Review of the Red Cross* 90, no. 872 (December 2008): 995–996, http://www.cicr.org/eng/assets/files/other/irrc-872-reports-documents.pdf. Examples of what might constitute this direct causal link include "capturing, wounding or killing military personnel [including through mines, or other time-delayed weapons]; damaging military objects; or restricting or disturbing military deployment, logistics and communication." International Committee for the Red Cross, "Direct Participation in Hostilities: Questions & Answers," June 2, 2009, http://www.icrc.org/eng/resources/documents/faq/direct-participation-ihl-faq-020609.htm.

14. Ibid.

15. An investigation into war crimes by the Sri Lankan government in its campaign against militant groups in 2009, including deliberate targeting of civilians, is described in International Crisis Group, *War Crimes in Sri Lanka*, Asia Report, no. 191, May 17, 2010, http://www.crisisgroup.org/en/regions/asia/south-asia/sri-lanka/191-war-crimes-in-sri-lanka.aspx.

16. Fuller documentation of attacks by Taliban and other nonstate armed groups against civilians can be found in United Nations Assistance Mission in Afghanistan and Afghanistan Independent Human Rights Commission, *Afghanistan Annual Report 2010: Protection of Civilians in Armed Conflict*, Kabul, Afghanistan (March 2011); Afghanistan Independent

Human Rights Commission, *A Campaign of Murder and Intimidation: Insurgent Abuses against Afghan Civilians*, Kabul, Afghanistan (December 2008), www.aihrc.org.af/AGEs_Completed_Report.pdf.

17. Ibid.

18. In addition, U.S. domestic legal provisions have criminalized an expanded number of indirect support activities. For example, section 805 of the USA PATRIOT Act expanded the scope for "material support for terrorism" to include "expert advice or assistance." Critics argued that the provision casts too wide a net, potentially leading to guilt by association.

19. Dapo Akande, "US/NATO Targeting of Afghan Drug Traffickers: An Illegal and Dangerous Precedent?" *Blog of the European Journal of International Law* September 13, 2009, http://www.ejiltalk.org/usnato-targeting-of-afghan-drug-traffickers-an-illegal-and-dangerous-precedent/.

20. Akande points to the Israeli Supreme Court case discussed earlier in the text, in which the Court found that "a person who sells food or medicine to an unlawful combatant is not taking a direct part, rather an indirect part in the hostilities. The same is the case regarding a person who aids the unlawful combatants by general strategic analysis, and grants them logistical, general support, *including monetary aid.*" *The Public Committee Against Torture in Israel v. The Government of Israel* (emphasis added).

21. Akande, "US/NATO Targeting of Afghan Drug Traffickers."

22. Ibid.

23. International Committee for the Red Cross, "Direct Participation in Hostilities: Questions & Answers."

The Civilianization of Armed Conflict: Trends and Implications

by Andreas Wenger and Simon J. A. Mason*

[...]

The nature of war has now clearly changed, and the role of civilians is central to this change. The terms 'civilians' and 'soldiers' are consequently no longer adequate and a plethora of new and more differentiated terms have been proposed, such as 'part-time terrorists', 'refugee warriors', or 'civilian augmentees'. The ambiguity of human intent and conduct and the ad hoc character of many organized groups using violence are illustrated, for example, by the owner of a tea shop in Sarajevo: 'Oh yes, I'll sit and sip tea with "them" in the daytime and take their money, but I may go out tonight to shoot them.'[4]

Efforts to clarify the notion of 'direct participation in hostilities' (DPH) are part of the necessary legal process of adapting to the changing nature of armed conflict.[5] Nevertheless, its meaning remains ambiguous, and no comprehensive definition has been achieved to date. Understanding the civilianization of conflict from a security policy point of view can help to put that notion into context—which is the aim of this article.

From a strategic point of view, the growing involvement of civilians in the conduct of international and non-international armed conflicts is linked to at least two trends:

1. the decline of inter-state wars, the revolution in military affairs, and the growing role of civilians in high-technology warfare; and

2. the growing relevance of intra-state armed conflict, the pervasiveness of civilian agency in such conflicts, and the blurring of lines between civilians and combatants.

After outlining these trends, we discuss how they merge in today's asymmetric conflicts. We then examine some of the implications for the ongoing discussion on 'direct participation in hostilities'. It seems useful to focus on 'conduct', rather than on 'membership' of an organized group, as the key criterion for differentiating between civilians and combatants. However, fine-tuning the legal concept alone will not solve the problem of insufficient differentiation between civilians and combatants. Various policy recommendations aimed at minimizing the blurring of lines between the civilian and the military domain on a more causal level are therefore also outlined.

One recommendation in particular is that governments must avoid outsourcing key security tasks to private security companies, especially in a state-building environment. They should use the double-edged sword of information warfare with the utmost care, as it threatens to blur the distinction between military and political responsibilities. Governments have to deal more comprehensively with complex and dynamic regional conflicts, instead of placing the highest priority on the seemingly more urgent task of fighting terrorism. The soft dimensions of security are pivotal, in contrast to relying too much on technological superiority. They require a better understanding of local-conflict dynamics and a greater focus on the human conscience as the key battle zone: winning hearts and minds is more important than the physical impact of force.

[...]

High-Technology Warfare Has Led to a Blurring of the Military and Civilian Domain

Today, the United States dominates the military playing field and alone has the option to project its military power almost instantaneously to every corner of the world. The current US dominance in terms of high-tech military forces originated in the 1970s, when Washington began to emphasize technology as a force multiplier in an effort to offset the quantitative superiority of the Soviet forces. As the RMA [revolution in military affairs] concept gained ground, the United States placed emphasis on the integration of advanced intelligence, surveillance and reconnaissance systems with stealthy long-range precision weapons systems in order to establish dominance in future battlefield engagements. The implications of the RMA for civilian participation in armed conflict are only tangentially addressed in the burgeoning literature on the military technological revolution—which is why some aspects are highlighted here.[9]

The development of a high-tech military force had major repercussions for the relationship between the military and the civilian spheres in at least two ways. First, as the technical complexity of modern weapons systems grew, civilian employees became progressively more important for maintaining and operating those systems. Under the paradigm of network-centric warfare the individual sensors, weapons platforms and control systems engaged in an attack could be geographically far apart and spread across continents.[10] Consequently civilian employees far from the actual battlefield also began to perform an increasingly direct and mission-critical support function in many military high-tech engagements. Civilian personnel who administer army battle command systems, communications systems and high-tech weaponry have become a highly specialized component of modern armed forces. They supplement military capabilities in areas of active military operations and are meanwhile an indispensable part of modern warfare.[11]

Second, the revolution in military affairs expanded the physical battlefield to include the virtual domain and ultimately the human mind. The object of warfare shifted from physical destruction of the adversary's military force to virtual control of the information space. The argument of RMA proponents was that speed, knowledge and precision would enable casualties to be minimized and wars to be rapidly ended. Information superiority, the argument continues, would maximize the political utility of force, reducing the friction inherent in warfare far enough to maintain public support for military operations. Control over the adversary no longer necessarily meant the physical control of objects, territory and personnel; virtual control over the opponent's capability to decide and act independently might be the far cheaper and politically more acceptable solution.[12]

In the context of their emphasis on information processes and content, RMA thinkers thus began to stress the importance of developing information warfare (IW) capabilities to downgrade an adversary's command, control, communications and intelligence systems. As the IW concepts broadened beyond the 'enabler paradigm', their highly problematic consequences for the relationship between the military and the civilian space became more visible. If IW targets the entire political, economic and military information infrastructure of an adversary across a continuum of operations between war and peace, then IW activities cannot but blur the boundaries between offence and defence and between war and peace.[13]

In fact, RMA thinkers began to realize over time that IW concepts were a double-edged sword. Modern societies depend heavily on reliable information and communication infrastructures, a problem that affects the military as well because it is heavily reliant on the civilian infrastructure. The risk of computer network attacks against civilian infrastructures highlights the fact that technology may end up being a source of vulnerability rather than the great force multiplier. The blurring of boundaries between civil and military responsibilities is also a critical issue in terms of the protection of a society's critical information infrastructures against cyber-attacks.[14]

THE RISE OF PRIVATE MILITARY AND SECURITY CONTRACTORS

The maintenance of a high-tech military force is very costly. This explains why the US military began to search for ways to increase its strategic, operational and tactical flexibility once the Cold War ended. After the Soviet Union and the Warsaw Pact had disappeared, the US military saw itself confronted with a very fluid and highly diffuse risk environment in which the tasks and functions of the military rapidly broadened. One way to increase flexibility is to rely on the flexibility of the market. So the US military began to outsource support functions more and more to private contractors, a development that was mirrored by the armed forces of many other countries.[15]

However, while outsourcing can increase flexibility, it tends to coincide with a loss of control, because private contractors are driven by a desire for money rather than for public goods such as peace, order and security. While states may be tempted to use private contractors as part of a foreign policy by proxy, farming out mission-critical functions to private military companies (PMCs) and private security companies (PSCs) may in reality weaken the unity of their command structures, result in a loss of control over the level of violence under their authority and/or undermine their control on legitimacy.[16]

The rise of PMCs and PSCs during the 1990s is therefore another factor that makes it more and more difficult to distinguish the civilian domain from the military domain. Security companies enjoy an unclear legal status in international and domestic law: should they be considered as business players, or as quasi-state entities acting on behalf of elected governments?[17] Furthermore, this is not only a problem for governments, because in today's complex conflict environments other players, including international organizations, NGOs and private industry, make growing use of the services of contractors.

Today, PMCs and PSCs offer an ever wider range of services. Most private contractors perform functions unrelated to the conduct of combat operations, but some are mandated to participate in major combat activities. Their assignments can range from support services (i.e. logistics) and consultancy (i.e. specialized expertise on technology and training) to the provision of personnel and specialized combat skills for defensive and offensive missions. The closer their functions are linked to the state monopoly on the use of force, the more problematic the engagement of private contractors is in terms of legitimacy. Furthermore, firms frequently offer a mix of services, making a distinction between tasks and their regulation more difficult. On the ground, functions are often very fluid in a rapidly changing conflict environment. Governments must ask themselves which functions can be outsourced and which are inherently governmental.[18]

In summary, inter-state wars have decreased since the end of the Cold War owing to structural and ideational factors, as reflected by the liberal and democratic peace theses. At a more operational level, the decrease in inter-state wars has gone hand in hand with the revolution in military affairs and the privatization of security tasks. Both of these trends have led to a blurring of the lines between civilians and combatants.

NOTES

[…]

4. Mary B. Anderson, *Do No Harm: How Aid Can Support Peace or* War, Lynne Rienner Publishers, Boulder/London, 1999, p. 25.

5. *Direct Participation in Hostilities*, Summary Report, International Committee of the Red Cross, Geneva, 31 December 2005, available at www.icrc.org/web/eng/siteeng0.nsf/html/ participation-hostilities-ihl-311205 (last visited 6 March 2009).

[…]

9. See e.g. John Arquilla and David F. Ronfeldt (eds.), *In Athena's Camp: Preparing for Conflict in the Information Age*, RAND, Santa Monica, 1996; Eliot Cohen, 'A revolution in military affairs', *Foreign Affairs*, Vol. 75 (2) (1996), pp. 37–54.

10. See e.g. Arthur K. Cebrowski and John J. Garstka, 'Network-centric warfare: its origin and future', *US Naval Institute Proceedings*, Vol. 124 (1) (1998), available at http://all.net/books/ iw/iwarstuff/www.usni.org/Proceedings/Articles98/PROcebrowski.htm (last visited 6 March 2009).

11. Geoffrey S. Corn, 'Unarmed but how dangerous? Civilian augmentees, the law of armed conflict, and the search for a more effective test for defining permissible civilian battlefield functions', *Journal of National Security Law & Policy*, Vol. 2 (2) (2008), p. 275, available at www.mcgeorge.edu/Documents/publications/jnslp/02_cornJCS111008%20PR.pdf (last visited 6 March 2009).

12. See e.g. Steven Metz and Douglas V. Johnson, *Asymmetry and US Military Strategy: Definition, Background, and Strategic Concepts*, Strategic Studies Institute, Carlisle, 2001.

13. For an excellent overview see Myriam Dunn Cavelty, *Cyber-Security and Threat Politics: US Efforts to Secure the Information Age*, Routledge, London, 2008, ch. 4, pp. 66–91; Edward Waltz, *Information Warfare: Principles and Operations*, Artech House, Boston, 1998.

14. See Dunn Cavelty, above note 13, ch. 5, pp. 91–121.

15. On the rise of private contractors see e.g. Peter W. Singer, *Corporate Warriors: The Rise of the Privatized Military Industry*, Cornell University Press, Ithaca, 2003; Fred Schreier and Marina Caparini, *Privatising Security: Law, Practice and Governance of Private Military and Security Companies*, Occasional Paper No. 6, Centre for the Democratic Control of Armed Forces, Geneva, 2005; Elke Krahmann, 'Security governance and the private military industry in Europe and North America', *Conflict, Security & Development*, Vol. 5 (2) (2005), pp. 247–68; Caroline Holmqvist, *Private Security Companies: The Case for Regulation*, SIPRI Policy Paper No. 9, Stockholm International Peace Research Institute, Stockholm, 2005.

16. We are indebted to Emmanuel Clivaz, who introduced the 'flexibility-control balance'

concept in a recent research note as a tool for analysing the impact of private contractors on the battlefield: Emmanuel Clivaz, 'Private contractors on the battlefield', ISN Case Studies, International Relations and Security Network (ISN), Zurich, September 2008, available at www.isn.ethz.ch/isn/Digital-Library/Publications/Detail/?id=93879&lng=en (last visited 6 March 2009).

17. Juan Carlos Zarate, 'The emergence of a new dog of war: private international security companies, international law, and the new world disorder', *Stanford Journal of International Law*, Vol. 34 (1998), pp. 75–162; Matt Gaul, 'Regulating the new privateers: private military service contracting and the modern marquee and reprisal clause', *Loyola of Los Angeles Law Review*, Vol. 31 (1998), pp. 1489–522; Christopher Kensey, 'Challenging international law: a dilemma of private security companies', *Conflict, Security and Development*, Vol. 5 (3) (2005), pp. 269–93.

18. Singer, above note 15.

*Andreas Wenger is professor of international and Swiss security policy and director of the Center for Security Studies at ETH (Eidgenössische Technische Hochschule) Zurich.

Simon J. A. Mason is a senior researcher working at the Center for Security Studies at ETH Zurich.

Andreas Wenger and Simon J. A. Mason, "The Civilianization of Armed Conflict: Trends and Implications," *International Review of the Red Cross* 90, no. 872 (December 2008): 835–43, 847–50.© ICRC.

Reprinted with the permission of Cambridge University Press.

NATO/Federal Republic of Yugoslavia "Collateral Damage" or Unlawful Killings? Violations of the Laws of War by NATO During Operation Allied Force

*by Amnesty International**

[…]

5.3 SERBIAN STATE TELEVISION AND RADIO: 23 APRIL

In the early morning of 23 April, NATO aircraft bombed the headquarters and studios of Serbian state television and radio (*Radio Televisija Srbije*—RTS) in central Belgrade. There was no doubt that NATO had hit its intended target. The building was occupied by working technicians and other production staff at the time of the bombing. There were estimated to be at least 120 civilians working in the building at the time of the attack.[45] At least 16 civilians were killed and a further 16 were wounded. A news broadcast was blacked out as a result. RTS broadcasting resumed about three hours after the bombing.

At the press conference later that day, NATO's Colonel Konrad Freytag placed this attack in the context of NATO's policy to "disrupt the national command network and to degrade the Federal Republic of Yugoslavia's propaganda apparatus." He explained: "Our forces struck at the regime leadership's ability to transmit their version of the news and to transmit their instruction to the troops in the field." In addition to housing Belgrade's main television and radio studios, NATO said the building "also housed a large multi-purpose communications satellite antenna dish."[46]

On the day of the attack Amnesty International publicly expressed grave concern, saying that it could not see how the attack could be justified based on the information available which stressed the propaganda role of the station. The organization wrote to NATO Secretary General Javier Solana requesting "an urgent explanation of the reasons for carrying out such an attack." In a reply dated 17 May, NATO said that it made "every possible effort to avoid civilian casualties and collateral damage by exclusively and carefully targeting the military infrastructure of President Milošević." It added that RTS facilities "are being used as radio relay stations and transmitters to support the activities of the FRY military and special police forces, and therefore they represented legitimate military targets."

At the Brussels meeting with Amnesty International, NATO officials clarified that this reference to relay stations and transmitters was to other attacks on RTS infrastructure and not this particular attack on the RTS headquarters. They insisted that the attack was carried out because RTS was a propaganda organ and that propaganda is direct support for military action. The fact that NATO explains its decision to attack RTS solely on the basis that it was a source of propaganda is repeated in the US Defence Department's review of the air campaign, which justifies the bombing by characterizing the RTS studios as "a facility used for propaganda purposes." No mention is made of any relay station.[47]

In an interview for a BBC television documentary, UK Prime Minister Tony Blair reflected on the bombing of RTS and appeared to be hinting that one of the reasons the station was targeted was because its video footage of the human toll of NATO mistakes, such as the bombing of the civilian convoy at Djakovica, was being re-broadcast by Western media outlets and was thereby undermining support for the war within the alliance. "This is one of the problems about waging a conflict in a modern communications and news world . . . We were aware that those pictures would come back and there would be an instinctive sympathy for the victims of the campaign."[48]

The definition of military objective in Article 52(2) of Protocol I, accepted by NATO, specifies that

"military objectives are limited to those objects which by their nature, location, purpose or use make an *effective contribution to military action* and whose total or partial destruction, capture or neutralization, in the circumstances ruling at the time, offers a *definite military advantage*." [emphasis added]

Amnesty International recognizes that disrupting government propaganda may help to undermine the morale of the population and the armed forces, but believes that justifying an attack on a civilian facility on such grounds stretches the meaning of "effective contribution to military action" and "definite military advantage" beyond the acceptable bounds of interpretation. Under the requirements of Article 52(2) of Protocol I, the RTS headquarters cannot be considered a military objective. As such, the attack on the RTS headquarters violated the prohibition to attack civilian objects contained in Article 52 (I) and therefore constitutes a war crime.

The authoritative ICRC *Commentary on the Additional Protocols of 8 June 1977 to the Geneva Conventions of 12 August 1949* interprets the expression "definite military advantage anticipated" by stating that "it is not legitimate to launch an attack which only offers potential or indeterminate advantages."[49] More recently the commentary on the German Military Manual states, "If weakening the enemy population's resolve to fight were considered a legitimate objective of armed forces, there would be no limit to war." And, further on, it says that "attacks having purely political objectives, such as demonstrating military power or intimidating the political leaders of the adversary" are prohibited.[50] British Defence doctrine adopts a similar approach: "the morale of an enemy's civilian population is not a legitimate target."[51]

It is also worth recalling in this context the judgment of the International Military Tribunal in Nuremberg in 1946 in the case of Hans Fritzsche, who served as a senior official in the Propaganda Ministry of the Third Reich, including as head of its Radio Division from November 1942. The prosecution asserted that he had "incited and encouraged the commission of War Crimes by deliberately falsifying news to arouse in the German People those passions which led them to the commission of atrocities." The Tribunal acknowledged that Fritzsche had shown in his speeches "definite anti-Semitism" and that he had "sometimes spread false news", but nevertheless found him not guilty. The Tribunal concluded its judgment in this case as follows:

"It appears that Fritsche [sic] sometimes made strong statements of a propagandistic nature in his broadcasts. But the Tribunal is not prepared to hold that they were intended to incite the German People to commit atrocities on conquered peoples, and he cannot be held to have been a participant in the crimes charged. *His aim was rather to arouse popular sentiment in support of Hitler and the German war effort.*"[52] [emphasis added]

On the issue of the legitimacy of attacking a television station in general, reference has been made to a list of categories of military objectives included in a working document produced by the ICRC in 1956, the Draft Rules for the Limitations of Dangers incurred by the Civilian Population in Time of War.[53] In paragraph (7) the list included "The installations of broadcasting and television stations." However, the French text of the Draft Rules made clear that such installations must be of "fundamental military importance."[54] Also, Article 7 of the Draft Rules stated that even the listed objects cannot be considered military objectives if attacking them "offers no military advantage."

Whatever the merit of the Draft Rules, it is doubtful that they would have supported the legitimacy of the attack on the RTS headquarters. In any case the Draft Rules were discussed at the 1957 International Conference of the Red Cross, for which they had been prepared, but in the following years the approach of drawing up lists of military objectives was abandoned in favour of the approach eventually adopted by Protocol I in Article 52.

The attack on the RTS headquarters may well have violated international humanitarian law even if the building could have been properly considered a military objective. Specifically, that attack would have violated the rule of proportionality under Article 51(5)(b) of Protocol I and may have also violated the obligations to provide effective warning under Article 57(2)(c) of the same Protocol.

Article 51(5)(b) prohibits attacks "which may be expected to cause incidental loss of civilian life . . . which would be excessive in relation to the concrete and direct military advantage anticipated." The ICRC Commentary specified that "the expression 'concrete and direct' was intended to show that the advantage concerned should be substantial and relatively close, and that advantages which are hardly perceptible and those which would only appear in the long term should be disregarded."[55] NATO must have clearly anticipated that civilians in the RTS building would have been killed. In addition, it appears that NATO realized that attacking the RTS building would only interrupt broadcasting for a brief period. SACEUR General Wesley Clark has stated: "We knew when we struck that there would be alternate means of getting the Serb Television. There's no single switch to turn off everything but we thought it was a good move to strike it and the political leadership agreed with us."[56] In other words, NATO deliberately attacked a civilian object, killing 16 civilians, for the purpose of disrupting Serbian television broadcasts in the middle of the night for approximately three hours. It is hard to see how this can be consistent with the rule of proportionality.

Article 57(2) (c) of Protocol I requires that "Effective warning shall be given of attacks which may affect the civilian population, unless circumstances do not permit." Official statements, issued prior to the RTS bombing, on whether NATO was targeting the media were contradictory. On 8 April, Air Commodore Wilby stated that NATO considered RTS as a "legitimate target in this campaign" because of its use as "an instrument of propaganda and repression." He added that radio and television would only become "an acceptable instrument of public information" if President Milošević provided equal time for uncensored Western news broadcasts for two periods of three hours a day.[57] And on the same day, General Jean Pierre Kelche, French armed forces chief, said at a press conference, "We are going to bust their transmitters and their relay stations because these are instruments of propaganda of the Milošević regime which are contributing to the war effort."[58]

But at the NATO press conference on the following day (9 April), when asked by a reporter for a clarification of NATO's policy on media in the FRY

NATO spokesperson Jamie Shea said: ". . . whatever our feelings about Serb television, we are not going to target TV transmitters directly . . . in Yugoslavia military radio relay stations are often combined with TV transmitters but we attack the military target. If there is damage to the TV transmitters, it is a secondary effect but it is not the primary intention to do that." Jamie Shea also wrote to the Brussels-based International Federation of Journalists on 12 April that "Allied Force targets military targets only and television and radio towers are only struck if they are integrated into military facilities . . . There is no policy to strike television and radio transmitters as such."

It appears that the statements by Wilby and Shea came after some members of the media had been alerted to the fact that an attack on the television station had already been planned. According to Eason Jordan, the President of CNN International, in early April he received a telephone call from a NATO official who told him that an attack on RTS in Belgrade was under way and that he should tell CNN's people to get out of there. Jordan told the official that loss of life at RTS would be significant and, given the short notice, unavoidable. The official persuaded NATO to abort the mission (apparently half an hour before the plane would have reached its target). Jordan believes that NATO's subsequent public threats against Serbian "propaganda" organs were made in order to minimize civilian casualties in a future attack.[59]

John Simpson, who was based in Belgrade for the BBC during the war, was among the foreign correspondents who received warnings from his headquarters to avoid RTS after the aborted attack. He believes that it was in response to the spreading of rumours about the aborted attack among the foreign media in Belgrade, that NATO issued the statements cited above.[60]

UK Prime Minister Tony Blair blames Yugoslav officials for not evacuating the building. "They could have moved those people out of the building. They knew it was a target and they didn't. And I don't know, it was probably for, you know, very clear propaganda reasons . . . There's no point—I mean there's no way of waging war in a pretty way. It's ugly. It's an ugly business."[61]

Amnesty International does not consider the statement against official Serbian media made by Air Commodore Wilby two weeks before the attack to be an effective warning to civilians, especially in light of other, contradictory statements by NATO officials and alliance members. As noted above, Western journalists have reported that they were warned by their employers to stay away from the television station before the attack, and it would also appear that some Yugoslav officials may have expected that the building was about to be attacked.[62] However, there was no warning from NATO that a specific attack on RTS headquarters was imminent. NATO officials in Brussels told Amnesty International that they did not give a specific warning as it would have endangered the pilots.

Some accounts in the press have suggested that the decision to bomb RTS was made by the US government over the objections of other NATO members. According to the writer Michael Ignatieff, "within NATO command allies were at loggerheads: with British lawyers arguing that the Geneva Conventions prohibit the targeting of journalists and television stations, and the US side arguing that the supposed 'hate speech' broadcast by the station foreclosed its legal immunity under the conventions." Due to the disagreement on the legality of the target "the British refused to take part in the bombing of the Serbian television station."[63] Others have reported French objections to the attack. Human Rights Watch has reported that an attack on RTS that was to take place on 12 April was postponed due to "French disapproval of the target."[64]

At the Brussels meeting a NATO official told Amnesty International that one nation judged RTS to be a legitimate target, without specifying the country in question. If this information is correct, it empties of all practical meaning NATO officials' assertion that a target deemed illegal by one nation would not be reassigned to another member. The case of RTS appears to indicate that NATO's way of dealing with such objections was to carry on bombing controversial targets without the participation of members who objected to the specific attacks. However, if in fact the UK or other countries did object and abstain from participating in this attack, they may not be absolved of their responsibility under international law as members of an alliance that deliberately launched a direct attack on a civilian object.

NOTES

45. Inter Press Service (IPS), "NATO and Serbian TV Accused of Rights Crimes", 19–26 October 1999.

46. NATO press conference, with Jamie Shea and Colonel Konrad Freytag, 23 April 1999.

47. US DoD, *Kosovo/Operation Allied Force After Action Report*, submitted to Congress 31 January 2000.

48. "Moral Combat—NATO at War", broadcast on BBC2 on 12 March 2000.

49. ICRC *Commentary on the Additional Protocols of 8 June 1977 to the Geneva Conventions of 12 August 1949*, para 2209.

50. Stefan Oeter, "Methods and Means of Combat" in *Handbook of Humanitarian Law in Armed Conflict*, Dieter Fleck, ed. Oxford University Press 1995.

51. Doubts about the lawfulness of attacking an object on propaganda grounds have been expressed, with specific reference to the RTS headquarters, by George Aldrich, who headed the US delegation at the diplomatic conference that led to the adoption of Protocol I: "[I]f the television studios . . . were targeted merely because they were spreading propaganda to the civilian population, even including blatant lies about the armed conflict, it would be open to question whether such use could legitimately be considered an effective contribution to military action." See "Yugoslavia Television Studios as Military Objectives", in *International Law FORUM du droit international*, Volume I, No. 3, September 1999, p. 150.

52. *American Journal of International Law*, Volume 41 (1947), p. 328.

53. See for example, Human Rights Watch, *Civilian Deaths in the NATO Air Campaign*, February 2000, p. 26. The list is referred to in the ICRC Commentary on the Additional Protocols, paragraph 2002, note 3.

54. The text of this paragraph in French is "Les installations des stations de radiodiffusion et de télévision, les centres téléphoniques et télégraphiques d'intérêt essentiellement militaire." In the English version, a semi-colon was inserted after the word "stations": "The installations of broadcasting and television stations; telephone and telegraph exchanges of fundamental military importance."

55. ICRC *Commentary on the Additional Protocols of 8 June 1977 to the Geneva Conventions of 12 August 1949*, para 2209.

56. "Moral Combat—NATO at War", broadcast on BBC2 on 12 March 2000.

57. NATO press conference, 8 April 1999.

58. Press conference of the (French) Minister of Defence and the Chief of Staff of the Armed Forces, 8 April 1999. (French original: "Et donc, nous avons décidé de nous en prendre aux relais radio, aux émetteurs radio, aux relais télévision, aux émetteurs télévision, car ces outils-là sont des outils de propagande de la part du régime de Monsieur Milošević, et qui vont dans le sens de la poursuite du combat.")

59. Communication to Amnesty International from Eason Jordan, President, CNN International, 8 March 2000.

60. Amnesty International interview with John Simpson, 31 January 2000.

61. "Moral Combat—NATO at War", broadcast on BBC2 on 12 March 2000.

62. See: "Death of a Makeup Girl" by Julian Manyon, in *The Guardian*, 30 April 1999, and "Des victimes du bombardement de la television serbe par l'Otan se retournent contre Sobodan Milosevic", *Le Monde*, 1 November 1999.

63. Michael Ignatieff, "Virtual War", *Prospect*, April 2000.

64. Human Rights Watch, *Civilian Deaths in the NATO Air Campaign*, February 2000, p. 26.

*Amnesty International is a leading international human rights organization.

Amnesty International, "NATO/Federal Republic of Yugoslavia: 'Collateral Damage' or Unlawful Killings? Violations of the Laws of War by NATO during Operation Allied Force," June 2000: "Case Studies: 5.3 Serbian State Television and Radio: 23 April," pp. 41–46. © Amnesty International, 1 Easton Street, London WC1X0DW, United Kingdom. http://www.amnesty.org.

Used by Permission.

US/NATO Targeting of Afghan Drug Traffickers: An Illegal and Dangerous Precedent?

*by Dapo Akande**

In August, the United States Senate Foreign Relations Committee, released a report ("Afghanistan's Narco-War: Breaking the Link Between Drug Traffickers and Insurgents") which confirmed that U.S. forces in Afghanistan are now mandated to kill or capture drug traffickers in Afghanistan who have links to the Taliban. The Taliban is estimated to receive between $70 million and $500 million dollars a year from the drugs trade and this money is said to play a critical role in financing the insurgency. Therefore, NATO (led on this issue by the US and the UK) consider it essential to starve the Taliban of the funds which make the insurgency in Afghanistan possible. However, targeting of individual drug traffickers or of drugs labs and other objects associated with the drugs trade raises some fundamental questions about who or what is a lawful target in armed conflict. The US and NATO's policy appears to be a regrettable return to the notion of "quasi combatants" and to the idea of total war in which persons or industries connected to the war effort become legitimate targets. Given that the International Criminal Court has jurisdiction over acts committed in Afghanistan and the Office of the Prosecutor has been collecting information in order to decide whether to open an investigation into alleged crimes committed in that country (see here and the discussion at Opinio Juris), US and NATO commanders ought to pay careful consideration to the legality of their targeting policy.

According to the report of the Senate Foreign Relations Committee:

two U.S. generals in Afghanistan said that the ROE [Rules of Engagement] and the internationally recognized Law of War have been interpreted to allow them to put drug traffickers with proven links to the insurgency on a kill list, called the joint integrated prioritized target list. The military places no restrictions on the use of force with these selected targets, which means they can be killed or captured on the battlefield; it does not, however, authorize targeted assassinations away from the battlefield. The generals said standards for vetting on the list require two verifiable human sources and substantial additional evidence. Currently, there are roughly 50 major traffickers who contribute funds to the insurgency on the target list. "We have a list of 367 'kill or capture' targets, including 50 nexus targets who link drugs and insurgency," one of the officers explained to the committee staff. [pp. 15–16]

The report goes on to explain that:

The authorization for using lethal force on traffickers caused a stir at NATO earlier this year when some countries questioned whether the killing traffickers and destroying drug labs complied with international law. Jaap de Hoop Scheffer, secretary general of NATO at the time, said filters had been put in place to make sure the alliance remains within the bounds of the law.

Indeed, this controversy within NATO is one which dates back to October 2008, when NATO defence ministers first agreed to allow forces in Afghanistan to target Afghan drug traffickers (see *Washington Post* report). However, the dispute intensified in January when it was reported in the German Magazine *Der Speigel* that NATO's Supreme Allied Commander Europe, American General John Craddock issued guidance to the German head of the NATO command center responsible for Afghanistan and the American General then in charge of the International Security Assistance Force (ISAF) in Afghanistan. Craddock wrote that it is "no longer necessary to produce intelligence or other evidence that each particular drug trafficker or narcotics facility in Afghanistan meets the criteria of being a military objective." Apparently, the respondents argued that such a policy would be illegal under international humanitarian law.

The furore generated by the January guidance must have had some effect as the policy outlined in the Senate Foreign Relations Committee differs in an important respect from the Craddock guidance. Craddock's guidance appear to countenance the targeting of any drugs trafficker or narcotics facility in Afghanistan without any need for a connection with the armed conflict going on there. It is now the case that targeted drug traffickers must have a proven link to the insurgency. It is difficult to think of an IHL argument that would legitimate the Craddock approach as that approach explicitly contemplates that the person or object need not be a military objective. The new approach, however, seeks to confine targeting of individuals not only to those who fund the Taliban insurgency but particularly to those found *on the battlefield* (whatever that may mean). Also, NATO's website confirms that ISAF may only engage in "the destruction of processing facilities and action against narcotic producers if there is a clearly established link with the insurgency."

However, the new approach raises questions about whether it is lawful to target a person or an object simply because they provide finance for armed forces or contribute to the sustaining the war effort. International humanitarian law clearly forbids making the civilians the object of an attack. This is the case both in an international armed conflict but also in a non-international armed conflict, which is what is taking place in Afghanistan (see Article 13(2) of Additional Protocol II (1977) to the Geneva Conventions (APII)). However, as with international armed conflicts, civilians who take a direct part in hostilities in non-international armed conflicts will lose their immunity from attack (Art. 13(3) APII). The key question with regard to the targeting of individual drug lords is whether they may be regarded as combatants (or fighters), or, alternatively, as civilians taking a direct part in hostilities. It is only if they fall into either of these categories that they become a legitimate target. Although IHL in non-international armed conflicts prohibits intentional targeting of civilians it has not been clear (both as a matter of law and in practice) who is a civilian or a combatant in such a conflict. Nevertheless, it is hard to see how Afghan drug lords can be regarded as combatants. To the extent that one is talking about drug traffickers who are not members of the Taliban but who simply fund the Taliban (eg by paying it protection money) these are clearly not fighters. They may act illegally but they are nevertheless civilians. Some NATO commanders have claimed that NATO is not targeting drug dealers with links to the Taliban but rather Taliban members with links to the drug trade. However, membership of the Taliban alone is not sufficient to constitute a person as a combatant or a fighter.

The ICRC's recent Interpretive Guidance on the Notion of Direct Participation in Hostilities (issued earlier this summer and commented on by me here) states that:

> For the purposes of the principle of distinction in non-international armed conflict, all persons who are not members of State armed forces or organized armed groups of a party to the conflict are civilians and, therefore, entitled to protection against direct attack unless and for such time as they take a direct part in hostilities. In non-international armed conflict, organized armed groups constitute the armed forces of a non-State party to the conflict and consist only of individuals whose continuous function it is to take a direct part in hostilities ("continuous combat function").

On this analysis, only those Taliban members who have a continuous combat function, i.e., whose function in the group it is to engage in hostilities, may be regarded as legitimate targets. Where a drug lord does not have such a function, he will not be a lawful target.

However, Taliban members or drugs lords may still be targeted where they take a direct part in hostilities. Perhaps this is what the US Senate Foreign Relations Report means when it says that the selected targets may be killed or captured *on the battlefield*. However, the notion of "direct participation in hostilities" is one on which there is not so much clarity. The ICRC's recent Interpretive Guidance on the Notion of Direct Participation in Hostilities goes some way in providing such clarity. Guidance V(2) of the ICRC's work points out that:

"there must be a direct causal link between the act and the harm likely to result either from that act, or from a coordinated military operation of which that act constitutes an integral part."

In the view of the ICRC, direct causation means that the harm in question must be caused in one causal step. Whether or not one agrees with this particular definition it is clear that direct participation means that it is the act (or the operation of which the act forms a part) which constitutes that participation which causes the actual harm to the enemy personnel or equipment. There is a distinction to be made between acts of participation in hostilities and acts which generally sustain the war effort. This is a crucial distinction as it may be the case that much activity in a state in armed conflict may go towards sustaining the war effort. To permit anyone who is involved in the war sustaining effort to be a direct target is to allow for unrestricted warfare—practically everyone could be a target. This would be a regressive move. Deplorable as their activities might be, IHL does not permit targeting of a drug trafficker simply on the basis of their drug trafficking and financing of the insurgency. More would be required for that person be considered as taking a direct part in hostilities. The Israeli Supreme Court accepted in the Targeted Killings case (para. 35) that providing monetary aid to belligerents does not constitute direct participation in hostilities.

For purposes of targeting, it matters little that drugs traffickers are engaging in illegal activity. The reason they are now being subject to targeting is not the illegality of their activity but the consequences of their conduct—that it funds the adverse party. From that perspective, their activity is no different to that of an executive in any industry (say, oil or manufacturing) which provides the bulk of the income of a belligerent State. Although some have argued (and still argued) that factories and objects connected with war sustaining industries are legitimate targets, I don't recall it being argued in the past that *individuals* connected with these industries are lawful targets. [...]

This leads to the question whether the Afghan poppy farms and drugs labs for converting the poppy paste to heroin are legitimate targets. As far as IHL is concerned the relevant questions are: (i) whether IHL applicable in non-international armed conflicts forbids the targeting of civilian objects and (ii) whether drug related objects belonging to members of the Taliban or which fund the Taliban are military objectives. While the ICRC Customary International Law study (Rule 7) says that the prohibition of attacks on civilian objects applies also in non-international armed conflicts, it is significant that such a prohibition is not contained in Additional Protocol II. Also, while Art. 8(2)(b)(ii) of the Statute of the International Criminal Court makes it a war crime to intentionally target civilian objects in an international armed conflict, Art. 8 omits to make such conduct a war crime in a non-international armed conflict.

Even if the prohibition against targeting civilian objects applies in the Afghanistan armed conflict, there is a question as to whether objects which contribute to funding a belligerent party are military objectives. To use the wording of Art. 52(2) of Additional Protocol I, the question is whether such objects make "an effective contribution to military action." The United States takes the view that objects are lawful targets where they "effectively contribute to the enemy's war-fighting/war-sustaining capability'" (*Annotated Supplement to the Commander's Handbook on the Law of Naval Operations*, paras. 5.3.1 and 8.2, reaffirmed in the Instruction No. 2 issued by the Dept of Defense for Military Commissions 2003). This interpretation is too broad and is rejected by scholars and by other States. It is generally considered that the contribution of an object to military action includes contribution to military action in general, however there must a proximate connection between the object and military action. The fact that an object provides the finances for military action is not sufficient. Otherwise, all facilities/industries that generate taxes for a State would be liable to attack in time of armed conflict. This would mean that practically all objects connected with economic production are liable to attack. To take such an approach would be a major reversal of the position of NATO allies other than the US—who have not hitherto taken this approach. Again, as far as the IHL prohibition of the targeting of civilian objects is concerned, it matters little that the object in question is being used in illegal activities. The reason for the targeting is that it is providing finance for the insurgency, in other words it is war-sustaining. If this were permissible, it would be permissible also for lawful activity and would be a regrettable return to a policy of total war.

However, there is another way of looking at the destruction of civilian property. This is the view that the destruction is permissible, not specifically by IHL, but is part of law enforcement in Afghanistan. NATO's website makes it clear that action by ISAF forces to destroy narcotics facilities can be undertaken only upon request of the Afghan Government. Thus, it could be argued that such destruction is simply assistance given by ISAF to the enforcement of Afghan criminal law. It is not uncommon that law enforcement officials destroy property in the process of law enforcement, eg the policeman who breaks down the door in the course of entering a house to make an arrest. In domestic law, where a seizure is made of illegal drugs, one would indeed expect law enforcement to destroy that property. The only applicable restraints would be the restraints imposed by human rights law. These restraints at least apply to the Afghan government and some would consider them as applying to the NATO forces too (I ignore for now the tricky question of the extra-territorial application of human rights treaties). These human rights restraints will require that the deprivation of property not be arbitrary and that it be in the public interest. Also proper procedure must be followed. As long as these principles are followed, governments are allowed to destroy property for the purposes of law enforcement. NATO may therefore be acting lawfully as it cannot be excluded, a priori, that action by military forces would fulfil these conditions.

Given that international (human rights) law would permit destruction by a government of civilian property in peacetime for the purpose of law enforcement, it would be surprising to have a blanket prohibition in time of internal armed conflict. This gives reason to be cautious about accepting that there is blanket prohibition of targeting civilian property in the customary IHL applicable to non-international armed conflicts. Of course this raises question about the relationship between IHL and human rights law. However, it would be odd for a government to find itself more restrained by international law in time of internal armed conflict than it would be absent such an armed conflict.

To conclude, NATO's targeting of individual Afghan drug dealers would clearly be unlawful, if based solely on their status as funders of the insurgency. However, the position is more complicated with regard to the destruction of poppy farms and drugs labs.

*Dapo Akande is university lecturer in public international law in the Oxford Law Faculty and co-director of the Oxford Institute for Ethics, Law and Armed Conflict.

Dapo Akande, "US/NATO Targeting of Afghan Drug Traffickers: An Illegal and Dangerous Precedent?" September 13, 2009, available at EJILTalk! http://www.ejiltalk.org/usnato-targeting-of-afghan-drug-traffickers-an-illegal-and-dangerous-precedent/.

IHL and Civilian Participation in Hostilities in the OPT

by the Program on Humanitarian Policy and Conflict Research, Harvard University*

INTRODUCTION

This policy brief reviews the legal questions associated with the participation of civilians in hostilities. This issue represents a critical challenge to the protection of civilians in current conflicts, particularly when hostilities are conducted in the midst of civilian populations and assets, and when non-state armed groups are engaged as central actors. This issue is also of particular relevance when the hostilities occur under occupation. While international law recognizes a basic right of self- determination for populations under occupation, it provides immunity against violence only to those not participating in hostilities. This apparent contradiction is at the core of the debate on the protection of civilians and raises a number of questions about the roles and rights of civilians in armed conflict, as well as the concept of participation in the war effort and the nature of hostilities. Is a member of a militant group necessarily a "combatant"? Can he or she be targeted according to the rules of international humanitarian law (IHL)? Is membership the key criterion, or are the actual acts of the individual the deciding factors of his or her status under the law? How can a civilian maintain or restore his or her protected status? Practitioners face these and related questions when developing policies for civilian protection in the occupied Palestinian territory (OPT).

[...]

A number of prominent scholars and practitioners today argue that the relevance of IHL to the protection of civilians rests on its ability to provide a clear rationale justifying the distinction between individuals who engage in hostilities—and as such become legitimate targets—from those who do not. In the view of such scholars, a substantive protection regime for civilians requires that the concept of participation in hostilities must be brought in line with current realities in the battlefield. In their view, the classical notion of distinction between civilians and combatants, embodied in the conventional mobilization of combatants in large uniformed contingents and the obligation to conduct military operations away from civilian centers, does not provide sufficient guidance in contemporary conflicts. In this reading, the drafting of the current treaties of IHL took place at a time when the categories of "combatant" and "civilian" were more clearly delineated than they are in today's conflicts. These scholars argue that state militaries now face a much more complex set of actors in the battle space: individuals who appear to enjoy immunity from attack under IHL, but who in fact occupy a new category between "innocent" civilians and regular combatants. They observe that militants nowadays in fact depend on their protected status as civilians to plan, prepare, and engage in hostilities.

Others argue that the rules of IHL did indeed anticipate the types of conflicts and actors we see today, and that the very clear legal separation between combatants and civilians should not be muddied by references to "new facts" or "changed paradigms" of warfare. These scholars argue that the legal understanding of civilian participation in hostilities has achieved the status of customary international law, and that all states are bound to limit their targeting of civilians who participate in hostilities to the narrow confines of existing law. In addition, these scholars and jurists note that any suggestion of a third category of actor in the battlefield, one between civilian and combatant, poses serious risks to all civilians caught up in armed conflict and diminishes the power of IHL as a clear set of rules for commanders making difficult decisions in the course of warfare.

For both sides of this debate, the Israeli-Palestinian conflict presents a key example and case study of their arguments. For those who argue that contemporary warfare has fundamentally changed, groups like Islamic Jihad and the military wing of Hamas present model cases of organized entities intent on utilizing terror tactics while enjoying the protection of civilian status. Others posit that militants in the OPT can be seen in light of existing IHL, and that the military must abide by strict rules of distinction and proportionality in targeting those civilians who directly engage in hostilities. This debate remains wide open, and for many, the stakes of accepting either argument are higher than ever. In this context, the International Committee of the Red Cross (ICRC) is conducting significant research on the issue, engaging international experts in a multi-stage process of deliberation and debate. In case of the OPT specifically, the Israeli Supreme Court has also explored this issue in detail in its decision on targeted attacks.[1]

Part I of this Policy brief examines the international legal framework applicable to the targeting of civilians who take a direct part in hostilities, in particular with reference to the recent Israeli Supreme Court decision. Part II defines the main components of direct participation of civilians. Part III addresses current uncertainties in the context of international and domestic law by suggesting three key questions for scholars and practitioners to consider in determining the lawfulness of targeting any given individual who is alleged to be taking a direct part in hostilities. Part IV concludes with a review of the current debate.

PART I: THE INTERNATIONAL LEGAL FRAMEWORK

This legal debate takes place within a politically charged environment, and in the case of the OPT, an ongoing military conflict. For some, the political nature of the debate diminishes the value of legal discussion as a plausible means for finding a solution to this dilemma. Yet, the law appears to shape the principles under which political and security decisions are made. Military commanders are trained on the basis of clear rules of engagement. Their decisions are informed by legal advisers in real time and may eventually be subject to review by a judicial body. While it may be the case that nuances of legal debate matter little in the theater of operations where military considerations and politics dictate the course of action, the law sets the vocabulary and planning framework within which military operations are devised, negotiated, and implemented. This distinction is relevant for practitioners, because most protection activities do not take place on the battlefield. Rather, these efforts address the legal responsibility of the higher echelons state and military leadership in the proper planning of operations. Hence, third party interventions to ensure protection of civilians will often be most effective at the level of the Ministry of Defense or Foreign Affairs.

In the current case, the legal distinction between civilians and combatants is understood by all parties as a core principle of humanitarian protection. This principle is enshrined in both treaty and customary law, and it applies to both non-international[2] and international armed conflict.[3] As one scholar noted nearly a century ago, "The separation of armies and peaceful inhabitants into two distinct classes is perhaps the greatest triumph of international law."[4] This general principle appears in the earliest texts of the laws of war and is expanded upon in Additional Protocol I of 1977, which holds that *"the civilian population and individual civilians shall enjoy general protection against dangers arising from military operations . . . the civilian population as such . . . shall not be the object of attack."*[5] Despite the fact that a number of prominent states, including Israel, are not party to the Additional Protocol, this aspect of the principle of distinction is widely recognized as binding customary international law (meaning that even states that have not signed the treaty are bound by those aspects that are recognized as customary).[6]

While requiring that civilians are to be protected, the law also recognizes the military imperatives of conducting effective and victorious operations. This principle, known as "military necessity," states that parties to the conflict can use all force necessary to achieve their military goals, unless such acts are prohibited by the law. In practice, this means that there is no obligation to arrest or to otherwise use lesser means to neutralize those who engage in hostilities. Combatants can be attacked at any time: they can be killed as they plan an attack, when they engage in hostilities in the battlefield, when they leave the battlefield, or even while they are sleeping in their barracks.[7] Only when a combatant surrenders or is otherwise put *"hors de combat,"* do attacks against him or her become illegal.

Civilians, on the other hand, benefit from immunity from attack. Inherent to this immunity and to the principle of military necessity is the prohibition on civilian engagement in hostilities. The language of Article 51(3) of the Additional Protocol is clear: *"Civilians shall enjoy the protection afforded by this Section unless and for such time as they take a direct part in hostilities."*[8] In this context, the immunity of civilians hinges on the circumstances of their participation and the way in which it is perceived and addressed. As such, the debate over civilian immunity is waged over the wording of this one sentence, in particular, the interpretation of "for such time as" and "direct part in hostilities." It also raises questions regarding the military responses to such participation, in terms of legitimate *means* of responding to an attack from a civilian, and legitimate *time frames* in which this response may take place. Can the military target these civilians at any time? Are they obliged to use lesser means to neutralize civilians participating in hostilities? Should they arrest these civilians whenever possible?[9]

[...]

Part II: The Meaning of "Unless and for Such Time as They Take a Direct Part in Hostilities"

However strong the position in treaty and customary IHL that civilians can only be targeted if they take a direct part in hostilities, the exact scope of the notions of "hostilities," "direct part[icipation]" and "for such time as" remains open to debate. The following analysis will consider each of these three elements in turn.

What Defines "Hostilities"

While it is clear that a civilian actively engaging in an armed attack would be targetable while in the heat of battle, the legal definition of what constitutes "hostilities" is not explicit. According to the Commentary on Article 51(3) of Additional Protocol I, "hostilities" include situations when a civilian undertakes hostile acts with or without the use of a weapon.[17] Hostile acts are "acts which by their nature and purpose are intended to cause actual harm to the personnel and equipment of the armed forces."[18] Similarly, the ICRC Model Manual specifies that, "[t]aking part in hostilities means engaging in hostile action against enemy armed forces but not [just] assisting in the general war effort."[19] Many experts have added that the definition of "hostilities" must also include activities aimed at the enemy in general, so as to include activities intended to harm civilians.[20] In the "targeted killings" case decided in December 2006, the Israeli Supreme Court considered "hostilities" to be "acts which by nature and objective are intended to cause damage to the army."[21]

Defining "Direct Participation"

While the law was intended to establish a requirement for a direct link between the contribution of a civilian and the conduct of a military operation, the ICRC Study on Customary International Humanitarian Law has concluded that there is no clear and uniform definition of "direct" participation in hostilities in state practice.[22]

Both the ICRC Commentaries and the ICTY have defined "direct" participation in hostilities as "acts of war which by their nature or purpose are likely to cause actual harm to the personnel and equipment of the enemy armed forces."[23] They further note that determining what is "direct" participation requires a margin of judgment because direct participation includes more than just combat and active military operations but at the same time must not be so broadly defined as to include the entire war effort.[24] At the ICRC Third Expert Meeting on the Notion of Direct Participation in Hostilities, some participants argued for a narrow definition of "hostilities" (i.e., violent acts) in order to maximize the number of civilians protected by the principle of distinction, while others argued that a broad interpretation of "hostilities" (i.e., acts that go beyond the use of violence) might strengthen the actual protection of civilians by offering clear incentives for non-combatants to stay away from the battlefield or any hostile activity.[25] There were disagreements at the ICRC Second Expert Meeting as to whether a civilian acting as a voluntary human shield, or gathering intelligence, would be considered to have taken a "direct part" in hostilities.[26]

The Inter-American Commission on Human Rights has distinguished between "direct" and "indirect" participation by stating that civilian activities which "merely support the adverse party's war or military effort" are indirect participation in hostilities. Such indirect activities include "selling goods to one or more of the armed parties, expressing sympathy for the cause of one of the parties or, even more clearly, failing to act to prevent and incursion by one of the armed parties." In contrast, direct participation involves "acts of violence which pose an immediate threat of actual harm to the adverse party."[27]

In the "targeted killings" case, the Israeli Supreme Court defined taking a "direct part" in hostilities broadly, to include not only the commission of attacks, but also direct support for the commission of such acts, including intelligence-gathering, the transportation of combatants, the operation, supervision, service to combatants or their weaponry,[28] enlisting or sending combatants to commit hostilities, and "deciding" and "planning" the attack. Those who enlist others, guide them and send them to commit terrorist acts are also seen as directly participating in hostilities.[29] "Targeted killings" of civilians who take such a "direct part" in hostilities may be lawful, subject to the Israeli Supreme Court's procedural requirements.[30] However, the Court classified the following as examples of "indirect" participation in hostilities: general strategic analysis, general support such as monetary aid, the selling of food or medicines, acting as an involuntary human shield, and distributing propaganda.[31] Civilians taking such an "indirect" part in hostilities would not lose their immunity from attack, and could not legally be the subject of a "targeted killing."

Temporal Element: "For Such Time As"

Beyond the qualitative contribution of a civilian to the hostilities, the concept of direct participation also has an important temporal element. This element is linked to the definition of "for such time as." In other words, the material contributions of a civilian to the hostilities do not by themselves remove the immunity against attack forever, but only *for such time as* this contribution effectively supports the conduct of hostilities. Hence, a civilian that has ceased to *engage* in acts of violence is again immune from attacks. Equally, a civilian who no longer provides *direct support* to the commission of an attack can no longer be targeted.

In its ongoing expert meeting process, the ICRC takes note of a consensus amongst participants that civilians are directly participating in hostilities while they are both *preparing for* and *returning from* combat activities.[32] In the "targeted killings" case, the Israeli High Court ruled that a civilian bearing arms (openly or concealed) who is on his way to the place where he will use them, or is using arms, or is on his way back from such a place, is taking "direct" part in hostilities.[33]

The ICRC Third Expert Meeting discussed four main approaches to targeting civilians "for such time as" they directly participate in hostilities: the specific acts approach, the affirmative disengagement approach, the membership approach, and the limited membership approach.[34] Each of these have anticipated strengths and weaknesses in practice, as discussed below.

The specific acts approach depends upon the scope of acts included in the concept of direct participation. It holds that when a civilian is participating in those acts, he or she can be targeted. Conversely, when he or she stops participating in those acts, he or she cannot be targeted, but must instead face standard law enforcement procedures, such as arrest or detention. Some participants at the ICRC Third Expert Meeting commended the parallel between this approach and the protection given to combatants if or when they alternate between active duty and civilian life.[35] The specific acts approach is alleged to mirror the intention of the drafters of AP I, yet it does not deal with the "revolving door" phenomenon. Supporters of expanding the scope of time for which a civilian may be targeted for taking a direct part in hostilities argue that a specific acts approach offers undue protection for a civilian who frequently takes a direct part in hostilities.

The affirmative disengagement approach permits the targeting of a civilian who takes a direct part in hostilities from the moment of his or her first specific act of direct participation until or unless he or she ceases such activity in a way which is *objectively recognizable* to opposing forces. This approach is alleged to deal with the problem of the "revolving door," and yet it presents possibly insurmountable intelligence difficulties. Targeting forces would need to monitor militants constantly for any act which constitutes affirmative disengagement. Unless a targeting force had up-to-date and verifiable information on every militant's every action, they would not know whether or not a given civilian had in fact disengaged from direct participation in hostilities. Therefore, in the absence of conclusive evidence, such a targeting force might well assume that any civilian who participates once in hostilities remains targetable for as long as the hostilities continue. Moreover, a civilian taking a direct part in hostilities may not know how to communicate his or her affirmative disengagement to the forces that might target him, nor to whom he should communicate it. There would be a strong disincentive for such a civilian to communicate his or her disengagement from hostilities for fear of reprisals, whether they be targeting, arrest, or detention. Moreover, the notion of "objectively" recognizable disengagement is difficult to define, and as Schmitt points out, the language of the affirmative disengagement approach relates strongly to the intention of the civilian—a subjective criterion.[36] If a civilian states his or her intention to cease providing strategic advice to a terrorist group, how would the targeting force know whether this is an objective cessation of participation?

The membership approach allows for the targeting of civilians who join armed groups for the duration of their membership in that armed group, using the rationale that such members pose an ongoing threat. The end of membership must be objectively communicated, posing the same intelligence problems as the affirmative disengagement approach above, especially given that many groups may not have official rosters of membership, uniforms, or centralized housing. The membership approach also poses specific problems in the context of the OPT, given the links between the political and social components (schools, hospitals, etc.) of Hamas and its armed wing. If a civilian were to support the political party Hamas through membership or financial contribution, this would not constitute taking a direct part in hostilities. A participant at the ICRC Third Expert Meeting noted that members of *armed groups* would not be civilians properly so-called, and that they might be targeted on the same terms as members of state armed forces.[37] However, the ICTY has ruled that membership of an armed group is not sufficient indication that a civilian is directly participating in hostilities for the purposes of targeting them with lethal force.[38]

The limited membership approach is narrower than the membership approach insofar as it does not permit the targeting of all members of armed groups at all times. It restricts the category of persons who can be targeted to the *fighting members* of the armed group. These individuals can be targeted even when they are not engaged in the specific acts of direct participation in hostilities: they are targeted on the basis of their membership and their active participation in combat operations. They only regain protection when they disengage in an objectively recognizable manner. Fighting members are defined functionally as those who can be identified with relative precision as regularly conducting hostilities, matching their function with those of traditional armed forces, i.e. command, war-fighting, logistics, and intelligence. Thus, under this approach, those members of organized armed groups that act as support personnel—cooks, secretaries, etc.—can not be continuously targeted on account of their membership. Like non-members, they are subject to a specific acts approach.[39] The limited membership approach therefore limits the capacity to target support personnel who are not taking a direct part in hostilities and narrows the substantive scope of targeting civilians who take a direct part in hostilities. The temporal scope is broader than that of the specific acts approach, but only for those civilians who take the most direct part in hostilities, that is, in organizing, planning, and conducting hostilities. The intelligence-based concerns remain for this approach, as for all four approaches, but the limited membership approach is preferable to the membership approach as it would avoid targeting the members or supporters of a political party such as Hamas who do not participate in armed groups.

With reference to non-international armed conflicts, the ICRC Commentary to Article 13(3) AP II notes that a civilian regains his immunity when he "no longer presents any danger for the adversary."[40] This introduces "threat" as one element of the temporal question: "for such time as." Ben-Naftali and Michaeli argue that "threat" is the rationale for the ability to target civilians and that when the threat is neither imminent nor severe, the civilian is not a legitimate target and alternative means should be used to prevent the threat from materializing.[41] This analysis does not use any of the four frameworks discussed above. An analysis based on a subjective criterion such as "threat" is yet more liable than the frameworks above to be expanded or contracted according to military discretion. However, if objective criteria were to be introduced for civilians' direct participation in hostilities, then the concept of "threat" could be given a verifiable objective meaning. Ben-Naftali and Michaeli acknowledge that "threat" should be refined to mean "imminent" or "immediate" threat, which does reduce its scope.[42]

In the "targeted killings" case, the Israeli Supreme Court noted that there is no international consensus regarding the meanings of the durational components of "takes a direct part in hostilities" and "for such a time as," and therefore such determinations need to be made on a case-by-case basis.[43] The court explained the two ends of the spectrum of possible situations when laying out its framework for assessing each potential target. On one end of the spectrum, a civilian who directly participates in hostilities once or even sporadically but later detaches himself from that activity, entirely or for a long period of time, regains protection. Such a civilian cannot be targeted for his or her past activities.[44] On the other end of the spectrum, when a civilian joins a terrorist organization (which becomes his "home") and, as part of his role as a member of this organization, engages in a *chain* of hostile acts with only short periods in between, he or she may be targeted for the entire duration of time it takes to complete that chain of hostile acts. This is because the rest between acts functions as preparation for the next activity. A militant should not be able to use the "revolving door" to find refuge to rest and prepare for his next attack.[45] Between these extreme cases, the court recognized there is considerable gray area, and that as such, each case must be determined individually upon examining the circumstances.

Part III: Analysis

Given that none of the key components of AP II Article 51(3)—"hostilities," "direct part" and "for such a time as"—has a settled meaning in international law, further criteria are needed to analyze the legality of attacks against civilians alleged to have taken a direct part in hostilities.

Based upon the above discussion, this section presents a short series of questions practitioners may want to consider in assessing the legality of an attack against a civilian.

- *Was this attack targeting a particular individual or was it an indiscriminate attack?* Indiscriminate attacks do not distinguish between civilian and military objects and are prohibited by Article 51(4) of Additional Protocol I. An air strike on a market or a beach which kills or injures civilians would likely be prohibited, both as a failure to distinguish between civilians and military objects, and because the deaths or injuries to civilians are disproportionate in relation to the military advantage anticipated from the attack.
- *Was the particular individual engaged in the use of force or otherwise providing a direct contribution to the use of force?* For example, an individual wearing an explosives belt, gathering intelligence for a suicide bombing, or engaged in conscripting or enlisting individuals to carry out a terrorist attack would qualify as a civilian taking a direct part in hostilities under the judgment of the Israeli High Court in the "targeted killings" case.
- *Was this direct participation or contribution taking place over time or was the participation only sporadic or unpredictable?* A civilian who consistently provides intelligence for militant operations might be considered to be taking a direct part in hostilities, whereas a taxi driver who transports militants to one meeting on one occasion would not lose his or her immunity from attack.

In recognition of the gray areas between clearly direct participation in hostilities and so-called indirect participation, the Israeli High Court set several procedural prerequisites for "targeted killings." First, proper information on the target is required; if there is any doubt as to whether the target in question is a civilian who is taking a direct part in hostilities, the operation must be abandoned. Second, using an analysis from international human rights law and Israeli domestic law rather than international humanitarian law, the High Court required that an attack should take place only if it was the least harmful means available to averting the threat posed by the target. Third, the targeted killings must not cause civilian deaths, injuries, or damage to civilian objects which are excessive to the military advantage anticipated from the attack. Fourth and finally, an investigation must be carried out following any targeted killing to review its legality or otherwise.[46]

PART IV: CONCLUSION

Recognizing that the law sets the vocabulary and framework within which military operations are devised, negotiated, and implemented, this policy brief analyzes the legal debates concerning the direct participation of civilians in hostilities. This is a significant issue relating to the protection of civilians in the OPT, where hostilities are often conducted in the midst of civilian populations, and non-state armed groups are central actors on the battlefield. There is a spectrum of opinion among scholars and practitioners concerning the lawfulness of targeting civilians who take a direct part in hostilities. Some argue that the classical IHL distinction between civilians who are immune from attack and must not participate in hostilities and combatants who both kill and can be killed is poorly adapted to the realities of modern warfare. In this view, state militaries increasingly face attack from a wide range of actors, including those who may appear to be civilians, and thus the existing rules must be modified or reinterpreted to meet a new context of warfare. Others argue that the clear separation of combatants and civilians must be maintained in order to maximize civilian protection and in order to maintain clarity of norms for militaries and civilians alike. These scholars and practitioners argue that there is no gray area or third category between combatants and civilians, and that the introduction of such a third category would undermine the very basis of civilian protection and IHL itself.

Although Israel has not ratified Additional Protocol I, it is bound by the principle of distinction as a matter of customary international law. However, the precise scope and application in customary international law of Article 51(3) AP I—which limits the principle of distinction by stating that civilians enjoy immunity from attack *"unless and for such time as they take a direct part in hostilities"*—remains a matter of debate among Israeli scholars and practitioners. This policy brief explores interpretations of "hostilities," "direct part," and "for such time as," and then formulates a set of questions to assist practitioners in assessing the scope of civilian protection set by this controversial legal norm.

Notes

1. For a detailed examination of the Israeli Supreme Court's judgment in the so-called "targeted killings" case, see the HPCR brief "On the Legal Aspects of "Targeted Killings" Review of the Judgment of the Israeli Supreme Court," May 2007, available online at http://www.ihlresearc:h.org/opt/pdfs/briefing3731.pdf.

2. Common Article 3 of the Geneva Conventions of August 12 1949; Additional Protocol II to the Geneva Conventions of August 12 1949, Relating to the Protection of Victims of Non-International Armed Conflicts (AP II), Article 13 (2).

3. *Supra*, note 1.

4. Roy S. Schondorf, "Extra-State Armed Conflicts: Is there a Need for a New Legal Regime?" *New York University Journal of Law and Politics*, Vol. 37, No. 1, Oct. 2005, p. 62, footnote 158.

5. *Supra*, note 2, AP II, Article 51 (1)(2).

6. Jean-Marie Henckaerts and Louise Doswald-Beck, eds., *Customary International Humanitarian Law* (Cambridge: Cambridge University Press, 2005), Rule 6.

7. W. Hayes Parks, "Air War and the Law of War," 32 A.F. L. Rev. 1, (1990), p. 143.

8. Additional Protocol I to the Geneva Conventions of 12 August 1949 relating to the Protection of Victims of International Armed Conflicts, 8 June 1977, Article 51, *available at*: http://www.icrc.org/ihl.nsf/FULL/470?OpenDocument. (Emphasis added.)

9. For an in-depth analysis of the international law relevant to civilians who take a direct part in hostilities, but without specific reference to the OPT, see Jean-Francouis Queguiner, *Direct Participation in Hostilities Under International Humanitarian Law*, HPCR Working Paper, November 2003, *available at* http://www.ihlresearch.org/ihl/feature.php?a=42.

[...]

17. Commentary on the Additional Protocols of 8 June 1977 to the Geneva Conventions of 12 August 1949, at 1943, *available at* http://www.icrc.org/ihl.nsf/COM/470-750065?OpenDocument [hereafter API Commentary].

18. API Commentary, *supra*, at 1942. Similarly, the ICRC Study on Customary IHL reports the Inter-American Commission on Human Rights as having stated that direct participation in hostilities is generally understood to mean "acts, which by their nature or purpose, are intended to cause actual harm to enemy personnel and *matériel*." (Inter-American Commission on Human Rights, Third Report on human rights in Colombia, cited in The ICRC Study on Customary IHL, at page 22).

19. Cassese, *Expert Opinion, supra*, paragraph 12 (quoting ICRC Model Manual, at paragraph 601).

20. "Targeted Killings," Judgment, paragraph 33; ICRC, Third Expert Meeting, *supra*, at 22–24; David Kretzmer, *Targeted Killing of Suspected Terrorists: Extra-Judicial Executions or Legitimate Means of Defense?*, 16 EUR. J. INT'L L. 171, (2005), at page 192, *available at*: http://www.ejil.org/journal/Vol16/No2/art1.pdf.

21. "Targeted Killings" case, Judgment, paragraph 33.

22. The ICRC Study on Customary IHL, *supra*, at 23.

23. ICRC Commentary on AP I, *supra*, at 1944. *Galic, supra*, at paragraph 48 (using almost identical language). Many experts have understood this as a requirement of causal proximity. *See, e.g.*, Michael N. Schmitt, "'Direct Participation in Hostilities' and the 21st Century

Armed Conflict," in *Crisis Management and Humanitarian Protection: Festschrift fur Dieter Fleck*, at page 509 (Berlin: BWV, Horst Fischer et al eds., 2004) *available at*: http://www. michaelschmitt.org/images/Directparticipationpageproofs.pdf.

24. ICRC Commentary on AP I, *supra*, at 1679.

25. ICRC, Third Expert Meeting, on the Notion of Direct Participation in Hostilities, Summary Report, October 23–25, 2005, *available at* http://www.icrc.org/Web/eng/siteeng0.nsf/htmlall/ participation-hostilities-ihl-311205/$File/Direct_participation_in_hostilities_2005_eng.pdf at pages 19–24.

26. ICRC, Second Expert Meeting: Direct Participation in Hostilities, Summary Report, at pages 5–7, October 25-26 2004, *available at* http://www.icrc.org/Web/eng/siteeng0.nsf/htmlall/ participation-hostilities-ihl-311205/$File/Direct_participation_in_hostilities_2004_eng.pdf.

27. Inter-American Commission on Human Rights, Third Report on Human Rights in Columbia, at 811 (1999).

28. "Targeted Killings" case, Judgment, paragraph 35; see also HPCR Policy Brief, *On the Legal Aspects of "Targeted Killings," supra*, pages 11–12.

29. "Targeted Killings" case, Judgment, paragraph 37.

30. HPCR Policy Brief, *On the Legal Aspects of "Targeted Killings," supra*, pages 13–15.

31. "Targeted Killings" case, Judgment paragraph 35.

32. Direct Participation in Hostilities, Webpage, ICRC, *available at* http://www.icrc.org/web/eng/ siteeng0.nsf/html/participation-hostilities-ihl-311205?opendocument. But Orna Ben-Naftali & & Keren R Michaeli (in "We Must Not Make a Scarecrow of the Law: A Legal Analysis of the Israeli Policy of Targeted Killings", in 36 Cornell International Law Journal (2003) 233 at 279) argue that "preparing to" and "returning from" should be only be included in direct participation in hostilities on a case-by-case determination of the military necessity and alternative means. See also Marco Sassòli, *Use and Abuse of the Laws of War in the "War on Terrorism," 22 LAW & INEQ. 195, 211–12 (2004): "[O]ne should not deduce from the fact that combatants may be attacked until they are hors de combat, that civilians who are suspected of planning to participate directly in hostilities, or who could resume a previous participation are legitimate targets."

33. "Targeted Killings" case, Judgment paragraph 34.

34. ICRC, Third Expert Meeting, on the Notion of Direct Participation in Hostilities, Summary Report, October 23–25, 2005, *available at* http://www.icrc.org/Web/eng/siteeng0.nsf/htmlall/ participation-hostilitiesihl-311205/$File/Direct_participation_in_hostilities_2005_eng.pdf.

35. ICRC Third Expert Meeting, *supra*, at 60.

36. Michael D. Schmitt, "Direct Participation in Hostilities and the 21st Century Armed Conflict," *supra*, at 519–20.

37. ICRC Third Expert Meeting, *supra*, at 63.

38. *Prosecutor v. Halilovic*, ICTY, Case No. IT-01-48-T, Judgment, Nov. 16, 2005, at paragraph 34, *available at* http://www.un.org/icty/halilovic/trialc/judgement/index.htm. It should be noted that these individuals could perhaps still be prosecuted under the reading of the ICTY for membership in an armed group, but they would not lose their immunity from attack as civilians as a result of this membership alone.

39. ICRC, Third Expert Meeting, *supra*, at 64–65.

40. ICRC Commentary to Additional Protocol II, at 4789, *available at* http://www.icrc.org/ihl.nsf/COM/475-760019?OpenDocument.

41. Ben-Naftali & Michaeli, *supra*, 278–279.

42. Ben-Naftali & Michaeli, *supra*, 278–279.

43. ISC, *Targeted Killings, supra*, at paragraph 39.

44. ISC, *Targeted Killings, supra*, 39–40.

45. ISC, *Targeted Killings, supra*, 39–40.

46. *Supra*, note 1.

*The **Program on Humanitarian Policy and Conflict Research** is an international research and policy program, based at the Harvard School of Public Health, that offers a multidisciplinary approach to new challenges in the field of humanitarian affairs.

Program on Humanitarian Policy and Conflict Research, "IHL and Civilian Participation in Hostilities in the OPT," Policy Brief, Harvard University, October 2007, available at http://www.hpcrresearch.org/sites/default/files/publications/ParticipationBrief.pdf.

Used by Permission.

Part 5:
Targeted Killings and Drones

One of the most publicly controversial tools in modern warfare has been state use of targeted killings. The nature and strength of global terrorism threats have made this a more tempting tactic for nations to use: disparate terrorist networks or individual terrorists who cannot be challenged on a traditional battlefield can be eliminated by a precision airstrike; a small, strike force team; or a single assassin. The development of unmanned aerial vehicles (drones) and other technology make it easier than ever for a state to target individuals in places where it does not have control of the territory or boots on the ground. As a result, targeted killings have taken place far from an open battlefield, often by intelligence or other civilian agents, and with a lack of public accountability that has led critics to allege that they are not legitimate tools of warfare but extrajudicial killings, killings beyond the law.

The use of targeted killings in counterterrorism campaigns sits at the crux of many of the problematic issues discussed in previous sections. Can states engage in an indefinite, global war against terrorism, such that they might be justified in targeting "combatants" anywhere in the world they are found? Do these tactics make it more or less likely that prohibitions on targeting civilians or restricting collateral damage will be effective? Should the use of drones to carry out these killings change concerns about the practice?

TARGETED KILLINGS FAR FROM THE BATTLEFIELD

From the assassination of Austrian Archduke Franz Ferdinand that sparked World War I, to the targeted killing of Japanese Admiral Isoroku Yamamoto, architect of the Pearl Harbor attack during World War II, political killings have long been a cause for and a consequence of warfare. Targeted killings are often confused with and described interchangeably with assassinations. Both share similar elements, in that they are premeditated attacks against a specific individual with an intent to kill, usually for political or strategic reasons. However, there are important differences. Assassinations are by definition illegal. They are peacetime extrajudicial killings, or murder. A targeted killing in contrast, may be legal if carried out by a warring party within the scope of an armed conflict, and provided all other rules of international humanitarian law (IHL) are complied with. These would include, for example, the principles of distinction, proportionality, and feasible precautions discussed in Part 3.

If a suspected combatant is killed in the midst of a war zone during a period of ongoing hostilities, the killing itself would be relatively uncontroversial (assuming IHL standards were met, as noted above). It would be a regular part of war. But what if the killing took place in a third country far from the battlefield, in what appeared to be a "peacetime" environment? Examples of this include:

- Since 2002, the United States has used drones to kill, or attempt to kill, suspected members of Al Qaeda and other affiliated groups in Yemen.
- Between 2004 and March 2011, U.S. drone strikes in Pakistan killed an estimated 1,555 to 2,450 people.[1]
- On May 1, 2011, U.S. Navy SEALs raided a compound in Abbottabad, Pakistan, and killed Al Qaeda leader Osama bin Laden.
- On January 20, 2010, covert Israeli agents killed Hamas military commander Mahmoud al-Mabhouh in a hotel room in Dubai, United Arab Emirates.

Were these lawful killings under the laws of war? At a minimum, the sovereignty of the host state may have been violated. These killings also provoke many of the same debates raised in earlier sections—whether a wartime versus a law enforcement paradigm is more appropriate for targeting terrorist networks (Part 2), and determinations of whether the person targeted was a combatant or a civilian directly participating in hostilities at the time (Parts 3 and 4).

State Sovereignty

As the above examples illustrate, targeted killings have been used on other states' territories, raising concerns about sovereignty violations. In general, states do not have the right to use armed force on another state's territory absent a declared armed conflict or the consent of that state. An exception to that is self-defense. Article 51 of the UN Charter reserves the right for a state to use force in response to an armed attack. While this would seem to be an easy catchall for targeting terrorists in any state that would not or could not apprehend them—for example, in a failed state such as Somalia—the scope of this "self-defense" rationale is murky, and may not apply in many of the situations in which states want to use targeted killings. For example, there is considerable debate about what threshold of violence or acts are necessary to qualify as an armed attack under Article 51, whether states can respond in self-defense to attacks by nonstate actors (particularly those un-affiliated with the host state), and whether pre-emptive or anticipatory attacks are permissible.[2]

Many of these issues arise in precisely the type of situations in which states would want to deploy targeted killings rather than other military or law enforcement means, for example, against terrorist individuals or groups. First, terrorist attacks generally do not meet the threshold of traditional armed conflict and thus individually may not constitute an armed attack. Second, nonstate actors like terrorist groups may not be directed by a state actor or even have any affiliation with any state actors so Article 51 self-defense would not be lawful according to some interpretations. Finally, states often want to act in advance to prevent terrorist attacks, rather than waiting for them to happen and then attacking. But the self-defense rationale has generally been interpreted to respond to an attack that has already occurred, or is at least imminent and certain.

Law Enforcement or Warfare Paradigm

In addition to these sovereignty questions, some have argued that the use of military force is inappropriate when there is no armed conflict present in the territory in which the targeted killing takes place. If there is no ongoing armed conflict, and thus no rationale for using military force, then those targeted are not combatants but just suspected criminals who should be apprehended according to law enforcement standards. Killing a criminal suspect outright under peacetime would violate countless domestic legal rules and international human rights norms.

This has been a common critique when targeted killings are used in campaigns against global terrorist networks, because of the ambiguity over the status of such counterterrorism campaigns and of individual terrorists, as well as the frequency that such killings might take place far from obvious battlefields. In particular, U.S. efforts to kill Al Qaeda and affiliated terrorists far from an open, declared battlefield through such targeted killings has revived debates (similar to those in Part 2) about whether the United States should be approaching its counterterrorism campaign through a warfare rather than a law enforcement paradigm. The letter from Anthony D. Romero, executive director of the American Civil Liberties Union (ACLU) to President Barack Obama argues that outside of an active battlefield, detaining individuals who are suspected terrorists is more appropriate outside of an active battlefield. He writes: "The entire world is not a war zone, and wartime tactics that may be permitted on the battlefields in Afghanistan and Iraq cannot be deployed anywhere in the world where a terrorism suspect happens to be located."[3] Romero argues that even if the United States might capture individuals anywhere in the world under an armed conflict rationale, killing an individual is a more serious deprivation of rights and should be used only as a last resort to stop an immediate threat.

Harold Hongju Koh, legal adviser to the U.S. Department of State, counters that the United States is in an armed conflict against terrorists (Al Qaeda and its affiliates) who may strike from anywhere in the world,[4] and thus they can be targeted anywhere they are found—including through targeted killings.

The article by Gabriella Blum and Philip Heymann suggests that states must be permitted to use targeted killings against terrorists globally given the high security threat they pose, but that these killings should be exceptional and subject to stricter limitations, including:

- only using force when the host state is "unable or unwilling" to stop the threat;[5]
- targeting only those affiliates of terrorist organizations who are actively and directly involved (for example, targeting a leader at the level of Osama bin Laden might be possible but not targeting any member of Al Qaeda);
- a higher obligation to limit collateral damage to civilians than in other operations.

Others have suggested other limits, perhaps borrowing more from traditional human rights and law enforcement standards applicable in peacetime, particularly when the strike takes place in a territory in which the state has control of its territory and rule of law is enforced.

Civilians or Combatants

Another critical point of tension over targeted killings is the status of those individuals being targeted. When targeted killings take place far from the battlefield, against individuals who look like civilians, it raises some of the questions about distinguishing civilians from combatants that dominated Part 4. The ACLU letter argues that those being targeted might not have clear membership ties to an armed party to a conflict. Those targeted might be civilians who supply the type of indirect support (financiers, etc.) that might be criminally liable, but would not make them combatants under IHL.

Another concern is that some of these targeted killings might target the wrong individuals altogether due to mistaken intelligence. As Part 3 suggested, in asymmetric warfare distinguishing civilians from combatants is often difficult, even with troops on the ground. Critics argue that it is even harder to gauge someone's identity or ensure that surrounding civilians are not indiscriminately or disproportionately targeted, with slim to no ground presence and (in the case of drone strikes) primarily signal intelligence to identify the target. The excerpt from the study by United Nations Special Rapporteur Philip Alston argues that the legality of targeted killings is "heavily dependent upon the reliability of the intelligence" used to target individuals, a point he questions: "It was clear during my mission to Afghanistan how hard it is even for forces on the ground to obtain accurate information. . . . International forces all too often based manned airstrikes and raids that resulted in killings on faulty intelligence."[6]

The ACLU letter also takes issue with the intelligence on which these killings are based. Romero points out, since September 11, "we have seen the government over and over again detain men as 'terrorists,' only to discover later that the evidence was weak, wrong, or non-existent. . . . This experience should lead you to reject out of hand a program that would invest the CIA or the U.S. military with the unchecked authority to impose an extrajudicial death sentence on U.S. citizens and others found far from any actual battlefield."[7]

The lack of transparency over targeting criteria and the inability of independent monitors or media to access many of these areas to verify who was targeted has increased suspicion that targeted killings might be striking the wrong targets or might be misused. Critics argue that decisions to kill someone using targeted killing undergo less scrutiny than a typical arrest and questioning process in most democratic countries. To an extent though, such standards depend on the above debates about whether targeted killings may be squarely justified under an armed conflict framework. Koh argues that because the United States is engaged in an armed conflict with Al Qaeda and its affiliates, the level of due process is sufficient, potentially even more than necessary: "[A] state that is engaged in an armed conflict or in legitimate self-defense is not required to provide targets with legal process before the state may use lethal force. Our procedures and practices for identifying lawful targets are extremely robust, and advanced technologies have helped to make our targeting even more precise."[8]

ATTACK OF THE DRONES

In some ways drones are simply the newest means of carrying out traditional tactics of warfare. Most drones are used for simple surveillance. Surveillance drones have become so common that U.S. military patrols in Afghanistan might carry small, hand-launch surveillance drones in their rucksacks. Though the higher resolution video and the ease of deploying such drones is a huge military advantage, the function itself is not that different from historical surveillance methods. As one United States Air Force colonel involved with drone usage commented in a CNN interview, "It's almost like what the hot air balloon was back in the Civil War for us. 'Hey, I can rise above and look around and see what the forces are doing on the battlefield.' So now we are just in the pioneering stage."[9]

Drones have gone beyond surveillance, however. Since 2002, the United States has used unmanned aerial vehicles for targeted killings in Pakistan, Yemen, and Somalia. The drones are piloted remotely, with those responsible for targeting and firing them often located in the United States. Like their surveillance counterparts, these drones are not carrying out a fundamentally different function from past warfare methods. Targeted killings, even in far-flung states, could be accomplished equally by other means, including covert intelligence or special operations (military) agents.

Yet despite the similar functions, there are some ways that using this type of weapon for targeted killings is new and troubling. Human rights monitors have argued that the use of drones exacerbates transparency concerns. As Alston and Hina Shamsi, a staff attorney in the ACLU's National Security Project, argued in a separate article related to UK drone usage in Afghanistan:

> Drones lend themselves to secrecy. Used without fanfare in remote and inaccessible areas, they are invisible to all but their potential victims. The military advantages are obvious, but so too are the potential rule-of-law problems. Unless governments voluntarily disclose information, human rights monitors and independent journalists are unable to verify claims that there are limited or no civilian casualties, let alone to weigh them against credible reports that hundreds of innocents have died.[10]

Drones are often prized because they can be operated remotely through computer interfaces, presenting little risk to the personnel manning them. Thus, while drones might achieve the same objective as a small, special operations or covert intelligence team, they present no risk to personnel and are substantially easier to deploy in foreign territory. Commentators worry that this remote-control targeting depersonalizes warfare in a way that may undermine natural limitations on killing. Alston points out that remote drone operation may tend toward a "play-station mentality" that would make those operating it oblivious to the human costs of killing.[11] Another concern may be that because drones are so "costless" to deploy, states may be more likely than they were in the past to conduct targeted killings on other states' territories, eroding the strength of prohibitions on use of force.

Finally, U.S. drone strikes have reportedly been carried out by civilian intelligence personnel, which has been controversial because there is an expectation under IHL that states will use regular military forces for armed attacks under an armed conflict paradigm. Alston argues that the use of civilian intelligence personnel to operate drones is not per se illegal, but those civilians doing so could be liable for criminal prosecution for murder. He notes that using covert civilian intelligence agents to carry these killings out *for the purpose* of skirting IHL requirements might also raise issues of state responsibility.

With the spread of drone technology, the use of targeted killings seems likely to increase. Yet the legal basis for such killings, and the constraints that must or should be imposed to limit potential harmful effects of these killings are still unclear. After going through the readings, think about how you would respond to the following issues.

- Do you think that states should be allowed to kill an individual they deem to be a combatant on the territory of another state? For example, would you consider it lawful for the United States to kill someone it deems to be a terrorist while that individual was located in Paris, France? What about in Somalia? Would your answer be any different if the individual was being detained rather than killed?

- One of the controversial aspects of targeted killings is that they may take place not only far from a battlefield but also when the individual does not appear to be engaged in any hostile actions. In a September 2011 speech, U.S. official John Brennan justified killing terrorists before any threat from them materializes because the "threats posed by non-state actors do not present themselves in the ways that evidenced imminence in more traditional conflicts. . . . [Al Qaeda] possesses the demonstrated capability to strike with little notice and cause significant civilian or military casualties."[12] Do you think the different nature of terrorist strikes justifies dispensing with traditional restraints on acting in self-defense only in response to an *imminent* threat?

- Do you agree that drones pose particular concerns versus other means of carrying out targeted killings because of the nature of the technology? If so, what aspects are most troubling?

- Some of the critiques of targeted killings and of drones in particular discuss the lack of transparency over how the killings are authorized and on what basis. What do you think states should have to disclose to justify targeted killings? Should such procedural requirements be mandated under IHL, under states' own domestic laws, as a matter of policy, or some combination?

Notes

1. New America Foundation, *The Year of the Drone: An Analysis of U.S. Drone Strikes in Pakistan, 2004–2010*, February 24, 2010, http://counterterrorism.newamerica.net/drones. The vast majority of drone strikes have taken place in the tribal areas of Pakistan, which are arguably under an armed conflict, although the Pakistan government maintains that they are not.

2. See Report of the Special Rapporteur on Extrajudicial, Summary or Arbitrary Executions, Philip Alston, Addendum: Study on Targeted Killings, May 28, 2010, A/HRC/14/24/Add.6, ¶¶37–45.

3. Letter from Anthony D. Romero, Executive Director, American Civil Liberties Union, to President Barack Obama, April 28, 2010.

4. The September 11 attackers were trained in camps in then-Taliban-controlled Afghanistan, but also planned and trained for the attacks out of cells in Germany and the United States.

5. The "unwilling or unable" standard has been proposed by many states, notably the United States, as the rationale for when a state could strike a nonstate actor on the territory of another state without their consent. However, this standard has not risen to the level of binding international law, and has been critiqued as too subjective a test. For more, see Report of the Special Rapporteur on Extrajudicial, Summary or Arbitrary Executions, Philip Alston, Addendum: Study on Targeted Killings, May 28, 2010, A /HRC/14/24/Add.6, ¶¶35, 41, 42; Ashley Deeks, "'Unwilling or Unable': Toward an Normative Framework for Extra-Territorial Self-Defense," *Virginia Journal of International Law* 52 (2012).

6. Report of the Special Rapporteur on Extrajudicial, Summary or Arbitrary Executions, Philip Alston, Addendum: Study on Targeted Killings, May 28, 2010, A /HRC/14/24/Add.6, ¶83.

7. Letter from Anthony D. Romero to President Barack Obama, April 28, 2010.

8. Address by Harold Hongju Koh, "The Obama Administration and International Law," speech given at the Annual Meeting of the American Society of International Law, Washington, DC, March 25, 2010, http://www.state.gov/s/l/releases/remarks/139119.htm.

9. Nic Robertson, "How Robot Drones Revolutionized the Face of Warfare," July 27, 2009, CNN.com, http://edition.cnn.com/2009/WORLD/americas/07/23/wus.warfare.remote.uav/.

10. Philip Alston and Hina Shamsi, "Killer Above the Law? Britain's Use of Drones in the War in Afghanistan Must Be in Accordance with International Law," *Guardian.co.uk*, February 8, 2010, http://www.guardian.co.uk/commentisfree/2010/feb/08/afghanistan-drones-defence-killing.

11. Report of the Special Rapporteur on Extrajudicial, Summary or Arbitrary Executions, Philip Alston, Addendum: Study on targeted killings, May 28, 2010, A /HRC/14/24/Add.6, ¶84.

12. John O. Brennan, "Strengthening Our Security by Adhering to our Values and Laws," speech given at the Harvard Law School, September 16, 2011, http://www.whitehouse.gov/the-press-office/2011/09/16/remarks-john-o-brennan-strengthening-our-security-adhering-our-values-an.

Letter from Anthony D. Romero, Executive Director, American Civil Liberties Union, to President Barack Obama

April 28, 2010

President Barack Obama
The White House
1600 Pennsylvania Avenue, N.W.
Washington, D.C. 20500

Dear Mr. President:

On behalf of the ACLU and its 500,000 members, I am writing to express our profound concern about recent reports indicating that you have authorized a program that contemplates the killing of suspected terrorists—including U.S. citizens—located far away from zones of actual armed conflict. If accurately described, this program violates international law and, at least insofar as it affects U.S. citizens, it is also unconstitutional.

The U.S. is engaged in non-international armed conflict in Afghanistan and Iraq and the lawfulness of its actions must be judged in that context. The program that you have reportedly authorized appears to envision the use of lethal force not just on the battlefield in Iraq, Afghanistan, or even the Pakistani border regions, but anywhere in the world, including against individuals who may not constitute lawful targets. The entire world is not a war zone, and wartime tactics that may be permitted on the battlefields in Afghanistan and Iraq cannot be deployed anywhere in the world where a terrorism suspect happens to be located. Your administration has eschewed the rhetoric of the "Global War on Terror." You should now disavow the sweeping legal theory that underlies that slogan.

Even in an armed conflict zone, individuals may be targeted only if they take a direct part in hostilities, for such time as they do so, or if they have taken up a continuous combat function. Propagandists, financiers, and other non-combat "supporters" of hostile groups cannot lawfully be targeted with lethal force. Applicable international humanitarian law also prohibits targeted killing except in order to prevent an individual's future participation in hostilities; fighters cannot be targeted solely as retribution for past actions. Furthermore, basic law-of-armed-conflict principles require that in such operations, civilians who are not taking direct part in hostilities must not be targeted, precautions must always be taken to spare the civilian population, anticipated civilian casualties must never be disproportionate to the expected concrete military advantage, and strikes must only occur when required by military necessity.

Outside armed conflict zones, the use of lethal force by the United States is strictly limited by international law and, at least in some circumstances, the Constitution. These laws permit lethal force to be used only as a last resort, and only to prevent imminent attacks that are likely to cause death or serious physical injury. According to news reports, the program you have authorized is based on "kill lists" to which names are added, sometimes for months at a time, after a secret internal process. Such a program of long-premeditated and bureaucratized killing is plainly not limited to targeting genuinely imminent threats. Any such program is far more sweeping than the law allows and raises grave constitutional and human rights concerns.

In a series of cases involving prisoners currently held by the U.S. at Guantanamo Bay, your administration has taken the position that the 2001 Authorization for Use of Military Force permits the detention of individuals captured anywhere in the world, even individuals who have no connection to the battlefield. For example, your administration has advanced that argument in the case of one of our clients—Mohammedou Salahi—who was detained in Mauritania. We do not think the AUMF can be read so broadly. In *Hamdi v. Rumsfeld*, the Supreme Court interpreted the AUMF consistently with international law, permitting the detention of a U.S. citizen captured in Afghanistan only because the detention of *battlefield* combatants was "so fundamental and accepted an incident to war as to be an exercise of the 'necessary and appropriate force' Congress has authorized the President to use." 542 U.S. 507, 518 (2004). But even if the AUMF could be read to authorize the *detention* of suspected terrorists apprehended far from any zone of actual combat, it is a far more radical thing to propose that the AUMF authorizes the extrajudicial *execution* of those people. Outside of armed conflict zones, human rights law and the Constitution prescribe strict limits on the use of lethal force, limits that are narrower than those applicable in armed conflicts, and narrower than the standards governing detention. Targeted killing of suspects away from the battlefield is not a "fundamental and accepted . . . incident to war." Based on the available information, neither does your targeted killing program appear to be an exercise of "necessary and appropriate force" used only as a last resort to prevent imminent threats. The AUMF may be broad, but the authority it granted was not limitless, and it cannot now be construed to have silently overridden the limits prescribed by international law.

The program you have reportedly endorsed is not simply illegal but also unwise, because how our country responds to the threat of terrorism will in large measure determine the rules that govern *every* nation's conduct in similar contexts. If the United States claims the authority to use lethal force against suspected enemies of the U.S. anywhere in the world—using unmanned drones or other means—then other countries will regard that conduct as justified. The prospect of foreign governments hunting and killing their enemies within our borders or those of our allies is abhorrent.

The program you have endorsed also risks the deaths of innocent people. Over the last eight years, we have seen the government over and over again detain men as "terrorists," only to discover later that the evidence was weak, wrong, or non-existent. Of the many hundreds of individuals previously detained at Guantánamo, the vast majority have been released or are awaiting release. Furthermore, the government has failed to prove the lawfulness of imprisoning individual Guantánamo detainees in 34 of the 48 cases that have been reviewed by the federal courts thus far, even though the government had years to gather and analyze evidence for those cases and had itself determined that those prisoners were detainable. This experience should lead you to reject out of hand a program that would invest the CIA or the U.S. military with the unchecked authority to impose an extrajudicial death sentence on U.S. citizens and others found far from any actual battlefield.

Sincerely,

Anthony D. Romero

Executive Director

*The **American Civil Liberties Union** is a national organization that works to preserve the rights and liberties that the Constitution and laws of the United States guarantee.

Letter from Anthony D. Romero, Executive Director, American Civil Liberties Union, to President Barack Obama, April 28, 2010, available at http://www.aclu.org/human-rights-national-security/letter-president-obama-regarding-targeted-killings.

Used by permission.

The Obama Administration and International Law[†]

by Harold Hongju Koh*

[...]

B. THE LAW OF 9/11

Let me focus the balance of my remarks on that aspect of my job that I call "The Law of 9/11." In this area, as in the other areas of our work, we believe, in the President's words, that "living our values doesn't make us weaker, it makes us safer and it makes us stronger."

We live in a time, when, as you know, the United States finds itself engaged in several armed conflicts. As the President has noted, one conflict, in Iraq, is winding down. He also reminded us that the conflict in Afghanistan is a "conflict that America did not seek, one in which we are joined by forty-three other countries ... in an effort to defend ourselves and all nations from further attacks." In the conflict occurring in Afghanistan and elsewhere, we continue to fight the perpetrators of 9/11: a nonstate actor, Al Qaeda (as well as the Taliban forces that harbored al Qaeda).

Everyone here at this meeting is committed to international law. But as President Obama reminded us, "the world must remember that it was not simply international institutions—not just treaties and declarations—that brought stability to a post-World War II world. ... [T]he instruments of war do have a role to play in preserving the peace."

With this background, let me address a question on many of your minds: how has this Administration determined to conduct these armed conflicts and to defend our national security, consistent with its abiding commitment to international law? *Let there be no doubt: the Obama Administration is firmly committed to complying with all applicable law, including the laws of war, in all aspects of these ongoing armed conflicts.* As the President reaffirmed in his Nobel Prize Lecture, "Where force is necessary, we have a moral and strategic interest in binding ourselves to certain rules of conduct ... [E]ven as we confront a vicious adversary that abides by no rules ... the United States of America must remain a standard bearer in the conduct of war. That is what makes us dif-

---

[†]Speech made at the Annual Meeting of the American Society of International Law on March 25, 2010, and was published at 2010 ASIL Proc. 207.

ferent from those whom we fight. That is the source of our strength." We in the Obama Administration have worked hard since we entered office to ensure that we conduct all aspects of these armed conflicts—in particular, detention operations, targeting, and prosecution of terrorist suspects—in a manner consistent not just with the applicable laws of war, but also with the Constitution and laws of the United States.

[...]

B. Use of Force

In the same way, in all of our operations involving the *use of force*, including those in the armed conflict with al Qaeda, the Taliban and associated forces, the Obama Administration is committed by word and deed to conducting ourselves in accordance with all applicable law. With respect to the subject of targeting, which has been much commented upon in the media and international legal circles, there are obviously limits to what I can say publicly. What I can say *is that it is the considered view of this Administration—and it has certainly been my experience during my time as Legal Adviser—that U.S. targeting practices, including lethal operations conducted with the use of unmanned aerial vehicles, comply with all applicable law, including the laws of war.*

The United States agrees that it must conform its actions to all applicable law. As I have explained, as a matter of international law, the United States is in an armed conflict with al Qaeda, as well as the Taliban and associated forces, in response to the horrific 9/11 attacks, and may use force consistent with its inherent right to self-defense under international law. As a matter of domestic law, Congress authorized the use of all necessary and appropriate force through the 2001 Authorization for Use of Military Force (AUMF). These domestic and international legal authorities continue to this day.

As recent events have shown, al Qaeda has not abandoned its intent to attack the United States, and indeed continues to attack us. Thus, in this ongoing armed conflict, the United States has the authority under international law, and the responsibility to its citizens, to use force, including lethal force, to defend itself, including by targeting persons such as high-level al Qaeda leaders who are planning attacks. As you know, this is a conflict with an organized terrorist enemy that does not have conventional forces, but that plans and executes its attacks against us and our allies while hiding among civilian populations. That behavior simultaneously makes the application of international law more difficult and more critical for the protection of innocent civilians. Of course, whether a particular individual will be targeted in a particular location will depend upon considerations specific to each case, including those related to the imminence of the threat, the sovereignty of the other states involved, and the willingness and ability of those states to suppress the threat the target poses. In particular, this Administration has carefully reviewed the rules governing targeting operations to ensure that these operations are conducted consistently with law of war principles, including:

- First, the principle of *distinction*, which requires that attacks be limited to military objectives and that civilians or civilian objects shall not be the object of the attack; and
- Second, the principle of *proportionality*, which prohibits attacks that may be expected to cause incidental loss of civilian life, injury to civilians, damage to civilian objects, or a combination thereof, that would be excessive in relation to the concrete and direct military advantage anticipated.

In U.S. operations against al Qaeda and its associated forces—including lethal operations conducted with the use of unmanned aerial vehicles—great care is taken to adhere to these principles in both planning and execution, to ensure that only legitimate objectives are targeted and that collateral damage is kept to a minimum.

Recently, a number of legal objections have been raised against U.S. targeting practices. While today is obviously not the occasion for a detailed legal opinion responding to each of these objections, let me briefly address four:

First, some have suggested that the *very act of targeting* a particular leader of an enemy force in an armed conflict must violate the laws of war. But individuals who are part of such an armed group are belligerents and, therefore, lawful targets under international law. During World War II, for example, American aviators tracked and shot down the airplane carrying the architect of the Japanese attack on Pearl Harbor, who was also the leader of enemy forces in the Battle of Midway. This was a lawful operation then, and would be if conducted today. Indeed, targeting particular individuals serves to narrow the focus when force is employed and to avoid broader harm to civilians and civilian objects.

Second, some have challenged *the very use of advanced weapons systems*, such as unmanned aerial vehicles, for lethal operations. But the rules that govern targeting do not turn on the type of weapon system used, and there is no prohibition under the laws of war on the use of technologically advanced weapons systems in armed conflict—such as pilotless aircraft or so-called smart bombs—so long as they are employed in conformity with applicable laws of war. Indeed, using such advanced technologies can ensure both that the best intelligence is available for planning operations, and that civilian casualties are minimized in carrying out such operations.

Third, some have argued that the use of lethal force against specific individuals fails to provide adequate process and thus constitutes *unlawful extrajudicial killing*. But a state that is engaged in an armed conflict or in legitimate self-defense is not required to provide targets with legal process before the state may use lethal force. Our procedures and practices for identifying lawful targets are extremely robust, and advanced technologies have helped to make our targeting even more precise. In my experience, the principles of distinction and proportionality that the United States applies are not just recited at meetings. They are implemented rigorously throughout the planning and execution of lethal operations to ensure that such operations are conducted in accordance with all applicable law.

Fourth and finally, some have argued that our targeting practices violate *domestic law*, in particular, the long-standing *domestic ban on assassinations*. But under domestic law, the use of lawful weapons systems—consistent with the applicable laws of war—for precision targeting of specific high-level belligerent leaders when acting in self-defense or during an armed conflict is not unlawful, and hence does not constitute "assassination."

In sum, let me repeat: as in the area of detention operations, this Administration is committed to ensuring that the targeting practices that I have described are lawful.

*Harold Hongju Koh is a legal adviser to the U.S. Department of State.

Harold Hongju Koh, "The Obama Administration and International Law," speech given at the Annual Meeting of the American Society of International Law, Washington, DC, March 25, 2010.

Used by Permission.

Law and Policy of Targeted Killing

*by Gabriella Blum and Philip Heymann**

I. INTRODUCTION

Imagine that the U.S. intelligence services obtain reliable information that a known individual is plotting a terrorist attack against the United States. The individual is outside the United States, in a country where law and order are weak and unreliable. U.S. officials can request that country to arrest the individual, but they fear that by the time the individual is located, arrested, and extradited the terror plot would be too advanced, or would already have taken place. It is also doubtful that the host government is either able or willing to perform the arrest. Moreover, even if it did arrest the suspected terrorist, it might decide to release him shortly thereafter, exposing the U.S. to a renewed risk. Should the United States be allowed to kill the suspected terrorist in the foreign territory, without first capturing, arresting, and trying him?

More than any other counterterrorism tactic, targeted killing operations display the tension between addressing terrorism as a crime and addressing it as war. The right of a government to use deadly force against a citizen is constrained by both domestic criminal law and international human rights norms that seek to protect the individual's right to life and liberty. In law enforcement, individuals are punished for their individual guilt. Guilt must be proven in a court of law, with the individual facing trial enjoying the protections of due process guarantees. Killing an individual without trial is allowed only in very limited circumstances, such as self- defense (where the person poses an immediate threat) or the immediate necessity of saving more lives. In almost any other case, it would be clearly unlawful, tantamount to extrajudicial execution or murder.

When agents of a state seek to engage in enforcement operations outside their own territory without consent of the foreign government, they are further constrained by international norms of peaceful relations and the respect for territorial boundaries among states. Ordinarily, when a criminal suspect finds refuge in another country, the United States would ask the other country for extradition to gain jurisdiction over him. Even interviewing a person outside of U.S. territory would be unlawful; executing him would be an extremely egregious offense. Violations of these norms run the risk of replacing law with force and spiraling international violence.

In wartime, governments may use deadly force against combatants of an enemy party, in which case the peacetime constraints are relaxed. But in war, the enemy combatants belong to another identifiable party and are killed not because they are guilty, but because they are potentially lethal agents of that hostile party. Moreover, soldiers are easily identified by the uniform they wear. Once in the uniform of an enemy state, any soldier, by commitment and allegiance, is a potential threat and thus a legitimate target, regardless of the degree of threat the soldier is actually posing at any particular moment: the relaxing, unarmed soldier, the sleeping soldier, the retreating soldier—all are legitimate military targets and subject to intentional targeting. No advance warning is necessary, no attempt to arrest or capture is required, and no effort to minimize casualties among enemy forces is demanded by law.

The identity and culpability of an individual not wearing a uniform but suspected of involvement in terrorism is far less easily ascertained. While combatants should not benefit from defying the obligation to distinguish themselves from civilians (wearing civilian clothes does not give a soldier legal immunity from direct attack), the lack of uniform does raise concerns about the ability to identify individuals as belonging to a hostile force.[1] Moreover, joining a military follows a distinct procedure that allows for a bright-line rule distinguishing between those in the military and those outside it (although it hides the dangerous responsibility of civilians who take part in hostile activity without being members of the armed forces). Joining a terrorist organization does not necessarily have a similar on/off switch; individuals might join the organization or support it in some ways or for some time, but then go back to their ordinary business without any ritual marking their joining or departing. Identifying individuals as terrorists grows more difficult as organizations, such as Al-Qaeda, become a network of small dispersed cells, or even individuals, making the association with a hostile armed group even more tenuous.

Despite these difficulties, both the United States and Israel (as well as several other countries) have made targeted killing—the deliberate assassination of a known terrorist outside the country's territory (even in a friendly nation's territory), usually (but not exclusively) by an airstrike—an essential part of their counterterrorism strategy. Both have found targeted killing an inevitable means of frustrating the activities of terrorists who are directly involved in plotting and instigating attacks from outside their territory.

Adopting a position on targeted killings involves complex legal, political, and moral judgments with very broad implications. Targeted killing is the most coercive tactic employed in the war on terrorism. Unlike detention or interrogation, it is not designed to capture the terrorist, monitor his or her actions, or extract information; simply put, it is designed to eliminate the terrorist. More than any other counterterrorism practice, it reveals the complexity involved in classifying counterterrorism operations either as part of a war or as a law enforcement operation.

A targeted killing entails an entire military operation that is planned and executed against a particular, known person. In war, there is no prohibition on the killing of a known enemy combatant; for the most part, wars are fought between anonymous soldiers, and bullets have no designated names on them. The image of a powerful army launching a highly sophisticated guided missile from a distance, often from a Predator drone, against a specific individual driving an unarmored vehicle or walking down the street starkly illustrates the difference between counterinsurgency operations and the traditional war paradigm. Moreover, the fact that all targeted killing operations in combating terrorism are directed against particular individuals makes the tactic more reminiscent of a law enforcement paradigm, where power is employed on the basis of individual guilt rather than status (civilian/combatant). Unlike a law enforcement operation, however, there are no due process guarantees: the individual is not forewarned about the operation, is not given a chance to defend his innocence, and there is no assessment of his guilt by any impartial body.

The uneasiness about classifying and evaluating targeted killings further grows as these operations are carried out outside an immediate battlefield, such as in Yemen, Pakistan, or Somalia. Justifying targeted killings in those countries faces the challenges of the constraints of peaceful international relations or else a potentially unlimited expansion of the geographical scope of the armed conflict beyond the immediate theater of war. There are slippery slope concerns of excessive use of targeted killings against individuals or in territories that are harder to justify. Recent reports about a U.S. "hit list" of Afghan drug lords, even though supposedly taking place in an active combat zone, have sparked criticism that drug lords, even when they finance the Taliban, do not fit neatly within the concept of "combatant," and must instead be treated with law enforcement tools.[2]

Concerns about the use of targeted killings grow as collateral harm is inflicted on innocent bystanders in the course of attacks aimed at terrorists. In war, collateral damage to civilians, if proportionate to the military gain, is a legitimate, however dire, consequence of war. In domestic law enforcement, the police must hold their fire if they believe that there is a danger to innocent bystanders, except where using lethal force against a suspect is reasonably believed likely to reduce the number of innocent deaths.

To make this tactic acceptable to other nations, targeted killings must be justified and accounted for under a set of norms that may not correspond perfectly to either peacetime or wartime paradigms, but is nonetheless respectful of the values and considerations espoused by both.

[…]

[…T]argeted killings, as they have been used by the United States in Yemen, Pakistan, and elsewhere, may well have been justified without ever relying on a "war on terrorism," but instead by being framed as an exceptional use of force in self-defense alongside peacetime law enforcement. Although Parks does not expound upon this point, from his equation of military action in peacetime with that of wartime, it seems he would accept some degree of collateral damage in a peacetime operation under similar logic of a wartime attack.

Choosing a peacetime framework with some allowance for military action is not free from difficulties. One obvious problem is that the "exceptional" use of force has been turned, in the context of the war on terrorism, into a continuous practice. In addition, the degree to which countries should be allowed to use force extraterritorially against non-state elements has been debated extensively by both international law and domestic law scholars. The implications of allowing the use of armed force to capture or kill enemies outside a country's own territory, and outside a theater of traditional armed conflict, may include spiraling violence, the erosion of territorial sovereignty, and a weakening of international cooperation.

Once the precedent is laid for a broad interpretation of Article 51 of the UN Charter, as existing alongside or as an exception to normal peacetime limitations, it becomes harder to distinguish what is allowed in peace from what is allowed in war. It is for these reasons that not everyone accepts Parks' legal reasoning, with critics arguing that any military attack on another country's territory, outside an armed conflict with that country, amounts to unlawful aggression. Thus, in the case of *Armed Activities on the Territory of the Congo*[25], the International Court of Justice, in a decision widely criticized, went as far as to rule that Uganda had no right to use force against armed rebels attacking it from the territory of the Democratic Republic of Congo. Recently, the U.N. Special Rapporteur on Extrajudicial, Summary, or Arbitrary Executions, concluded that reliance on the exceptional self-defense argument under Article 51 in support of targeted killings "would diminish hugely the value of the foundational prohibition contained in Article 51."[26]

Even if justified as an exception to a peacetime paradigm, one obvious pre-condition for the legality of targeted killing operations outside a theater of war, in consideration of the other countries' sovereignty, must be that the state in whose territory the terrorist resides either consent to the operation by the foreign power (as in the case of the collaboration between the United States and Yemen) or else would be unable or unwilling to take action against the terrorist (as in the case of targeted killings in Gaza). On some rare occasions there may be an overwhelming necessity to act without the immediate possibility of obtaining the other country's consent.

Note that under a law enforcement model, a country cannot target any individual in its own territory unless there is no other way to avert a great danger. If so, if the Yemeni authorities can capture a terrorist alive, they cannot authorize the United States to engage in a targeted killing operation in its territory or execute one on its own.

To sum up, targeted killings of terrorists by both the United States and Israel have been justified under a war paradigm: in the American case, by treating terrorists as (unlawful) combatants; in the Israeli case, by treating terrorists as civilians who are taking direct part in hostilities. It seems that a persuasive argument can also be made that under some conditions, targeted killings of suspected terrorists can be justified on the basis of a law enforcement paradigm. When conducted in the territory of another country, targeted killing must be based on a self-defense exception to the international law prohibition on the use of force, and in consideration of that other country's sovereignty, should only be executed if that other country either consents to the operation or else is unable and unwilling to interdict the terrorist.

In the conclusion of this chapter, we set forth what the legitimate contours of the use of targeted killing must be. We conclude that they seem to fit both a more constrained war paradigm and a more lax law enforcement paradigm (although the latter suits more sporadic and measured use of the tactic). For present purposes it should be noted that if we take the Israeli Supreme Court's decision as controlling, then the conditions for the legitimacy of targeted killings of terrorists in the armed conflict between Israel and Palestinian militants are not very different from those that would apply under a law enforcement model. Both would allow the targeted killing of some terrorists in Gaza and both would prohibit—or place greater constraints—on the targeting of suspected terrorists outside a conventional theater of war if the alternative of capture was feasible.

[...]

V. Conclusions

Targeted killing operations display more clearly than any other counterterrorism tactic the tension between labeling terrorism a *crime* and labeling it an *act of war*. If a terror attack is simply a crime, counterterrorism forces would follow the same laws and rules as the Chicago or Miami police department do in fighting crime, where intentional killing could rarely if ever be lawful, other than where necessary in a situation immediately requiring the defense of self or others, or in making an arrest of an obviously dangerous felon. From the perspective of international peacetime relations, targeted killings face even greater legal constraints when targeting a terrorist outside the state's jurisdiction.

If a terrorist plan is an act of war by the organization supporting it, any member of any such terrorist organization may be targeted anytime and anywhere plausibly considered "a battlefield," without prior warning or attempt to capture.

Known or anticipated collateral damage to the innocent is generally prohibited in law enforcement, but is legitimate within the boundaries of proportionality in fighting wars. In fighting crime, the government's obligation to protect its citizens applies to all citizens—criminals and innocents. In fighting wars, the government's primary obligation is to its own citizens, with only limited concern for the well-being of its enemies.

Assuming, as we do, that states do have a right to defend themselves against acts of terrorism, targeted killings cannot be always illegal and immoral. But because terrorism is not a traditional war, nor a traditional crime, its non-traditional nature must affect the ethical and strategic considerations that inform targeted killings, the legal justification behind them, and the choice of targets and methods used to carry them out.

As we have shown, targeted killings may be justified even without declaring an all-out "war" on terrorism. A war paradigm is overbroad in the sense that it allows the targeting of any member of a terrorist organization. For the United States, it has had no geographical limits. When any suspected member of a hostile terrorist organization—regardless of function, role, or degree of contribution to the terrorist effort—might be targeted anywhere around the world without any due process guarantees or monitoring procedures, targeted killings run grave risks of doing both short-term and lasting harm. In contrast, a peacetime paradigm that enumerates specific exceptions for the use of force in self-defense is more legitimate, more narrowly tailored to the situation, offers potentially greater guarantees for the rule of law. It is, however, harder to justify targeted killing operations under a law enforcement paradigm when the tactic is used as a continuous and systematic practice rather than as an exceptional measure.

Justifying targeted killings under a law enforcement paradigm also threatens to erode the international rules that govern peacetime international relations as well as the human rights guarantees that governments owe their own citizens.

Whichever paradigm we choose as our starting point, greater limitations than those offered by the Parks memorandum or that are currently operating in the American targeted killings program should be adopted. The limits set by the Israeli Supreme Court—ironically, within the paradigm of wartime operations—are a good place to start.

First, the tactic should not be used unilaterally by the endangered state if the host country of the terrorists is willing and able to act on its own to arrest or disable in a timely manner the source of the threat. Host country cooperation in capture and extradition must be the first alternative considered. That is, targeted killings must only be carried out as an extraordinary measure, where the alternative of capture or arrest is unfeasible.

Second, only those who are actively and directly involved in terrorist activities are legitimate targets; not every member of a terrorist organization is or should be.

Third, the fact that terrorists do not wear uniforms should not give them an unfair legal advantage over soldiers in uniform in the sense of immunity from deliberate attack. But their lack of uniform does raise legitimate concerns about the ability to ensure the correct identification of the target, in terms of personal identity as well as specific culpability. Any targeted killing operation must therefore include mechanisms in its planning and execution phases that would ensure an accurate identification. Such mechanisms need not involve external judicial review; judges are neither well situated nor do they have the requisite expertise to authorize or reject an operation on the basis of intelligence reports. Rather, the system should be based on verified and verifiable intelligence data from different and independent sources, careful monitoring, and safety mechanisms that would allow aborting the mission in case of doubt.

The concern about collateral damage requires specific attention. Unlike ordinary battlefield strikes, the fact that the targeting forces have control over the time, means, and methods of strike mandates that a heightened degree of care should be exercised to choose an occasion and means that will minimize collateral harm to uninvolved individuals, especially where the operations are carried out outside an immediate conflict zone. In those cases, we believe that where innocent civilians suffer collateral damage, those injured should generally be compensated.

Finally, the aggression of the targeted killing tactic mandates its measured use in only the most urgent and necessary of cases. The government's interest should be to tame violence, not exacerbate it. Where alternatives exist, they should be pursued, not just as a matter of law but also as a matter of sound policy.

NOTES

1. One such famous case took place in July 1973, when the Israeli Mossad assassinated an innocent Moroccan waiter in Lillehammer, Norway, mistaking him for a member of the Black September faction responsible for the Munich massacre.

2. For a report on the U.S. "hit list," see Craig Whitlock, *Afghans Oppose U.S. Hit List of Drug Traffickers*, WASH. POST, Oct. 24, 2009, *available at* http://www.washingtonpost.com/wp-dyn/content/article/2009/10/23/AR2009102303709.html.

[. . .]

25. Armed Activities on the Territory of the Congo (Dem. Rep. Congo v. Uganda), 2005 I.C.J. 116 (Dec. 19).

26. Special Rapporteur on Extrajudicial, Summary or Arbitrary Executions, *Report of the Special Rapporteur on Extrajudicial, Summary or Arbitrary Execution: Study on Targeted Killings*, ¶41, *delivered to the Human Rights Council*, U.N. Doc. A/HRC/14/24/Add.6 (May 28, 2010), *available at* http://www2.ohchr.org/english/bodies/hrcouncil/docs/14session/A.HRC.14.24.Add6.pdf.

*Gabriella Blum is assistant professor of law at Harvard Law School.

Philip Heymann is the James Barr Ames Professor of Law at Harvard Law School.

Gabriella Blum and Philip Heymann, "Law and Policy of Targeted Killing," *Harvard National Security Journal* 1 (June 27, 2010): 145–70. Copyright 2010.

Report of the Special Rapporteur on Extrajudicial, Summary or Arbitrary Executions

Addendum: Study on Targeted Killings

by Philip Alston*

E. WHO MAY CONDUCT A TARGETED KILLING

70. Reported targeted killings by the CIA have given rise to a debate over whether it is a violation of IHL for such killings to be committed by State agents who are not members of its armed forces. Some commentators have argued that CIA personnel who conduct targeted drone killings are committing war crimes because they, unlike the military, are "unlawful combatants", and unable to participate in hostilities. This argument is not supported by IHL. As a threshold matter, the argument assumes that targeted killings by the CIA are committed in the context of armed conflict, which may not be the case. Outside of armed conflict, killings by the CIA would constitute extrajudicial executions assuming that they do not comply with human rights law. If so, they must be investigated and prosecuted both by the US and the State in which the wrongful killing occurred. The following discussion assumes, without accepting, that CIA killings are being conducted in the context of armed conflict.

71. Under IHL, civilians, including intelligence agents, are not prohibited from participating in hostilities. Rather, the consequence of participation is twofold. First, because they are "directly participating in hostilities" by conducting targeted killings, intelligence personnel may themselves be targeted and killed. Second, intelligence personnel do not have immunity from prosecution under domestic law for their conduct. They are thus unlike State armed forces which would generally be immune from prosecution for the same conduct (assuming they complied with IHL requirements). Thus, CIA personnel could be prosecuted for murder under the domestic law of any country in which they conduct targeted drone killings, and could also be prosecuted for violations of applicable US law.

72. It is important to note that if a targeted killing violates IHL (by, for example, targeting civilians who were not "directly participating in hostilities"), then regardless of who conducts it—intelligence personnel or State armed forces—the author, as well as those who authorized it, can be prosecuted for war crimes.

73. Additionally, unlike a State's armed forces, its intelligence agents do not generally operate within a framework which places appropriate emphasis upon ensuring compliance with IHL, rendering violations more likely and causing a higher risk of prosecution both for war crimes and for violations of the laws of the State in which any killing occurs. To the extent a State uses intelligence agents for targeted killing to shield its operations from IHL and human rights law transparency and accountability requirements, it could also incur State responsibility for violating those requirements.[121]

[...]

G. THE USE OF DRONES FOR TARGETED KILLING

79. The use of drones for targeted killings has generated significant controversy. Some have suggested that drones as such are prohibited weapons under IHL because they cause, or have the effect of causing, necessarily indiscriminate killings of civilians, such as those in the vicinity of a targeted person.[142] It is true that IHL places limits on the weapons States may use, and weapons that are, for example, inherently indiscriminate (such as biological weapons) are prohibited.[143] However, a missile fired from a drone is no different from any other commonly used weapon, including a gun fired by a soldier or a helicopter or gunship that fires missiles. The critical legal question is the same for each weapon: whether its specific use complies with IHL.

80. The greater concern with drones is that because they make it easier to kill without risk to a State's forces, policy makers and commanders will be tempted to interpret the legal limitations on who can be killed, and under what circumstances, too expansively. States must ensure that the criteria they apply to determine who can be targeted and killed—i.e., who is a lawful combatant, or what constitutes "direct participation in hostilities" that would subject civilians to direct attack—do not differ based on the choice of weapon.

81. Drones' proponents argue that since drones have greater surveillance capability and afford greater precision than other weapons, they can better prevent collateral civilian casualties and injuries. This may well be true to an extent, but it presents an incomplete picture. The precision, accuracy and legality of a drone strike depend on the human intelligence upon which the targeting decision is based.

82. Drones may provide the ability to conduct aerial surveillance and to gather "pattern of life" information that would allow their human operators to distinguish between peaceful civilians and those engaged in direct hostili-

ties. Indeed, advanced surveillance capability enhances the ability of a State's forces to undertake precautions in attack.[144] But these optimal conditions may not exist in every case. More importantly, a drone operation team sitting thousands of miles away from the environment in which a potential target is located may well be at an even greater human intelligence gathering disadvantage than ground forces, who themselves are often unable to collect reliable intelligence.

83. It was clear during my mission to Afghanistan how hard it is even for forces on the ground to obtain accurate information. Testimony from witnesses and victims' family members, showed that international forces were often too uninformed of local practices, or too credulous in interpreting information, to be able to arrive at a reliable understanding of a situation.[145] International forces all too often based manned airstrikes and raids that resulted in killings on faulty intelligence. Multiple other examples show that the legality of a targeted killing operation is heavily dependent upon the reliability of the intelligence on which it is based.[146] States must, therefore, ensure that they have in place the procedural safeguards necessary to ensure that intelligence on which targeting decisions are made is accurate and verifiable.

84. Furthermore, because operators are based thousands of miles away from the battlefield, and undertake operations entirely through computer screens and remote audio-feed, there is a risk of developing a "Playstation" mentality to killing. States must ensure that training programs for drone operators who have never been subjected to the risks and rigors of battle instill respect for IHL and adequate safeguards for compliance with it.

85. Outside the context of armed conflict, the use of drones for targeted killing is almost never likely to be legal. A targeted drone killing in a State's own territory, over which the State has control, would be very unlikely to meet human rights law limitations on the use of lethal force.

86. Outside its own territory (or in territory over which it lacked control) and where the situation on the ground did not rise to the level of armed conflict in which IHL would apply, a State could theoretically seek to justify the use of drones by invoking the right to anticipatory self-defence against a non-state actor.[147] It could also theoretically claim that human rights law's requirement of first employing less-than-lethal means would not be possible if the State has no means of capturing or causing the other State to capture the target. As a practical matter, there are very few situations outside the context of active hostilities in which the test for anticipatory self-defence—necessity that is "instant, overwhelming, and leaving no choice of means, and no moment of deliberation"[148]—would be met. This hypothetical presents the same danger as

the "ticking-time bomb" scenario does in the context of the use of torture and coercion during interrogations: a thought experiment that posits a rare emergency exception to an absolute prohibition can effectively institutionalize that exception. Applying such a scenario to targeted killings threatens to eviscerate the human rights law prohibition against the arbitrary deprivation of life. In addition, drone killing of anyone other than the target (family members or others in the vicinity, for example) would be an arbitrary deprivation of life under human rights law and could result in State responsibility and individual criminal liability.

[...]

Notes

121. In response to Freedom of Information Act litigation seeking the legal basis for alleged CIA targeted killings, the CIA has said that it cannot even confirm or deny the existence of any records because that information is classified and protected from disclosure. See Letter from CIA Information and Privacy Coordinator, 9 March 2010, available at http://www.aclu.org/national-security/predatordrone-foia-cia-letter-refusing-confirm-or-deny-existence-records.

[...]

142. Murray Wardrop, Unmanned Drones Could be Banned, Says Senior Judge, The Telegraph, 6 July 2009.

143. The general prohibition under IHL is against weapons that violate the principle of distinction or cause unnecessary suffering. See HPCR Commentary, section C.

144. Michael N. Schmitt, Precision Attack and International Humanitarian Law, 87 Int'l Rev. Red Cross 445 (Sept. 2005).

145. A/HRC/11/2/Add.4, paras. 14–18, 70.

146. See, e.g., Israel Ministry of Foreign Affairs Website, "Findings of the inquiry into the death of Salah Shehadeh" http://www.mfa.gov.il/MFA/Government/Communiques/2002/Findings%20of%20the%20inquiry%20into%20the%20death%20of%20Salah%20Sh.

147. Infra III.B.

148. See R.Y. Jennings, The Caroline and McLeod Cases, 32 Am. J. Int'l L. 82, 92 (1938).

*Philip Alston is John Norton Pomeroy Professor of Law at New York University School of Law and co-chair of the law school's Center for Human Rights and Global Justice.

United Nations, Human Rights Council, Report of the Special Rapporteur on Extrajudicial, Summary or Arbitrary Executions, Philip Alston, May 28, 2010, A /HRC/14/24/Add.6. paras. 70–73; 79–86.

Part 6:
Globalization, State Responsibility, and Future Threats

So far, many of the articles in this volume have examined how international humanitarian law (IHL) has been tested by the rise of terrorism and insurgency as the dominant modes of modern warfare. Authors in this final section challenge us to think about how broader trends of economic globalization, technological development, and shifting global power balances have impacted the regulation of war. Has the focus on threats due to terrorism or other forms of irregular warfare obscured attention from other equally serious threats from transnational crime, human trafficking, or others? What can we learn from exploring the problems that have arisen in addressing these other transnational issues? What are the costs of trends toward outsourcing war, either to privatized soldiers and military companies (sometimes considered to be mercenaries) or to robots? Though each author in this section deals with very different sets of issues in the international security realm, they all question how evolving global economic and power dynamics and technological advances test the basic structure of state and individual accountability that IHL regulation depends upon.

GLOBALIZATION, SOVEREIGNTY AND 21ST CENTURY CONFLICT

Globalization has made national boundaries less important, limiting state abilities to control the spread of transnational threats like global terrorism or transnational crime. Meanwhile, increased transnational flows of goods and information, together with technological innovation have made increasingly advanced weapons of war more affordable and accessible to nonstate actors. Now private actors ranging from private security companies to terrorist networks, can exercise significant war-making powers.[1]

These developments have not only changed the nature of threats in 21st century conflict but also have complicated the international system's ability to control or regulate war. Many of the provisions of IHL are premised on a system in which the state is dominant and has a monopoly on force. When many of the principle threats facing the international system are initiated by nonstate actors who cannot or will not be bound by international legal treaties, state-centric IHL provisions may be difficult, if not impossible, to enforce. Because of this, two of the authors in this section suggest that greater attention to how global economic and social changes affect sovereignty and state responsibility might be the key to developing more effective international regulation of transnational threats.

In the first article, Moisés Naím argues that undue focus on the "global war on terrorism" has obscured attention from five other "wars" stemming from globalization that pose an equal threat to the international system. These are the threats of drug and arms trafficking, intellectual property violations, trafficking of humans, and money laundering. Like the challenges posed by asymmetric warfare, these wars are not new, but Naím argues that they have "boomed" with the onset of globalization. Common features of these other wars illustrate that challenges to IHL in recent years are part of the broader phenomenon of the breakdown of sovereign control and the inability of governments to deal with transnational threats fueled by global market forces. "These five wars stretch and even render obsolete many of the existing institutions, legal frameworks, military doctrines, weapons systems, law enforcement techniques, and even basic definitions on which we have relied for years," he argues.[2] He suggests that reconceptualizing state sovereignty, ownership, and tools of regulation will be critical to addressing (if not winning) these wars, and by analogy, to resolving modern issues in regulating conflict.

The article by E. L. Gaston also grapples with sovereignty issues but focuses on how a breakdown in state responsibility for misconduct in warfare has affected one particular sector, the fast-growing privatized military and security sector. The widespread use and high-profile abuses of private military and security companies (PMSCs) during the U.S.-led interventions in Iraq and Afghanistan sparked proposals for stronger regulation and control. Gaston argues that the focus on specific misconduct or criminal behavior by those working for PMSCs, or efforts to fold them into the centuries-old international prohibition on "mercenaries," has distracted from the more fundamental threat posed by the rise of PMSCs. She argues that the widespread use of PMSCs by both state and nonstate actors poses a problem because it delinks state accountability from acts committed in conflict. The solution, she suggests, is not to focus on the liability of PMSC companies or individuals, but to focus on restoring that link to state responsibility. She suggests creating specific prohibitions or standards applicable when states use PMSCs as an extension of their military forces, in the vein of other IHL controls on "means and methods" of warfare.

FROM STATE TO INDIVIDUAL CONTROLS: FUTURE ROBOTICS AND TECHNOLOGY

The final article in this section, "Building a Better WarBot: Ethical Issues in the Design of Unmanned Systems for Military Applications," by Robert Sparrow, explores how changes in technology might undermine not only state control and responsibility but also more elemental human controls on warfare.

Though drones are the "new weapon" that has garnered the most attention, robotics is playing an increasing role in many modes of modern warfare. Peter W. Singer, a leading scholar in the field, notes: "By the end of 2004, there were 150 robots on the ground in Iraq; a year later there were 2,400; by the end of 2008, there were about 12,000 robots of nearly two dozen varieties operating on the ground in Iraq."[3] For example, small, motorized devices called "Pack-bots" have been sent ahead of troops in places like Iraq and Afghanistan to scout out a location that might be an ambush, or to defuse improvised explosive devices (IEDs) or unexploded ordnance. Automated antiaircraft cannons routinely form part of U.S. base defenses; with a reaction speed faster than humanly possible, they shoot down incoming artillery barrages. Another recently tested, more advanced form of robotics, the Special Weapons Observation Reconnaissance Detection System, is an armed battlefield robot that can take on many of the combat functions of a regular soldier.[4]

Sparrow examines how wider deployment of autonomous or semiautonomous robotic weapons might affect controls on the use of force. Are robots more or less likely to refrain from unnecessary killing or destruction, or to avoid killing civilians? On the one hand, autonomous robots would not feel compassion or sympathy, and thus would never be restrained from killing by such emotions. Even robots that keep a "human in the loop" and are remotely operated by humans may be less restrained by human empathy. Like Philip Alston, who critiqued drones in the previous section, Sparrow is concerned that the use of remotely operated robots depersonalizes war, eroding some of the operator's psychological limitations on the use of force. On the other hand, many deaths in war are caused by simple mistakes, which robots are less likely to make. Plus, while they may lack compassion, they also would not kill out of anger or fear the way a soldier under pressure might.

Wider deployment of robots—particularly autonomous robots—may also have serious consequences for the mechanisms IHL uses to regulate warfare. Theoretically, robots could be programmed to apply IHL principles such as proportionality and distinction. With increasing advancements in visual recognition software, they could one day recognize a targeted combatant as well as a human soldier can. However, as Sparrow points out, this would not eliminate the risk of civilian casualties or, potentially, war crimes. When a robot kills a civilian who should be held accountable, he asks? Should it be the "commander" of the robot's unit? The company that manufactured or designed the robot? Without being able to ascribe personal or command responsibility for certain actions, IHL regulations become almost impossible to enforce.

CONCLUSION

The articles in this compendium have tried to address whether twenty-first-century conflict is fundamentally "new," and whether IHL can successfully regulate and constrain 21st century conflict. Authors in past sections have explored these questions by looking at IHL's interaction with the threats and challenges prominent in the past decade: from irregular warfare, like terrorism or insurgent war, to new technologies, like precision warfare and unmanned weaponry. Authors have disagreed about whether these aspects make 21st century warfare critically different from past eras of warfare and whether a revision of existing IHL rules (in whole or in part) is merited.

Authors in this section suggest a more fundamental difficulty for regulating 21st century conflict. Globalization and technological change have not just made it more difficult to apply IHL rules as they are currently written. They have eroded states' abilities to control and regulate threats and to enforce *any* system of rules. Emerging technologies and threats such as cyber warfare, unmanned weaponry, and integration of robotics into warfare may further undermine state and individual controls on warfare in the future.

Given these background conditions, could *any* "rewrite" of the laws of war be effective in regulating 21st century conflict? In view of the many challenges to IHL application described in this and other sections, a pessimistic response cannot be ruled out. Yet perhaps today's challenges are no more or less insurmountable than those faced by other generations: in every era, international actors have tried to control and regulate warfare, only to meet as many failures as successes. In light of this, attempts to limit unnecessary suffering in warfare may seem Sisyphean. Looking forward, the only thing that seems certain is the increasing lethality and destructiveness of warfare. As long as this trend continues, efforts to limit the scourge of war will likely continue to be imperfect, but absolutely essential.

As you read the three articles in this section, think about some of the broader effects of the phenomena being discussed in contrast to the concerns raised by authors in previous sections.

- Naím argues that existing institutions and regulatory mechanisms within the international system are broken and no longer work in the modern, globalized era. But rather than concluding that regulation is impossible, he suggests that the international community must and can come up with new rules and systems for regulating the transnational crimes, conflict, and abuse he examines. Given not only his analysis but other pieces in this compendium, do you share his optimism? Why or why not?

- In trying to prod "new thinking" about how to regulate 21st century threats, Naím argues that some of the products of globalization could be used to develop new controls on international threats: "[I]nstead of using bureaucracies to curb the excesses of these markets, it would be better to use market incentives. For example, it is clear that in some cases technology can do a better job of protecting intellectual property rights than patents, lawyers, and courts."[5] Do you find his arguments compelling? Can market forces or technology replace international legal mechanisms in terms of enforcement?

- Gaston argues that the more serious consequence of states' outsourcing wartime functions to private actors is that it delinks state accountability from actions in war. In some ways, this argument is similar to Sparrow's concern about responsibility for robots' actions. Do you agree with them that outsourcing war to private actors or machines poses particular problems for state accountability? Both authors propose suggestions for restoring the link between state responsibility and the conduct of either PMSCs or robots. Do you find their solutions convincing?

- Some argue that greater robotics use and automation in warfare would result in better civilian protection because of robots' precision targeting and surveillance aspects, and their remove from personal risk. Similar arguments about the potential of technology to improve IHL compliance have been made in past sections, for example, with regard to precision weapons. Do you think that the benefits of such advances can outweigh their destructive power or the way they override other controls on uses of force? Or, as previous authors in this compendium have argued, do such advances merely give the illusion of a costless war, reducing the pressure for states or the individuals manning these weapons to avoid resort to the use of force?

NOTES

1. The 1994 Rwandan genocide, in which more than 800,000 minority Tutsis were killed over the course of about 100 days, was perpetrated almost exclusively by ordinary civilians, not members of organized armed forces or groups. Many were killed using machetes, knives, or other simple household weapons.

2. Moisés Naím, "The Fourth Annual Grotius Lecture: Five Wars of Globalization," *American University International Law Review* 18, no. 1 (2002): 17.

3. Peter W. Singer, "Military Robots and the Laws of War," *New Atlantis* (Winter 2009): 25–45.

4. Ibid.

5. Naím, "The Fourth Annual Grotius Lecture," 18.

Five Wars of Globalization

*by Moisés Naím**

The criminal events of September 11 injected into the national conversation concepts that until then had been used mainly within small groups of experts. Concepts like "asymmetrical war," "transnational terrorist networks," "sleeper cells," or "military tribunals" leapt from specialized journals to the Teleprompters of news anchors and from dry government reports to opinion columns in newspapers and magazines everywhere. The tragedy also made the general public painfully aware of how vulnerable governments were to the activities of small groups of like-minded individuals determined to achieve their goals. The world now knows that small groups of highly motivated individuals can successfully overcome governmental attempts to constrain, eliminate, or neutralize them. Government forces, and particularly armies, are designed to confront other armies, not stateless, decentralized, civilian networks with military training that move freely and stealthily across national borders.

The spotlight on al Qaeda and religious, particularly Islamic, terrorism, has obscured the fact that the war on terrorism is just part of all the five global wars where governments are pitted against international networks of stateless civilians. Governments everywhere have long been trying to stamp out, or at least curb, the illegal international trade in drugs, arms, intellectual property, people, and money.

These five wars are more than just different examples of a growing tide of "transnational crime." These "wars" have many common characteristics, drivers, and outcomes.[1] Looking at them as different expressions of a broader phenomenon fueled by globalization yields interesting insights into the challenges the world is facing in terms of security, politics, economics, and international relations in general. The implications for international law are, of course, enormous.

I. THE FIVE WARS

In the last decade, and way before the war on terrorism monopolized everyone's attention, every day the media gave us—and still gives us—the dispatches from the front lines of the five wars. Pick any newspaper anywhere in the world, any day and you will find news about illegal migrants, a drug bust, smuggled weapons, laundered money, or a story about the speed and effectiveness with which counterfeiters have copied the latest Gucci bag or Microsoft product. The statistics of the resources—financial, human, institutional, technological —deployed in these wars have reached orders of magnitude that are hard to fathom. So do the numbers of victims. The anecdotes about the tactics and tricks or the violence used by the combatants boggle the mind. The "globality" of these five wars was unimaginable just a decade ago. The fact that they are part of the same phenomenon and that they are driven by the same global trends is not, however, typically found in the reports from the front. Before discussing their commonalties let me first briefly describe each of the five wars.

A. The War on Drugs[2]

The best known, of course, is the war on drugs. The violence in the battles and skirmishes in this war seems only to be exceeded by the profits involved. Retail sales of illicit drugs are about $150 billion a year, roughly equivalent to half the total sales of the pharmaceutical industry worldwide. The U.S., for example, spends between $35 to 40 billion each year on the war on drugs, most of it on interdiction and intelligence. Increases in governmental resources and effectiveness seem to be immediately matched by increases in the drug cartels' creativity and boldness.[3] In March of 2002, for example, a tunnel was found under the U.S.-Mexican border that was used to move tons of drugs to the U.S. and billions of dollars in cash back.[4] Commercial jetliners, private submarines and all types of boats, planes and vehicles are customarily deployed by the drug cartels. One of the unintended consequences of the war in Afghanistan is a bumper harvest in poppies that has authorities in Europe and the U.S. bracing for a flood of opium and heroin in their markets.[5] The U.S.-crafted Plan Colombia has already displaced coca production and processing labs to neighboring Ecuador and Peru.[6] Britain's High Commission in Jamaica says that one in ten passengers flying to the U.K. from that island is smuggling drugs.[7] The war on drugs, protracted, global, costly, and murderous, does not show any sign of abating or of an imminent victory on the part of governments.

Even when the top leaders of drug cartels are captured or killed by police, authorities are quick to point out that the vacuum left in the market will soon be filled by one or more of their rivals. This happened when Colombian kingpin Pablo Escobar Gaviria was killed by the police a few years back and was what most likely happened after the arrest of one of the Arellano Felix brothers— leaders of one of Mexico's main drug trafficking networks—in early 2002.[8]

Most Americans know this. According to Pew Research Center poll conducted in February of 2001, three out of four Americans believe that "we are losing the drug war."[9]

B. The War Against Arms Trafficking[10]

Drugs and arms often go together. In 1999, ten thousand of the assault rifle Automat Kalashnikova 1947, or the infamous AK-47, originally bought for the Peruvian Army in Jordan were parachuted to the FARC [Revolutionary Armed Forces of Columbia] guerrillas in Colombia—a group closely allied to drug growers and traffickers.[11] According to the United Nations ("UN"), small arms fueled forty-six of the forty-nine largest world conflicts of the last decade and the UN also estimates that about half of all these weapons are from illegal sources. Of the 550 million small arms and light weapons in circulation today, only eighteen million [about three percent] are used by government, military, or police forces.[12] Speaking only of AK-47s, the weapon of choice for most guerrilla groups, there are fifty to eighty million units in circulation today throughout the world.[13] The weapon is officially manufactured in fourteen countries, but illegal production has become quite common and as a result its price has plummeted to about $100 in Nicaragua for example.[14] In 1986, the price of an AK-47 in Kolowa, a town in Kenya, was fifteen cows. Today is just four cows.[15]

Illicit trade in small arms is estimated to be responsible for one thousand deaths a day worldwide and more than eighty percent of the victims are women and children.[16] Governments have long tried to control the illicit trade in arms but we have yet to find a determined rogue state, a guerilla movement, a terrorist organization, or a criminal cartel that cannot procure the arms it needs. After procuring the weapons, they seldom seem to lack a steady supply of munitions for them.

And it is not just small arms. Governments are also at war with the international traffickers of weapons of mass destruction.[17] The actual supply of stolen nuclear materials and technology or biological and chemical "weapons" may still not be very large. But there is no doubt that the potential demand for these materials and technology is there, it is huge and it is growing.[18] The world does not lack secessionist conflicts, civil wars, or ethnic disputes where one of the parties would be more than willing to resort to a weapon of mass destruction to completely recast the situation to its advantage. A huge and soaring demand and a constrained supply means exorbitant prices. These, in turn, mean exorbitant incentives to satisfy this pent up demand. While historically the design and production of weapons of mass destruction was in the hands of governments and required huge capital investments, this is no longer the case. The technology to produce weapons of mass destruction is not any more the monopoly of governments and the capital and the infrastructure needed to produce them are no longer outside the realm of possibilities of the private sector.[19] Therefore, it is not prudent to assume that biological, chemical, and Internet "weapons" can only be produced by governments. Moreover, the historical record shows how difficult it is to contain the dissemination of technology and know-how once it becomes available, especially to non-state actors. The tools and trends of globalization facilitate this proliferation.

C. The War Against the Illegal Trade of Intellectual Property

The war that governments are waging against the international trade in stolen intellectual property used in producing weapons is just one front of the larger war they are fighting to curb the production and trade of pirated software, bootlegged movies, records, and medicines and a panoply of other counterfeited goods and branded services. The International Intellectual Property Alliance estimates that in 2001, $9.4 billion were lost to copyright piracy.[20] When the estimates for other forms of theft and illegal commerce of intellectual property are added, the sums involved are as staggering as the speed at which intellectual property is copied and illegally merchandized internationally. In 2001, two days after recording the voice track of a movie in Hollywood, actor Dennis Hopper was in Shanghai where a street vendor sold him an excellent, but pirated, copy of the movie with his voice already on it. "I don't know how they got my voice into the country before I got here" he said.[21] In 1993, a piracy group called DrinkOrDie founded in Russia with leaders operating from bases in Australia and the U.S. "released" its own [pirated] version of Windows 95 operating system three days before Microsoft's official release.[22] Forty percent of Procter and Gamble shampoos, sixty percent of Honda motorbikes, eighty percent of all DVD's, and ninety-four percent of the brand name software sold in China in 2001 were pirated.[23]

The problem is not only confined to software, fake Prada bags, popular toys, expensive watches, and Cuban cigars. Industrial valve makers in Italy are worried that their $2 billion a year export market is being eroded by counterfeit valves made in China and sold in world markets with the same Italian brand names but a price that is forty percent cheaper.[24] Cheaper copies of electrical goods and engine and car parts also account for a booming market. Nor is the problem only confined to China. The piracy rate of business software in Japan and France is forty percent, in Greece and South Korea it is about sixty percent, and in Germany and Britain it hovers around thirty percent. The average for the world has been increasing and in 2001 reached an all time high of thirty-seven percent.[25] Technology is obviously boosting both the demand and the supply of illegally copied products. Users of Napster, the Internet technology that allows anyone, anywhere to download and reproduce copyrighted music for free grew from zero to twenty million in just one year.[26] The courts in some countries have acted to stem this trend but it does not seem safe to assume that in the long run governments, lawyers and courts will trump technologies designed to facilitate using other people's intellectual property for free. Napster emulators have already occupied the market that was opened once Napster's offerings were curbed by legal actions. See for example www.Kazaa.com.[27]

D. The War Against Traffickers of People

In the same way that the illegal trade in drugs and arms are often intertwined, the international distribution of counterfeited merchandise is also closely related to the international trafficking of people. The man or woman that sells a Louis Vuitton bag or a Cartier watch in the streets of Florence or New York for a tenth of its price in stores is probably an illegal alien. Very likely, he or she was transported across several continents by a network of traffickers in humans that has a strategic alliance with another network that specializes in the worldwide and illegal copying, manufacturing, and distribution of high-end, branded products.

Alien smuggling is a $7 billion a year business and according to the UN is the fastest growing business of organized crime.[28] Approximately 150 million people or roughly 2.5 percent of the world's population live today outside their countries of origin.[29] This number has doubled since 1965 and the data shows that legal and illegal migration is accelerating. Many are voluntary migrants that enlist the help of smuggling rings to help them enter illegally another country.[30] Others instead, are trafficked—that is bought and sold internationally—as commodities. The U.S. Congressional Research Service ["CRS"] reckons that each year between seven thousand to two million people, the majority of them women and children, are trafficked across international borders.[31] Thirty-five percent are under the age of thirty-five.[32] Girls from villages in Nepal and Bangladesh are sold to brothels in India for $1,000.[33] UNICEF estimates that 200,000 children are enslaved by cross border smugglers in Central and West Africa.[34] According to the CRS, trafficking in people is now the third most important source of revenue for international criminal networks, after drugs and guns.[35] Initially tempting the victims with offers of jobs or, in the case of children, with offers of adoption in wealthier countries, human traffickers then keep them in subservience through physical violence, debt bondage, passport confiscation, and threats of arrest, deportation, and violence against the victims' families back home.[36]

Governments everywhere are enacting tougher immigration laws and have boosted both their budgets and their technologies to fight the flow of illegal aliens. In response, individuals desperate to leave countries rife with political instability, civil war, or with a bleak economic future and the international networks that exploit the enormous demand for illegal immigration are using increasingly bold and imaginative tactics to defeat the efforts of governments. The booming numbers of Moroccans smuggled last year into Spain, Mexicans, Central Americans, and Chinese into the U.S., Albanians into Italy, or Eastern Europeans and Turks into Germany indicate that governments are far from winning this war.[37]

E. The War Against Money Laundering

One reason why governments are not winning and in some cases even losing ground in their efforts to contain the international commerce in drugs, arms, pirated goods, and people is because there is just too much money being made in these activities. These enormous quantities of money are also traded internationally and illegally, and governments are also at war against illegal money traffickers. The profits of those involved in these wars are not, of course, the only sources of money laundered internationally. In general, this giant pool of money consists of any funds that owners want to hide from governments, creditors, business partners, or family members—such as the proceeds of tax evasion, corruption, gambling and other forms of crime—and each year it is estimated to equal around two to five percent of the global GDP. This means that governments are trying to detect and contain the international trade of between $800 billion to $2 trillion each year.[38]

The U.S. Treasury estimates that it loses $70 billion a year through offshore tax evasions just by individuals, while developing countries lose about $50 billion a year in taxes through these modalities. In 1998, $74 billion were transferred from Russian banks to overseas accounts. Of that amount, $70 billion went to accounts at banks in the small island-state of Nauru.[39] The following year, Nauru's banks were used to illegally move $7.5 billion from Russia to the Bank of New York.[40]

Among nation states, Nauru is of course neither the only nor the most important player. The Cayman Islands, with a population of 35,000, is home to almost

600 banks and trust companies, more than 2,200 mutual funds, 500 insurance companies, and 45,000 foreign businesses. Its banking system has almost $700 billion in assets. In more traditional Switzerland, banks have $2.3 trillion under management, more than half owned by foreigners.[41]

Again, faced with this growing tide, governments have stepped up their efforts to clamp down on rogue international banking, tax havens, and money laundering. While some progress has been made, advances in information and communication technology, the limits of sovereignty, greed, and globalization are conspiring against the governmental efforts to limit and regulate the illegal international trade in money.

II. What Do These Five Wars Have in Common?

A lot. Perhaps their most salient common characteristic is that they are not new. In one form or another they all have been part of the human experience since time immemorial. But one other aspect that they have in common is that they all have boomed in the last decade, propelled by the collection of forces we call globalization.

But these five wars also share other important traits.

First: They all pit governments against market forces. Each of the five wars consists of one or more government bureaucracies fighting to contain the disparate, uncoordinated actions of thousand of independent, stateless organizations motivated by the huge profits that can be obtained by exploiting international price differentials, a huge, unsatisfied demand, or the cost advantages produced by theft. Hourly wages for a Chinese cook are far higher in Manhattan than in Fujian.[42] A gram of cocaine in Kansas City is 17,000 percent more expensive than in Bogota.[43] Fake Italian valves are forty percent cheaper because the counterfeiters do not need to cover the costs of developing the product.[44] A well-funded guerrilla group will pay anything to get the weapons it needs. In each of these five wars the incentives to successfully overcome government imposed limits to trade are, simply, enormous.

Second: They are not bound by geography. Where is the theater or the front line of the war on drugs. Is it Colombia or Miami? Myanmar or Milan? Where are the battles against money launderers being fought? In Nauru or in London? Is China the main theater in the war against the infringement of intellectual property or are the trenches of that war to be found on the Internet? If so what is the Internet equivalent of trench wars or guerrilla warfare?

Third: Governments are at a disadvantage in these wars. While their enemies can exploit the advantage of moving freely between jurisdictions, nations are bound by sovereignty, borders, and international law. States have to rely on centralized, hierarchical, Weberian bureaucracies to fight against highly mobile, decentralized networks of highly motivated individuals. A senior official at the Central Intelligence Agency once told me: "in my experience it was often easier for international gangs to move people, money, and weapons internationally than it was for us to re-assign assets inside the U.S. government agencies."

Fourth: In each of the five wars the government side is not winning and in some of them it is in fact losing. Drugs, weapons, pirated products, illegal aliens, and opportunities to illegally move, hide, and launder money internationally have not become scarcer despite governmental efforts to do so.

III. WHY ARE GOVERNMENTS NOT WINNING THE FIVE WARS?

Globalization has done more to empower international criminal networks than governments. Globalization and other changes that characterized the end of the last decade made available to the public—and therefore to the groups acting in these wars—the technologies, resources, and possibilities that until the early 1990's were often only available to governments. The Tamil Tigers, for example, obtained night-vision goggles and Global Position Satellite devices to direct their projectiles before the Sri Lankan military against which they were fighting.[45] The telecommunication and logistics infrastructure of drug traffickers, counterfeiters, or smugglers of people is often superior to that of the regulatory and law enforcement agencies of most countries. The information and communication technology, the sophisticated financial instruments, and the myriad of new financial institutions that exist today make the regulation of international flows of money a daunting task. The imminent, large-scale introduction of e-money—cards with microchips that can store large amounts of money and thus can be easily transported outside regular channels or simply exchanged among individuals—will make this task all the more daunting.

But it is not just technology that boosts the capabilities of criminal networks. More porous borders, a larger number of countries, many new democracies with institutions that are vulnerable to being captured or heavily influenced by criminal gangs, higher levels of international travel, trade, and investment, more civil wars and weak or even failed states are also some of the legacies of the 1990's that create advantages for the networks fighting the five wars.

IV. WHAT TO DO?

The nature of these five wars, of their combatants, and of the technical, economic, political, legal, and social trends that give them strength suggest five avenues for governments that seek to make progress.

First, develop more flexible notions of sovereignty. Governments need to recognize that restricting the scope of multilateral action for the sake of protecting their sovereignty is often a moot point. Their sovereignty is compromised, in some cases even daily, by the stateless networks that break their laws and cross their borders to conduct their business. In a recent example, the Venezuelan government denied authorization for U.S. planes to fly over Venezuelan territory in order to monitor the air routes commonly used by narco-traffickers.[46] The fact that the planes of the drug traffickers violated Venezuelan territory on a daily basis was given less importance than the symbolic value of asserting national sovereignty over the air space.

Second, strengthen existing multilateral institutions. The global nature of these wars means that no government, regardless of its economic power, political influence, or military superiority will make much progress acting alone. If this seems obvious, then why does INTERPOL, the multilateral agency in charge of fighting international crime, have a total staff of 373, only 120 of which are police officers, and an annual budget of $23 million, less than the price of a single boat or plane used by drug traffickers?[47] In fact, EUROPOL, INTERPOL's European equivalent, has a staff of 338 and a budget of $44 million.[48]

One of the reasons why INTERPOL is not better funded and staffed is because its 178 member governments do not trust each other.[49] Many assume, and perhaps rightly so, that the criminal networks they are fighting have penetrated the police departments of other countries and it would not therefore be prudent to share information with them or with INTERPOL. Others fear that today's allies can easily become tomorrow's enemies. Others have legal impediments to sharing intelligence with other nation states or, what is an even more formidable barrier, the organizational culture and habits of their intelligence services and law enforcement agencies makes it almost impossible for them to collaborate effectively with other agencies. But these are institutional obstacles that can and must be overcome, if only through painful experience; they are not an adequate justification for inaction.

Third, devise new mechanisms and institutions. These five wars stretch and even render obsolete many of the existing institutions, legal frameworks, military doctrines, weapons systems, law enforcement techniques, and even basic definitions on which we have relied for years.

The concept of war "fronts" defined by geography or the definition of "combatants" according to the Geneva convention;[50] the functions of intelligence agents, soldiers, police officers, customs agents or immigration officers need rethinking and adaptation to the new realities. The notion that ownership is essentially a physical reality and not a "virtual" one or that money can only be issued by sovereign nations will also need adjustments.

Fourth, where possible, move from repression to regulation. Beating market forces is next to impossible. In some cases, this reality may mean that governments will need to move from repressing the market to regulating it. In others it may mean that instead of using bureaucracies to curb the excesses of these markets, it would be better to use market incentives. For example, it is clear that in some cases technology can do a better job of protecting intellectual property rights than patents, lawyers, and courts. Powerful encryption techniques and other such technologies can better protect software or a CD from being copied in Ukraine than forcing Ukraine to develop a reliable and transparent system to enforce patents and copyrights and trademarks.

Note that I have not called these four points "solutions" but "avenues." This is because I am trying to sound very tentative, and even experimental. I don't think anyone can offer definitive solutions to these problems because our understanding of their nature, scope, and interconnections is still very primitive.

The central message of this lecture is that we have entered into new territory, one that demands new maps, new approaches—in short new thinking

In this sense, I thought that it was appropriate to conclude by quoting Christopher Weeramnatry and Nathaniel Berman who in the First of these Grotius Memorial Lectures and as opening tribute to Hugo Grotius said:

"It was an unprecedented situation that faced the newly emerging states of Grotius's time. Detached from their traditional moorings to church, empire, and a higher law, they were groping for new principles of conduct and interrelationship to provide a compass for the tempestuous waters that lay ahead.

Grotius rose to the occasion—a towering intellect with a passionate vision of an ordered relationship among nations—a relationship based not on the dogma of religion or the sword of conquest, but on human reason and experience. He based his principles largely on knowledge gleaned a posteriori from the experience of history, not on a priori pronouncements prescribing in advance how humanity should behave."[51]

We obviously are in dire need of one or more towering intellects who, like

Grotius, can rise to the occasion and provide the world with ideas that will en-sure international stability and prosperity.

Thank you very much.

NOTES

1. *See generally* R.T. NAYLOR, WAGES OF CRIME (2002); LINNEA P. RAINE & FRANK J. CILLUFO, GLOBAL ORGANIZED CRIME—THE NEW EMPIRE OF EVIL (1994) (providing an introduction to this topic).

2. *See generally* MIKE GRAY, DRUG CRAZY—HOW WE GOT INTO THIS MESS AND HOW WE CAN GET OUT (1998) (providing further information on this topic).

3. *See Stumbling in the Dark*, ECONOMIST, July 26, 2001, at S3 (stating that, when calculated using retail prices, the illegal drug market is most likely the world's largest illicit market), *available at* http://www.economist.com (last visited Sept. 20, 2002).

4. *See* Kevin Sullivan, *Drugs Worth "Billions' Moved Through Tunnel*, WASH. POST, Mar. 1, 2002, at A1 (explaining that investigators are referring to the 1200 foot tunnel as one of the most lucrative drug-smuggling mechanisms that drug agents have ever discovered along the U.S.-Mexican border).

5. *See* Marc Kaufman, *Surge in Afghan Poppy Crop is Forecast; World Drug Control Authorities Consider Force and Funds to Limit Production*, WASH. POST, Dec. 25, 2001, at A22 (discussing Afghanistan's poppy production, which has earned Afghanistan the notoriety of being the world's largest illicit opium supplier).

6. See Claire Marshall, *Peru Set to be Drug Leader*, BBC NEWS (Feb. 11, 2001) (discussing Plan Colombia's influence on drug trafficking in Peru), at http://news.bbc.co.uk/1/hi/world/americas/1176452.stm (last visited Sept. 20, 2002).

7. See John Steele & David Millward, *Britain Hit by Cocaine Flights from Jamaica*, DAILY TELEGRAPH (London), Apr. 1, 2002, at P5 (noting that Jamaican drug couriers are potentially smuggling as much as thirty kilograms of cocaine into the United Kingdom on each flight); *see also Jamaican Drug Mules 'Flooding' UK*, BBC NEWS, Jan. 3, 2002 (relating that the U.K.'s Deputy High Commissioner in Jamaica has suggested that the number of Jamaican drug smugglers from Jamaica could be higher than previously estimated), *at* http://news.bbc.co.uk/1/hi/uk/1739808.stm (last visited Sept. 20, 2002).

8. See E. Lynne Walker & Marisa Taylor, *Outsiders May Make Move on Drug Cartel*, SAN DIEGO UNION-TRIB., Mar. 13, 2002, at A1 (explaining that several Mexican drug traffickers might take advantage of the power vacuum that resulted after authorities arrested Benjamin Arellano Felix, leader of a prominent Mexican drug cartel). *See generally* LUIS ASTORGA, DRUG TRAFFICKING IN MEXICO: A FIRST GENERAL ASSESSMENT (UNESCO MOST Discussion Paper No. 36, 1999) (providing an overview of Mexican drug trafficking), at http://www.unesco.org/most/astorga.htm (last visited Oct. 4, 2002).

9. *See* PEW RESEARCH CENTER FOR THE PEOPLE & THE PRESS, INTERDICTION AND INCARCERATION STILL TOP REMEDIES (2001) (noting that public opinion regarding the drug war has not changed since the late 1980s), *at* http://people-press.org/reports/display.php3ReportID=16 (last visited Oct. 4, 2002).

10. For an introduction to this topic see Running Guns: The Global Black Market in Small Arms (Lora Lumpe ed., 2000).

11. *See* Douglas Farah, *Colombian Rebels Tap E. Europe for Arms-Guerrillas' Firepower Superior to Army's*, WASH. POST, Nov. 4, 1999, at A1 (discussing the weapons supply that the Revolutionary Armed Forces of Colombia ("FARC") has purchased from sources in the former Soviet Union and Eastern Europe).

12. *See* Kofi A. Annan, Small Arms, Big Problems, Remarks at the United Nations Conference on the Illicit Trade in Small Arms and Light Weapons in All Its Aspects (July 9–20, 2001), *in* INT'L HERALD TRIB., July 10, 2001, at 9 (reporting on the dangers that small arms pose to the world).

13. *See* Margaret Coker, *Illegal Small Weapons Pose Global Threat*, SEATTLE POST-INTELLIGENCER, July 9, 2001, at A1 (relating that the AK-47 is the most widely used variety of small arms).

14. *See* Michael Reid, *Central America Still in the Grip of War's Dangerous Legacy*, GUARDIAN (London), Aug. 20, 1993, at 10 (commenting that in Managua's market, an AK-47 and four magazines sell for less than one hundred dollars); see also Annan, supra note 12 (adding that the direct and indirect costs of small arms violence is estimated to be between $140 and $170 billion per year in Latin America alone).

15. *See* Karl Vick, *Small Arms' Global Reach Uproots Tribal Traditions*, WASH. POST, July 8, 2002, at A1 (discussing how the AK-47, the assault weapon of choice, is changing tribal warfare in Kenya).

16. *See* Annan, *supra* note 12 (illustrating that an AK-47 is so easy to purchase that it sells for as little as fifteen dollars or for a bag of grain).

17. *See Weapons of Mass Destruction: The New Strategic Framework*, 7 U.S. FOREIGN POLICY AGENDA 2, 5–6 (2002) (discussing the spread of chemical and biological weapons and the threat these weapons pose to the world), at http://usinfo.state.gov/journals/itps/0702/ijpe/ijpe0702.pdf (last visited Sept. 20, 2002).

18. *See, e.g.*, Bill Miller, *Panel Questions New Agency's Intelligence Powers*, WASH. POST, June 10, 2002, at 2 (noting that Homeland Security Director Tom Ridge believes that al Qaeda terrorists want to use nuclear, biological, and chemical weapons against the United States).

19. *See, e.g.*, Richard Lloyd Parry, *Sarin Cult "Doing Nuclear Research,"* INDEPENDENT (London), Apr. 3, 1995, at 14 (reporting that the Aum Shinri Kyo Cult that released sarin gas in the Tokyo subway killing eleven people and injuring over five thousand was also engaging in biological and nuclear weapons research).

20. International Intellectual Property Alliance ("IIPA"), USTR 2002 "Special 301" Decisions and IIPA Estimated U.S. Trade Losses Due to Copyright Piracy (In Millions of U.S. Dollars) and Estimated Levels of Copy Right Piracy for 2000-2001, at 1 (2002) (reporting that $9.4 billion were lost to copyright piracy in 2001), at http://www.iipa.com/pdf/2002 Jul11 USTRLOSS.pdf (last visited Oct. 4, 2002).

21. *Fast Track Avenue of the Americas*, FIN. TIMES (London), Jan. 25, 2002, at 13 (indicating that if the story is true, this act might "rate as one of the fastest examples of piracy"). According to Dennis Hopper, "it was an excellent copy too." Id.

22. *See* Philip Shenon, *Guilty Plea by Suspect in Web Theft*, N.Y. TIMES, Feb. 28, 2002, at C5 (reporting that one of DrinkOrDie's leaders pled guilty to a federal conspiracy charge nine years after the group released a pirated copy of Windows 95 two weeks prior to the software's public release); *see also* WIKIPEDIA, DRINKORDIE (stating that the DrinkOrDie Network

is considered criminal for its copyright infringement), *at* http://www.wikipedia.com/wiki/ DrinkOrDie (last modified May 11, 2002).

23. *See* IIPA & Office of U.S. TRADE REPRESENTATIVE, SPECIAL 301 REPORT, 16–17 (2002) (describing China's high levels of piracy and counterfeiting and its efforts to enforce intellectual property rights), http://www.ustr.gov/reports/2002/special301-report.pdf (last visited Oct. 4, 2002).

24. *See* Peter Marsh, *Fakes are Blotting the Horizon in Italy's Valley of the Valves: Chinese Counterfeit Goods Have Reached Europe's Valve Sector*, FIN. TIMES (London), Mar. 20, 2001, at 35 (noting that not only do Italian companies lose sales because of counterfeit valves, the inferior quality of the copied valves damages the company's reputation).

25. *See Global Software Piracy Rate Flattens to 37 Percent*, May 21, 2001 (reporting on the piracy rates in the six major world regions and estimating that software piracy groups copied one of every three business software applications released during the previous year), *at* http:// dc.internet.com/news/article.php/769381 (last visited Sept. 20, 2002).

26. *See* Vickie L. Feeman et al., *Napster: Innocent Innovations or Egregious Infringement? Revenge of the Record Industry Association of America: The Rise and Fall of Napster*, 9 VILL. SPORTS & ENT. L. FORUM 35, 35 (2002) (discussing the Napster's technology and the intellectual property issues that evolved from it).

27. This website, which provides applications for file-sharing, boasts that 130 million Kazaa Application Desktops have been downloaded so far (last visited Sept. 29, 2002).

28. *See* NAT'L SEC'Y COUNCIL, ALIEN SMUGGLING, INTERNATIONAL CRIME THREAT ASSESSMENT (2002) (noting that migrant smuggling involves four million people worldwide), http://clinton4.nara.gov/WH/EOP/NSC/html/documents/pub45270/ pub45270chap2.html (last visited Sept. 20, 2002).

29. *See UN Warns of Migrants' Miserable Lot*, BBC NEWS, Dec. 18, 2001 (adding that many of the 150 million aliens that live out of their country experience discrimination and substandard living conditions), *at* http://news.bbc.co.uk/1/hi/world/1716899.stm (last visited Sept. 20, 2002).

30. *See* WORLD RESOURCES INST., WORLD RESOURCES 1998-99 (1998) (describing that the annual growth rate of immigration is mostly attributed to the migration of peoples from developing countries), http://www.wri.org/trends/migratio.html (last visited Sept. 20, 2002).

31. *See* Francis T. MIKO, TRAFFICKING IN WOMEN AND CHILDREN: THE U.S. AND INTERNATIONAL RESPONSE (CONG. RES. SERVICE, Report 98-649C, 2002) (distinguishing between human trafficking and human smuggling, in that smuggling involves knowingly purchasing an illegal service to gain access into a foreign country), *available at* http://usinfo.state.gov/topical/global/traffic/crs0510.htm (last visited Sept. 20, 2002).

32. *See id.* (relating that many trafficked woman are only teenagers).

33. *See id.* (explaining that India is a source of and a destination for trafficked women).

34. *See* U. N. OFFICE FOR DRUG CONTROL AND CRIME PREVENTION FACT SHEET ON HUMAN TRAFFICKING (2002) ("International organized crime has taken advantage of the freer flow of people, money, goods and services to extend its own international reach."), *at* http://www.undcp.org/odccp/trafficking fact sheet.html (last visited Sept. 20, 2002).

35. *See* MIKO, *supra* note 31 (estimating that each year, between one and two million people are trafficked worldwide).

36. *See id.* (noting that gangs from China, Asia, Mexico, Central America, Russia, and other former Soviet Union countries are the leading traffickers of people).

37. *See* NAT'L SEC'Y COUNCIL, *supra* note 28 (according to the U.S. government estimates, 500,000 to 600,000 illegal migrants who entered the United States in 1999 were Mexican and 225,000 were from Central America).

38. *See* William F. Wechsler, *Follow the Money*, FOREIGN AFF., July–Aug. 2001, at 40, 45 (describing the problem of the globalization of money laundering, tax evasion, and rouge banking and explaining that underregulated banking systems facilitate abuses of money laundering and tax evasion).

39. *See id.* at 47–48 (describing how rogue banking affects the world stage through the illegal transfer of money from Russia to Naru and explaining that one single bank from Nauru ordered a transfer of three billion dollars from Russia).

40. Wechsler, *supra* note 38, at 40, 48.

41. *See id.* at 42 (detailing the size and scope of the financial industries in the Cayman Islands and Switzerland).

42. *Hoping Their Kids Could Do Better*, NEWSDAY, July 3, 1990, at 8 (discussing the plight of Chinese immigrants in New York City).

43. *See generally* Michael Massing, *Pervasive Influence of Crack May Make Drug War Useless*, L.A. DAILY NEWS, Oct. 1, 1989, at V1 (describing how cocaine use is spreading across the United States).

44. *See* Marsh, *supra* note 24 (reporting that counterfeit valves looked identical to the originals and were selling abroad for significantly less).

45. Janaki Bahadur Kremmer, *Tamil Conflict at India's Doorstep*, CHRISTIAN SCI. MONITOR, May 16, 2000, at 6. *See generally* David M. Rothenberg, *Negotiation and Dispute Resolution in the Sri Lankan Context: Lessons from the 1994–1995 Peace Talks*, 22 FORDHAM INT'L L.J. 505, 510–37 (1998) (reviewing the history of the Sri Lankan ethnic conflict).

46. *See Venezuela Presidents Denies US Request to Use Venezuela Air Space for Narcotics Flights at U.S. Scrambles to Replace the Loss of Panama for Counterdrug Efforts*, 15 INT'L ENFORCEMENT L. REP. 270, 270-71 (1999) (explaining why Venezuela objected to the United States' request to monitor its airspace in counterdrug efforts).

47. *See* INTERPOL, FACT SHEETS: INTERPOL—AN OVERVIEW (detailing updated statistics on Interpol activity and productivity), *available at* http://www.interpol.int/Public/Icpo/FactSheets/FS200101.asp (last visited Sept. 23, 2002).

48. *See* Judy Dempsey, *Europol Labours to Forge Bonds Among EU's Crimefighters*, FIN. TIMES (London), Feb. 28, 2002, at 7 (citing Europol's problems with budget, staff, and cooperation between EU member states). *See generally* EUROPOL, THE EUROPEAN POLICE OFFICE: FACT SHEET (listing the updated numbers of the Europol staff and budget), *available at* http://www.europol.eu.int/facts/en.htm (last visited Sept. 23, 2002).

49. *See generally* MALCOLM ANDERSON, POLICING THE WORLD: INTERPOL AND THE POLITICS OF INTERNATIONAL POLICE CO-OPERATION 186-94 (1989) (discussing Interpol's shortcomings as a multinational agency, including problems of sovereignty and trust between nations).

50. *See Diplomatic Conference on Reaffirmation and Development of International Humanitarian Law Applicable in Armed Conflict: Protocols I and II to the Geneva Conventions*, 16 I.L.M. 1391, 1410 (1977) (detailing the articles of the Geneva Convention, including the definition of a "combatant").

51. Christopher Weeramantry, *The Grotius Lecture Series*, 14 AM. U. INT'L L. REV. 1515, 1516 (1999).

*Moisés Naím** is a senior associate in the international economics program at the Carnegie Endowment for International Peace.

Moisés Naím, "The Fourth Annual Grotius Lecture: Five Wars of Globalization," *American University International Law Review* 18, no. 1 (2002): 1–18.

Mercenarism 2.0? The Rise of the Modern Private Security Industry and Its Implications for International Humanitarian Law Enforcement

*by E. L. Gaston**

[...]

III. Contrasting PMSCs and Mercenaries: An Argument for a Different Treatment

Much of the public attention and legal debates surrounding PMSCs [private military and security companies] have been focused on reports of serious criminal misconduct by "trigger-happy" private security contractors in Iraq and Afghanistan.[31] The negative reputation of PMSCs and their private sector status have led some commentators to compare PMSCs to mercenaries, and to suggest that they in turn should be banned under the existing international legal prohibition on mercenary activity.[32] However, the corporate form of private military and security companies, and the advanced independent capabilities that go with that corporate form, not only distinguish them from mercenaries of the past but may also create additional challenges for the international system. These significant differences make it a legal stretch for the standing mercenary definitions to be applied to these actors, and also counsel against treating security companies that pose a very different, and in many ways more significant, threat to the international system with the same legal solution that was applied to mercenaries of the past.

Much of the controversy surrounding PMSCs has been due to frequent reports of unpunished criminal misconduct, human rights abuses, and potential war crimes by PMSC personnel. In the 1990s, DynCorp employees hired to represent the U.S. contingent in the U.N. Police Task Force in Bosnia were involved in a sex-trafficking scandal.[33] During many of its operations in Africa, the private military firm Executive Outcomes was criticized for using cluster bombs and other military methods that were questionable under international humanitarian law.[34] In the context of PMSC involvement in Iraq, security contractors employed as interrogators by CACI International and Titan were involved in the Abu Ghraib prison abuses.[35] A few months after Abu Ghraib, a video surfaced on the Internet showing Aegis contractors on patrol in Iraq apparently arbitrarily shooting at Iraqi civilians.[36] In February 2007, a former CIA contractor named David Passaro was convicted in U.S. federal court for beating an Afghan prisoner to death.[37] In the fall of 2007, Blackwater contractors came under heavy fire for the apparently unjustified killing of 17 Iraqi civilians in September 2007 while they were providing mobile convoy protection for USAID employees.[38] Investigations spurred by this Blackwater incident revealed evidence of even more widespread, and perhaps unjustified, attacks against Iraqi civilians or Iraqi civilian property.[39]

Beyond these more serious incidents of abuse, many have argued that PMSC contractors in Iraq and Afghanistan generally treated local civilians disrespectfully and exacerbated local hostility to coalition operations.[40] As one journalist described it,

> Blackwater's thugs with guns now push and punch Iraqis who get in their way: Kurdish journalists twice walked out of a Bremer press conference because of their mistreatment by these men. . . . There is a disturbing increase in reports that mercenaries are shooting down innocent Iraqis with total impunity.[41]

In Afghanistan, the PMSC originally hired to protect Afghan President Hamid Karzai, DynCorp, was fired because of repeated incidents of disrespect or abuse to local Afghans.[42] The fact that DynCorp actually suffered some financial repercussions for misconduct on the Karzai contract is notable because for most incidents PMSCs and their employees have suffered no legal or financial consequences. Of the thousands of PMSC contractors that have served in Iraq and Afghanistan since 2001, only one has ever been prosecuted.[43]

The misconduct of some PMSC actors has led them to be compared with mercenaries.[44] Similarly negative historical connotations of mercenaries, and their association with widespread misconduct and abuse, led to the existing international law prohibition on mercenary activities. The use of "guns for hire" or other private actors has been longstanding practice in warfare and was traditionally unquestioned under international law.[45] No provisions explicitly prohibiting mercenarism existed in the Hague Conventions,[46] the original Geneva Conventions,[47] or in customary international humanitarian law prior to World War II.[48] Mercenaries were considered a legitimate means of warfare until post-World War II, when they became actively involved in many of the post-colonial struggles for independence.[49] In addition to being associated with severe human rights abuses and other war crimes in those post-colonial struggles, the use of mercenaries was increasingly delegitimized because it potentially prolonged certain conflicts and undermined international principles of self-determination.[50] As a result of this negative historical experience, the push for international provisions criminalizing mercenarism came primarily from post-colonial African states and often over the objection of Western states.[51] A series of regional African conventions and statements condemning mercenaries set the first legal precedents for a ban on mercenaries,[52] ultimately resulting in the 1989 U.N. Convention Against Recruitment, Use, Financing, and Training of Mercenaries ("U.N. Convention Against Mercenaries"), which went into effect in 2001.[53] In addition, African delegates to the negotiations on the additional protocols to the Geneva Conventions pushed through a provision in Protocol I (article 47) that denied mercenaries the privileges of lawful combatants.[54]

Although the mercenary ban is firmly established in IHL,[55] it is one of the weaker provisions.[56] Outside of the community of African states that championed it, the mercenary ban has never received the type of widespread support that would make enforcement likely. In addition, the legal standards within these instruments are difficult to meet, and the enforcement provisions are themselves weak. To illustrate, the Protocol I provision on mercenaries does not make it a crime *per se* to be a mercenary, but simply permits the detaining party to deny any captured mercenary prisoner-of-war status as an unlawful combatant.[57] The U.N. Convention Against Mercenaries goes one step further and does make it a crime to be a mercenary, but enforcement of this crime depends on implementing legislation by the relevant state party.[58] Another important limitation on the effect of these instruments is that neither Protocol I nor the U.N. Convention Against Mercenaries has explicit provisions making state use of mercenaries an offense.[59] Although such provisions were proposed, Western states rejected them, arguing that states are incapable of controlling the actions of their nationals abroad.[60] Finally, many commentators have suggested that the reason the international mercenarism prohibition has been under-enforced is that the definition of a mercenary in these instruments is unworkable.[61] The definition is composed of six cumulative elements, including that the individual is not a national nor a resident of a party to the conflict, has not been sent by a state that is not a party to the conflict, has been "specially recruited" to fight in that conflict, has taken direct part in the hostilities, and is primarily motivated by a desire for "material compensation substantially in excess" of that paid to regular armed forces to the conflict.[62] The motive element renders categorization as a mercenary particularly problematic, since an individual found to meet all of the other five elements of the definition can easily claim some motivation other than money.[63]

This mercenary definition would be particularly difficult to apply to the majority of private security contractors.[64] For example, many of the private security contractors playing supporting or defensive roles may not meet the requirement that a mercenary be specifically recruited to and actually take "direct part" in the conflict.[65] The difficulty of drawing a clear distinction between when security contractors are engaged in direct combat activity and when they are not would make this element even more difficult to establish. It would also be difficult to establish that these contractors' motivation was solely a desire for substantial financial gain;[66] many PMSCs are former soldiers with extensive service to their countries, and even if they are not actually motivated by a sense of patriotic duty, it may be difficult to prove otherwise. In the specific context of Iraq or Afghanistan, security contractors who are citizens of either the United States or coalition partners would be disqualified under the provision concerning nationals of a party to the conflict. Iraqi or Afghan nationals hired by these countries would similarly be disqualified under the provision excepting a resident to a territory controlled by a party to the conflict.[67]

In addition to these legal enforcement issues, the differences between mercenaries and modern private security actors, as well as the unique threats posed by the latter, justify different treatment. While the ban on mercenarism was driven mostly by the historical experience of a few states, it is possible to extrapolate some doctrinal rationales for its criminalization. Cherif Bassiouni, a prominent scholar in the origins and classification of international criminal law, justifies the crime of mercenarism as an extension of the crime of aggression and a threat to international peace and security.[68] The crime of aggression usually refers to any use of force by states not justified by self-defense or authorized by the United Nations.[69] Since mercenaries are by definition those individuals who are not citizens of a party to the conflict, their participation may be construed as the participation of a neutral in an armed conflict, which may constitute a crime of aggression. The availability of mercenary actors for state action may also be considered a threat to the overall enforcement of international humanitarian law because many of the constraints on the use of force and on the conduct of hostilities are based on state-centered restrictions; to the extent that states can evade these restrictions by outsourcing to individuals who are at best ambiguously liable under the laws of war, the overall framework of enforcement may be weakened. The high incidence of human rights abuses and war crimes among mercenary armies historically may also make the practice of mercenarism a sufficiently significant threat to the international system.[70]

The corporatization of privatized force, as well as the advanced independent capabilities that go with that corporate form, has the potential to exponentially increase many of these threats. First, the corporate form and independence of

PMSCs more seriously erode the monopoly on force than did mercenarism. Unlike PMSCs, mercenaries provided limited services—little more than additional manpower to existing combat operations.[71] Through the corporate form, though, PMSCs can independently provide sustained and complex operations, in-depth training and advisory services, and extensive logistical and operational support—capabilities that any amalgamation of individual mercenaries could never have achieved. Nonstate actors can now buy military force capabilities that previously might have been possible almost exclusively through a state-supported military.[72] Even where PMSCs are hired by state actors, the corporation itself usually retains immediate control and supervision of its contractors, thus reducing the control that states have over their own warfare and the overall level of state-based control over uses of force.[73]

The advanced capabilities of PMSCs may also enable state violence that would otherwise not have been possible because of political or resource constraints. Small or weak states that might otherwise not have been able to raise an army or to build certain advanced capabilities over time can instead buy such capabilities from PMSCs.[74] For example, in 1992, the weakened Sierra Leonean government could not defeat advancing Revolutionary United Front rebels on its own but was able to hire Executive Outcomes to do so.[75]

Even for states that do have advanced military capabilities, the availability of advanced capabilities in the private sector that can appear to operate independently of the state may enable it to get around certain domestic political constraints. Hiring PMSCs as force multipliers allows states to purchase additional manpower and capabilities without incurring political costs or having to raise support for citizen participation.[76] PMSCs often do not attract the same media attention and public scrutiny as enlisted soldiers or other state actors would. If a PMSC is killed in an operation overseas it does not garner the same headlines as if an enlisted soldier were killed. Deploying PMSCs, even large and sustained units of PMSCs, to train, assist, or advise foreign governments may not raise the same congressional or popular political checks that deploying an equivalent number of military or civilian officials would. For example, throughout the 1990s, the Clinton Administration increasingly outsourced U.S. involvement in Colombian anti-narcotic campaigns to PMSCs in order to avoid congressional troop ceilings and other domestic constraints on U.S. involvement.[77] Moreover, because of their independent capabilities, PMSCs can provide extra manpower and resources without requiring the bureaucratic overhead or decisionmaking processes that might typically accompany such uses of force by democratic states. The thousands of private contractors in Iraq act as an important force multiplier for U.S. operations not only because they provide more manpower without the political costs of sending more troops but also because the U.S. government can manage these additional capabilities with fewer bureaucratic resources or institutional hurdles.

Hiring PMSCs to act in their place may also allow states to avoid political costs at an international level, thus unhinging some of the informal, normative restraints on uses of force. For example, during the conflict in the Balkans in the mid-1990s, the United States wanted to intervene to stop some of the immediate fighting but because of its role in peace negotiations, could not afford to lose the appearance of neutrality.[78] Instead, it engineered the hiring of U.S.-based Military Professional Resources Incorporated ("MPRI") to help train Croat forces so that they could become a better counterweight against Serb aggression in the Krajina region.[79] While this use of PMSCs was arguably beneficial for the international community in that instance (because it stopped immediate fighting and loss of life), the ability of outside states to intervene in conflicts without international political costs is not a positive development. In many cases, the interference of outside actors, many of whom do not share the same interests as the warring parties or as those civilians caught in the conflict, may prolong the conflict or complicate peaceful resolution.

In addition to reducing checks on state uses of force, the independence of PMSCs may erode state responsibility for the conduct of war making and more generally weaken international humanitarian law compliance. Because of their independence from state militaries, most PMSCs are beyond the reach of international humanitarian law regulations. Article 43 of Protocol I suggests that an individual must be formally incorporated into the armed forces of a state before that state can be held legally responsible for that individual as a combatant.[80] Although some contractors may be carrying out traditional military functions or be de facto integrated into the armed forces of a state, they are rarely, if ever, formally incorporated into the armed forces of a state as required by article 43. A second possibility is that PMSCs might be considered a militia or volunteer corps fighting on behalf of their state-client, under article 4(A) of the Third Geneva Convention.[81] However, it is unlikely that most PMSCs satisfy the requirement in article 4(A) that they carry arms openly and wear a fixed distinctive sign.[82]

As a result, many PMSC violations of international humanitarian law do not carry the same consequences for state clients as they would if carried out by a member of that state's military. After the United States hired MPRI to train Croat forces during the conflict in Bosnia, MPRI reportedly provided direct planning, assistance, and perhaps even engagement for one particularly bloody

Croat advance that later raised charges of war crimes for the Croat commanders involved.[83] The United States received no criticism for helping one side to engage in further combat, much less for the potential human rights or war crimes that resulted from this assistance. Because they are less likely to be held responsible, states have fewer incentives to establish the same rigorous accountability and oversight measures that they use for their professional militaries and that may prevent many international humanitarian law violations. Where misconduct does occur, states have fewer incentives to enforce international humanitarian law provisions against those individuals. PMSCs hired by states essentially create a corporate shield against state liability for contractors' actions.[84] DynCorp employees hired to help provide the U.S. contribution for the International Police Task Force in Bosnia were found to be extensively involved in sex trafficking in 1998.[85] U.S. officials escaped with barely any criticism despite awareness by the Department of Defense of continuing violations as late as 2003.[86] With few, if any, legal consequences for the misconduct of these privatized parts of the force, states have fewer incentives to prevent and check any violations of international law than they would if this private outsourcing of legal liability was not possible. Although the increasing public criticism of the misconduct of many PMSCs in Iraq may reverse the trend, the initial lack of legal pressure for the United States to prevent and control PMSC misconduct may also have contributed to the lack of domestic prosecutions and weak contract oversight for PMSC activities in Iraq and Afghanistan.[87]

Finally, one additional, emerging threat that PMSCs may pose to the international system stems from a combination of the purposes for which they have been hired and from the accountability problems described above. The increasing use of PMSCs in post-conflict operations may undermine the long-term stability of the region or country in which they are operating—a threat to international peace and security that the individual mercenary did not pose. PMSCs are increasingly given extensive responsibilities in the reconstruction and stabilization of post-conflict environments, including protecting and helping to implement major infrastructure and construction projects, maintaining and operating refugee camps, or simply working with other international actors involved in reconstruction and development initiatives.[88] This means that many of the elements for establishing long-term stability in a country may be placed in the hands of actors whose profit motivations push them to focus more on short-term cost effectiveness than on the potential long-term consequences of their actions. For example, many PMSCs operating in a country resort to bribery or black-market trade as the most expedient means of getting the equipment and licenses they need.[89] A generous characterization of such practices would be that since PMSCs do not have the same privileges and immunities that the United Nations, the local government, or other foreign actors have in these countries, they often have little choice but to work within the existing rules and conditions. Within conflict or post-conflict zones with fragile to nonexistent legal structures, that often means operating extra-legally. Critics might argue that PMSCs do not care if they reinforce these negative elements so long as they can fulfill their contract with a higher profit margin. Whichever rationale is true, the effect is that PMSCs often are involved in other violations of international and domestic laws.[90] As a result, despite being hired to reinforce security and stability, their presence may inadvertently reinforce the criminal elements within that society.

[...]

V. CONCLUSION

Actors in the modern security industry are not simply revamped mercenaries. Their resources and their increasingly prominent roles in humanitarian aid, contingency operations, and other military or security operations worldwide present unique and perhaps more troubling challenges for international peace and security. In particular, their corporate form brings with it advanced, independent capabilities that may disable domestic and international restraints on the use of force and may weaken the degree of state responsibility for holding those engaged in its military and security operations responsible for IHL and human rights violations. While these are significant threats to the international system, market forces have consistently been pushing these actors to operate openly and within the constraints of international and domestic law. This is particularly true for those PMSCs whose target clients are credible international actors who care about reputational costs and international legal compliance. Therefore, developing a principle under IHL that would require state clients to establish mechanisms for ensuring that any PMSC to which they outsource complies with international and domestic legal norms and regulations may significantly address the more serious threats posed by PMSCs.

The international community should attempt to define whether and to what extent it considers the private security industry to be a threat and develop a coordinated response. The current ambiguous status, lack of coordinated regulation, and outdated definitions of mercenarism only exacerbate the current threats posed by this industry. If IHL is not able to adapt to these threats by recognizing the role of these nonstate actors in state uses of force, then the availability of such advanced, independent force capabilities may seriously undermine much of the validity and effectiveness of the current state-centered mechanisms governing the use of force.

Notes

[. . .]

31. *See, e.g.,* Editorial, *The Folly of Using Mercenaries in Iraq,* Int'l Herald Trib., Nov. 6, 2007, at 8 (critiquing American use of "trigger-happy bodyguards" and arguing that "gun-toting mercenaries . . . run around Iraq without any clear legal tether"); Sue Pleming, *Blackwater Involved in 195 Iraq Shootings,* Reuters, Oct. 2, 2007, *available at* http://www.reuters.com/articl ePrint?articleId=USN273998922007 1002 (noting public investigations uncovering evidence of PMSC misconduct against Iraqi civilians and their property).

32. *See supra* note 2.

33. *See* Robert Capps, *Crime Without Punishment,* Salon.com, June 27, 2002, http://dir.salon.com/ story/news/feature/2002/06/27/military/index.html?pn=1.

34. Singer, *supra* note 8, at 116 (noting Executive Outcomes' use of napalm, cluster bombs, and fuel-R air explosives); Nathaniel Stinnett, *Regulating the Privatization of War: How To Stop Private Military Firms from Committing Human Rights Abuses,* B.C. Int'l & Comp L. Rev. 211, 215 (2005) (reporting that Executive Outcomes commanders gave orders to their pilots to "kill everybody" without regard to the civilian population).

35. *See* Stockman, *supra* note 1; Joel Brinkley & James Glanz, *Contract Workers Implicated in February Army Report on Prison Abuse Remain on the Job,* N.Y. Times, May 4, 2004, at A6.

36. *See* Sean Rayment, *"Trophy" Video Exposes Private Security Contractors Shooting Up Iraqi Drivers,* Telegraph.co.uk, Nov. 26, 2005, at 10, *available at* http://www.telegraph.co.uk/news/ main.jhtml?xml=/news/2005/11/27/wirq27.xml&sSheet=/news/2005/11/27/ixworld.html.

37. *See* Weigl, *supra* note 1.

38. *See* Glanz & Rubin, *supra* note 1.

39. *See, e.g.,* Pleming, *supra* note 31.

40. Hamida Ghafour, *Afghans Are Fed Up with Security Firm: Residents of a Kabul Neighborhood Say They Feel They Are Under Occupation as DynCorp Barricades a Street and Conducts Searches,* L.A. Times, Sept. 27, 2004, at A3; Editorial, *The Folly of Using Mercenaries in Iraq, supra* note 31, at 8 (arguing that the United States' use of unaccountable "trigger-happy bodyguards" "wiped out whatever residual sense of legitimacy Iraqis may have still attached to the U.S. mission").

41. Robert Fisk, *Saddam in the Dock: So This Is What They Call the New, Free Iraq,* Indep. on Sunday (London), July 4, 2004, at 12.

42. *See* Interview with senior political officer, UNAMA, in Kabul, Afg. (Jan. 18, 2007) (on file with author); Interview with a manager of an American PSC, in Kabul, Afg. (Jan. 14, 2007) (on file with author); Interview with two senior/commanding officers of an American PSC, in Kabul, Afg. (Jan. 12 & 14, 2007) (on file with author); Interview with legal affairs representative of an American PSC, in Washington, D.C. (Nov. 10, 2006) (on file with author).

43. Ned Parker, *U.S. Restricts Movement of Its Diplomats in Iraq; The Limits Come as a Shooting by a Convoy's Guards Is Investigated,* L.A. Times, Sept. 19, 2007, at A1 (noting that CIA contractor David Passaro is the only contractor convicted of civilian abuse in Iraq or Afghanistan).

44. *See supra* note 2.

45. *See, e.g.*, Singer, *supra* note 8, at 20–29, 33–34 (describing the historical hiring of mercenaries by ancient Greek and Roman armies, by the Italian city states to fight in the Crusades, by European monarchs and feudal lords from the Middle Ages through the Thirty Years' War, and by the British Empire in conflicts overseas, among others); Wm. C. Peters, *On Law, Wars, and Mercenaries: The Case for Courts-Martial Jurisdiction over Civilian Contractor Misconduct in Iraq*, 2006 BYU L. Rev. 367, 377–81 (2006) (describing U.S. use of civilian contractors throughout its military history).

46. *See* Katherine Fallah, *Corporate Actors: The Legal Status of Mercenaries in Armed Conflict*, 88 Int'l Rev. Red Cross 599, 603–04 (2006) (noting that the Hague Conventions have no explicit provisions on mercenaries but that Hague Convention V may have implications for mercenaries by providing that individuals from neutral states who take up arms on behalf of a belligerent lose the privileges of neutrality).

47. Geneva Convention Relative to the Protection of Civilian Persons in Time of War, Aug. 12, 1949, 6 U.S.T. 3516; Geneva Convention Relative to the Treatment of Prisoners of War, Aug. 12, 1949, 6 U.S.T. 3316 [hereinafter Geneva POW Convention]; Geneva Convention for the Amelioration of the Condition of Wounded, Sick and Shipwrecked Members of Armed Forces at Sea, Aug. 12, 1949, 6 U.S.T. 3217; Geneva Convention for the Amelioration of the Conditions of the Wounded and Sick in Armed Forces in the Field, Aug. 12, 1949, 6 U.S.T. 3114.

48. Article 9 of the Brussels Conference of 1874, which represented customary international law at the time, incorporated mercenaries into the laws of war as irregular combatants. *See, e.g.*, Fallah, *supra* note 46, at 603–04; Bohunka O. Goldstein, *Mercenarism, in* 1 International Criminal Law 439, 445–46 (M. Cherif Bassiouni ed., 2d ed. 1999).

49. *See, e.g.*, Goldstein, *supra* note 48, at 445 (suggesting that mercenaries attracted by adventure and money joined whichever rebel group, foreign power, or government paid the most); Lyal S. Sunga, The Emerging System of International Criminal Law: Developments in Codification and Implementation 183–85 (1997) (stating that European powers hired mercenaries to maintain influence over former colonies because it was taboo to retain direct influence after World War II).

50. *See* Goldstein, *supra* note 48, at 457 (arguing that the rise of mercenaries in Africa was a threat in part because mercenaries engaged in the killing and torturing of civilians and prisoners); Office of the U.N. High Comm'r for Human Rights, Fact Sheet No. 28, The Impact of Mercenary Activities on the Right of Peoples to Self-Determination 7–11 (2002), *available at* http://www.ohchr.org/english/about/publications/docs/factsheet28.pdf.

51. *See, e.g.*, G.A. Res. 3103, ¶ 6, U.N. GAOR, 28th Sess., Supp. No. 30, U.N. Doc. A/9030 (1973) (condemning the use of mercenaries by "colonial and racist regimes" against the self-determination movements of former colonies); James Cockayne, *The Global Reorganization of Legitimate Violence: Military Entrepreneurs and the Private Face of International Humanitarian Law*, 88 Int'l Rev. Red Cross 459, 475–76 nn.48–49 (2006).

52. *See generally* Goldstein, *supra* note 48, at 442–43 (summarizing the international law developments leading to the creation of the United Nations Working Group on the Use of Mercenaries as a Means of Violating Human Rights and Impeding the Exercise of the Right of Peoples to Self-Determination); Organization of African Unity, Convention for the Elimination of Mercenarism annex II, July 3, 1977, O.A.U. Doc. CM/817 (XXIX), *reprinted in* Documents of the Organization of African Unity 58 (Gino J. Naldi ed., 1992); Riley Martin, *Mercenaries and the Rule of Law*, 17 Rev. Int'l Comm'n Jurists 51 (1977) (describing the June 1976 trial of thirteen British, American, and Argentinean citizens in Angola on

grounds of mercenarism as a crime under customary international law); Organization of African Unity, Int'l Comm'n of Inquiry on Mercenaries, Draft Convention on the Prevention and Suppression of Mercenarism art. 4, Luanda, June 1976, *reprinted in* Paul W. Mourning, *Leashing the Dogs of War: Outlawing the Recruitment and Use of Mercenaries*, 22 VA. J. INT'L L. 589, 615 (1982) (seeking to deny mercenaries the status of lawful combatants).

53. Convention Against Mercenaries, *supra* note 3; *see also* Goldstein, *supra* note 48, at 443–44 (describing momentum toward and driving forces within the negotiations toward the Convention Against Mercenaries).

54. Protocol I, *supra* note 3, art. 47. This provision was included despite the objections of many Western states. *See* Fallah, *supra* note 46, at 604–05 (describing the origin of the provisions on mercenaries in the Additional Protocol I to the Geneva Convention); *see also* FRITS KALSHOVEN & LIESBETH ZEGVELD, CONSTRAINTS ON THE WAGING OF WAR: AN INTRODUCTION TO INTERNATIONAL HUMANITARIAN LAW 90 (2003) (noting that article 47 was only included as a concession to African states); Edward Kwakwa, *The Current Status of Mercenaries in the Law of Armed Conflict*, 14 HASTINGS INT'L & COMP. L. REV. 67, 68 & n.7 (1990) (noting that one of the reasons the United States cited for not ratifying Protocol I was the provision on mercenaries).

55. *See* Lindsey Cameron, *Private Military Companies: Their Status Under International Humanitarian Law and Its Impact on Their Regulation*, 88 INT'L REV. RED CROSS 573, 579 & n.21 (2006) (noting that the International Committee for the Red Cross has found the Protocol I definition of a mercenary to be part of customary international law, although the United States has long rejected this view).

56. The crime of mercenarism was not included in the 1996 Draft Codes of Crimes adopted by the International Law Commission, largely because it was not considered widespread or severe enough to justify the status of a grave threat to peace and security. See Goldstein, *supra* note 48, at 444–45 nn.31–33 (noting the objections of Austria, the Netherlands, Norway, and the United Kingdom in particular to elevating mercenarism to the status of a "grave offense"). Under the Rome Statute, mercenarism is not listed as a crime. Rome Statute of the International Criminal Court, July 17, 1998, 2187 U.N.T.S. 90 [hereinafter Rome Statute].

57. *See* Cameron, *supra* note 55, at 577–79.

58. Convention Against Mercenaries, *supra* note 3, art. 3(1) ("A mercenary, as defined in article 1 of the present Convention, who participates directly in hostilities or in a concerted act of violence, as the case may be, commits an offence for the purposes of the Convention."). Articles 7 and 9 of the Convention Against Mercenaries deal with the obligation of states parties to take necessary measures for the implementation of the Convention and to establish jurisdiction within its territory for offenses described in the Convention. *Id.* arts. 7, 9.

59. See Goldstein, *supra* note 48, at 454.

60. *Id.*

61. As one commentator famously noted, the definition of a mercenary in these instruments is so unworkable and riddled with loopholes that "any mercenary who cannot exclude himself from this definition deserves to be shot—and his lawyer with him." GEOFFREY BEST, HUMANITY IN WARFARE: THE MODERN HISTORY OF THE INTERNATIONAL LAW OF ARMED CONFLICT 374 n.83 (1980); *see also* Sarah Percy, *Mercenaries: Strong Norm, Weak Law*, 61 INT'L ORG. 367, 369–70 (2007) (postulating reasons for which the prohibition on mercenaries might be so weak, including lack of support by powerful Western countries, a weak definition of mercenaries, and failure to address the PMSC problem). *See generally* Francoise Hampson, *Mercenaries: Diagnosis Before Prescription*, XXII NETH. Y.B. INT'L L. 3, 14–16 (1991) (arguing that the six-

point definition of a mercenary is "unworkable"). Instead of relying on the rarely enforced ban on mercenarism, prosecutions have largely been based on domestic criminal laws. *See, e.g.,* Fallah, *supra* note 46, at 611 & n.47 (citing the case of French mercenary Bob Denard who was ultimately convicted under French law of "belonging to a gang who conspired to commit a crime" for his part in aiding rebels to attempt a coup in the Comoros Islands).

62. Protocol I, *supra* note 3, arts. 47.2(a)–(f). For a more detailed analysis, See Kwakwa, *supra* note 54, at 70–74.

63. Singer, *supra* note 13, at 529 (arguing that the motivation element of the definition of a mercenary makes it "unworkable" because the "intent to fight exclusively for profit is often unknowable, and as it lacks good objective proxies, it is difficult to prove").

64. *See, e.g.,* Emanuela-Chiara Gillard, *Business Goes to War: Private Military/Security Companies and International Humanitarian Law,* 88 INT'L REV. RED CROSS 525, 568–70 (2006) (discussing in depth the reasons for which many PMSCs would not meet the six-point cumulative definition of a mercenary).

65. See Protocol I, *supra* note 3, art. 47.2 (a)–(b); Convention Against Mercenaries, *supra* note 3, art. 1(a).

66. See Protocol I, *supra* note 3, art. 47.2(c); Convention Against Mercenaries, *supra* note 3, art. 1(b).

67. See Protocol I, *supra* note 3, art. 47.2(d); Convention Against Mercenaries, *supra* note 3, art. 1(c).

68. M. CHERIF BASSIOUNI, INTRODUCTION TO INTERNATIONAL CRIMINAL LAW 144–45 (2003); *see also* G.A. Res. 48/92, pmbl., U.N. Doc. A/RES/48/92 (Dec. 20, 1993) (classifying use of mercenaries as a threat to peace).

69. BASSIOUNI, *supra* note 68, at 136–37; U.N. Charter art. 3935; Rome Statute, *supra* note 56, art.5.2; Int'l Law Comm'n, *Second Session, Principles of International Law of the Charter and Judgment of the Nuremberg Tribunal,* 4 INT'L ORG. 714, 717–19 (1950) (Nuremberg Principles VI).

70. *See* Goldstein, *supra* note 48, at 457.

71. It is important to note that the traditional soldier-for-hire mercenaries are not extinct. During the Kosovo war, the Kosovo Liberation Army ("KLA") hired mercenaries at $4,000 a month. Mercenaries fighting on the Serbian side were compensated by being promised free rein to pillage any area territory they conquered. SINGER, *supra* note 8, at 42–44.

72. At least one commentator has already suggested that philanthropists like Bill Gates or George Soros should fund a PMSC intervention in Darfur—an idea that despite its good intentions may have troubling consequences for the state monopoly on force. Max Boot, *A Mercenary Force for Darfur,* WALL ST. J., Oct. 25, 2006, at A14.

73. *See, e.g.,* Major Karen L. Douglas, *Contractors Accompanying the Force: Empowering Commanders with Emergency Change Authority,* 55 A.F. L. Rev. 127, 135–36 (2004) (arguing that military field commanders have less control over the conduct of their force because contractors take orders only from their contracting company or from the contracting officer in Washington, D.C.); Minow, *supra* note 7, at 1008–13 (noting that extensive outsourcing, combined with under-supported oversight, makes it hard for governments to retain control of costs and management of projects).

74. United Nations Comm'n on Human Rts., *Report on the Question of the Use of Mercenaries as a Means of Violating Human Rights and Impeding the Exercise of the Right of Peoples to Self-Determination,* ¶¶ 116–17, U.N. Doc. E/CN.4/1994/23 (Jan. 12, 1994) (*prepared by* Special

Rapporteur Enrique Bernales Ballesteros); *see also* SINGER, *supra* note 8, at 174–75 (noting that the availability of such force may also lead to more state conflicts by upsetting traditional power balances and deterrence effects).

75. *See supra* notes 15–16 and accompanying text.

76. AVANT, *supra* note 8, at 68 ("Through proxies, state leaders can affect conditions abroad without mobilizing broad support for troops or (sometimes) even money. Policy changes can be instituted with the input of a very few actors, circumventing the domestic institutional processes."); Jon D. Michaels, *Beyond Accountability: The Constitutional, Democratic, and Strategic Problems with Privatizing War*, 82 WASH. U. L.Q. 1001, 1040–41 (2004); Clifford Rosky, *Force, Inc.: The Privatization of Punishment, Policing, and Military Force in Liberal States*, 36 CONN. L. REV. 879, 939 (2004); Peter W. Singer, *Outsourcing War*, 84 FOREIGN AFF. 119, 125 (2005).

77. Thomas Catan et al., *Private Companies on the Frontline*, FIN. TIMES, Aug. 12, 2003, at A15 (suggesting that the United States' Plan Colombia was politically feasible only because of a lack of press coverage of any PMSC deaths or incidents that arose); Michaels, *supra* note 76, at 1024–25 nn.58–59 and accompanying text (noting how the Clinton Administration increasingly used PMSCs like DynCorp and MPRI to evade congressional limitations and public criticism for counter-narcotic operations in Colombia).

78. SARAH PERCY, INT'L INST. FOR STRATEGIC STUD., REGULATING THE PRIVATE SECURITY INDUSTRY 12–13 (2006); Michaels, *supra* note 76, at 1025–29 nn.61–82 and accompanying text.

79. PERCY, *supra* note 78, at 12–13; Michaels, *supra* note 76, at 1025–29 nn.61–82 and accompanying text.

80. *See* Protocol I, *supra* note 3, art. 43.3 ("Whenever a Party to a conflict incorporates a paramilitary or armed law enforcement agency into its armed forces it shall so notify the other Parties to the conflict."); *see also* Cameron, *supra* note 55, at 583–84.

81. *See* Geneva POW Convention, *supra* note 47, art. 4(A)(2).

82. *See id.* art. 4(A)(2)(b)–(c). For a fuller discussion of whether some, but certainly not all, private security or military contractors could qualify as combatants under article 4(A)(2), *See* Cameron, *supra* note 55, at 584–87; Michael N. Schmitt, *War, International Law, and Sovereignty: Re-evaluating the Rules of the Game in a New Century—Humanitarian Law and Direct Participation in Hostilities by Private Contractors or Civilian Employees*, 5 CHI. J. INT'L L. 511, 527–32 (2005).

83. *See* Michaels, *supra* note 76, at 1028.

84. *See* Singer, *supra* note 76, at 133 (noting that hiring PMSCs allows the United States to engage in activities that otherwise would not be politically feasible because it can always deny "direct participation" and engage without any "limiting public oversight or debate").

85. *See, e.g.*, Capps, *supra* note 33.

86. *See, e.g.*, DEP'T OF DEF. OFFICE OF THE INSPECTOR GEN'L, ASSESSMENT OF DOD EFFORTS TO COMBAT TRAFFICKING IN PERSONS: PHASE II—BOSNIA-HERZEGOVINA AND KOSOVO 20 n. 14 (2003), *available at* http://www.dodig.osd.mil/fo/foia/HT-Phase_II.pdf [hereinafter DoD Inspector General Report]; Capps, *supra* note 33; Robert Capps, *Outside the Law*, SALON.COM, June 26, 2006, http://dir.salon.com/Rstory/news/feature/2002/06/26/bosnia/index.html.

87. *See* Parker, *supra* note 43 (noting that only one contractor has been prosecuted for misconduct in Iraq or Afghanistan); Broder & Rohde, *supra* note 20 (noting past oversight issues in U.S. PMSC contracts and recent U.S. reform proposals).

88. *See supra* notes 19–30 and accompanying text.

89. For example, within Afghanistan, many PMSCs can get around domestic regulations by bribing Afghan officials. PMSCs often also work with local warlords to guarantee protection or to recruit local hires for their projects. *See, e.g.*, U.S. INST. OF PEACE, ESTABLISHING THE RULE OF LAW IN AFGHANISTAN 117 (2004), *available at* http://www.usip.org/pubs/specialreports/sr117.pdf (exploring how bribery and corruption within the judiciary and other administrative agencies undermine the rule of law in Afghanistan); Interview with U.S. Embassy-Kabul official, in Kabul, Afg. (Jan. 14, 2007) (on file with author) ("It's easy to circumvent any local regulations. The normal system [in Afghanistan] is more bribing than rule of law. . . . PSCs are in tight with Afghani officials."); Interview with Deputy Special Representative in Afghanistan, Council of the European Union, in Kabul, Afg. (Jan. 15, 2007) (on file with author) (noting that the push for new Afghan regulations on PMSCs has been thwarted because enforcement is "highly subject to corruption. . . . [It comes down to] buying off the right minister."); Interview with Senior Political Officer, UNAMA, in Kabul, Afg. (Jan. 18, 2007) (on file with author); Interview with British PSC manager, in the Serena Hotel lobby, Kabul, Afg. (Jan. 18, 2007) (on file with author) (stating that PMSCs get around domestic regulations through the black market and that some Afghan officials have a financial interest in the black market).

90. Bribing local officials and associating with criminal gangs are both violations of international law. *See* BASSIOUNI, *supra* note 68, at 154, 158.

*E. L. Gaston is a human rights lawyer working on Open Society Institute's Regional Policy Initiative in Afghanistan and Pakistan.

E. L. Gaston, "Mercenarism 2.0? The Rise of the Modern Private Security Industry and Its Implications for International Humanitarian Law Enforcement," *Harvard International Law Journal* 49 (Winter 2008): 228–39. Copyright 2008.

Building a Better WarBot: Ethical Issues in the Design of Unmanned Systems for Military Applications

*by Robert Sparrow**

[. . .]

DESIGNING FOR THE LAW OF ARMED CONFLICT

The ethical use of UMS in armed conflict, like that of other weapons, will need to be governed by the Law of Armed Conflict (LOAC) (Gulam & Lee 2006; Klein 2003; Lazarski 2002). The details of the application of the LOAC to the operation and design of UMS is a matter for military lawyers (Dalton 2006; Gulam & Lee 2006; Royal Australian Air Force 2004, p. 74–75). However, several core requirements of the law of armed conflict do place significant constraints on the ethical use and design of these systems and are therefore worth considering here.

Can Robots Meet the Criteria of Discrimination and Proportionality?

It is clear that, at a bare minimum, any ethical use of UMS will need to comply with the principles of discrimination (Bender 2005) and proportionality, which derive from the just war doctrine of *jus in bello* (Schmitt 2005). That is to say, UMS must be capable of discriminating between legitimate and illegitimate targets and of applying force proportionate to the pursuit of legitimate military ends (Arkin 2007, p. 2). These are perhaps the principal design challenges involved in the future development of UMS, especially UMS that are intended to have the capacity to operate autonomously.

One possible "work around" these problems is to deploy UMS in such a way as to exclude the possibility that they will attack illegitimate targets. For instance, armed sentry robots could patrol inside a perimeter fence with suitable warnings on it to prevent any possibility of non-combatant presence (Arkin 2007, pp. 92–3). However, it may be difficult to reliably prevent robots from acquiring illegitimate targets in this way, especially during wartime. Moreover, limiting the use of UMS to circumstances where they will not come into contact with non-combatants will severely limit their military value. John Canning

(2005 & 2006) has championed another version of this approach, in which autonomous weapon systems would be tasked with targeting only enemy weapon systems rather than enemy warfighters, thus minimising the chance of killing non-combatants. Similar problems seem likely to beset this approach. In many circumstances, it will be difficult to distinguish, for instance, an armed tribesman carrying an AK-47 because this is the local cultural practice, from a hostile insurgent. There is also the danger that the number of non-combatants killed when an attack is launched against an enemy weapon system (for instance, a mortar fired from a hospital car park) will be such as to render the force used disproportionate. Unwillingness to risk these outcomes, on the other hand, will significantly limit the context in which automated weapon systems may ethically be used.

Another possible solution—to the problem of *discrimination* at least—is to try to equip the systems themselves with the capacity to make the requisite judgements as to when a target is legitimate (Arkin 2007). Some weapon systems, including anti-tank, anti-aircraft, anti-ship, and counter-fire systems, may be capable of distinguishing between military and civilian targets. If the target recognition algorithms on weapons of this sort are sufficiently reliable, it might appear that there would be fewer ethical barriers to deploying them (Arkin 2007).

However, even with these weapons there is the possibility that a potential military target may have indicated its desire to surrender or may no longer pose sufficient military threat to be a legitimate target of attack (Fielding 2006). The fact that the principle of discrimination is extremely context-dependent suggests that autonomous weapon systems would have to have a very high level of autonomy indeed to be able to make the judgements necessary in order comply with its requirements. Similarly, decisions about what constitutes a level of force *proportionate to the threat* posed by enemy forces are extremely complex and context dependent and it seems unlikely that machines will be able to make these decisions reliably for the foreseeable future. Barring some remarkable breakthrough in artificial intelligence research, it will therefore be necessary to include a human "in the loop" before deploying lethal ordnance from a UMS in order to ensure that the use of UMS does not violate the LOAC in this regard (Gulam & Lee 2006; Fitzsimonds & Mahnken 2007; Kenyon 2006, p. 43).

If the application of UMS is going to rely on a "human in the loop" in order to ensure that it complies with the requirements of discrimination and proportionality, the operation of UMS must provide their operators with sufficient information to be able to make the necessary judgements reliably. Given the limited situational awareness available to operators of UMS (Kainikara 2002;

Mustin 2002) this may require that operators have access to independent sources of information about the nature of the targets they are attacking. This, in turn, has implications for the nature and capacities of the communication systems that are required in order to be able to use UMS ethically (Thorton 2005).

Locating Responsibility

As I have argued more extensively elsewhere (Sparrow 2007), the application of the law of armed conflict to the use of UMS requires that a clear chain of responsibility can be established between the consequences of any such use and the person who is responsible for them (Arkin 2007, pp. 76–83; Asaro 2007; Foster 2006). If violations of ethical standards occur, it must be possible to identify the sources of violation in order that such violations can be addressed and, if necessary, the relevant party criticised, disciplined, or prosecuted. This will be a significant challenge given that multiple parties may be involved in the operations of UMS (Featherstone 2007; Sullivan 2006).

The need to be able to determine responsibility for the activities of UMS has implications for engineers, roboticists, and computer scientists working on UMS in at least three dimensions.

Firstly, the designers are an obvious and important possible endpoint for the allocation of responsibility for the consequences of the operation of these systems. Thus, for instance, if a design error in a UMS results in the killing of civilians or friendly forces then the designers will be partially responsible for these deaths. That the designers of UMS might be—and might be held to be—responsible for the deaths of innocents should serve as a reminder of the gravity of their role and an incentive for them to perform this role diligently.

Secondly, a concern for the attribution of responsibility will have implications for the appropriate organisation of the process of designing and operating unmanned systems, which should be such as to clearly allocate responsibility for each distinct function of the mechanism and also for the function of the system as a whole. If a problem arises with the operations of an unmanned weapon system, it must be possible to identify those responsible (Marino and Tamburrini 2006). Of course, this is but one instance of the application of more general principles of good design of complex systems and of good project management. However, this fact does not render their application any less important in this instance. Moreover, the requirement that it must be possible to identify those responsible for systems failures will be especially demanding if an unmanned weapon system has the capacity to operate in a "fully autonomous" mode, in which case it will be necessary to *assign* responsibility for the outcomes of the actions of the machine in this mode to appropriate parties (Marino and Tamburrini 2006), which may include the commanding officer and/or those who have designed/programmed the UMS.[9]

Thirdly, the capacity to sustain a chain of responsibility during the operations of UMS is itself an important criteria of good design of these systems. Thus, for instance, "ethical" systems will have robust communications linking them with their operators and will have mechanisms in place to record telemetry data in order that problems with—and responsibility for—the operations of the systems can be identified when necessary.

"Designing Out" War Crimes

The combination of a number of features of UMS may function to lower the psychological, social, and institutional barriers to the commission of war crimes. In particular, the geographic and psychological distance between the operator and the UMS may make it easy for the operator to perform actions that they would not perform if they were physically present in the battlespace (Cummings 2004; Cummings 2006; Graham 2006; Ulin 2005). As a result, they may be more likely to attack illegitimate targets or to use a disproportionate amount of force in attacking legitimate targets.

Of course, this possibility exists with any long-range weapon. Modern warfighters already possess a godlike power to call down destruction from the skies upon their enemies. Telescopic sights, night-vision goggles, and other targeting systems already distance those exercising lethal force from the human beings their actions affect. These existing technologies may therefore already serve to lower some of the psychological barriers to illegitimate killing (Dunlap 1999; Shurtleff 2002).

However, the use of UMS is likely to exacerbate this distancing effect whilst at the same time increasing "contact" with the enemy. In particular, UAVs may make surveillance ubiquitous on the battlefield and also extend it throughout the entire territories of the warring states. The operators of the Predator UAV can watch people going about their daily activities in real time from half a world away. The Predator UAV flies at such a height and produces so little engine noise that those being tracked via this system may have no idea that they are under observation (Fulghum 2003; Kaplan 2006). Watching targeting video taken from the Predator (available via YouTube!) one is struck by the bizarre sense of intimacy this footage generates (Blackmore 2005, p. 202).[10] One description of the Predator UCAV in action recounts how it is possible for the operators to observe individuals in Afghanistan walking outside to defecate and confirm that they have done so by the infrared traces of the faeces they have left behind (Kaplan 2006). Yet the explosions that inevitably follow in the footage that I have watched seem entirely unreal, flickerings on a cathode ray screen made trivial by their similarity to images we have seen a thousand times before in film and on television. By simultaneously increasing the amount of contact with the enemy whilst distancing warfighters from them, UMS may contribute to weapons operators coming to see enemy combatants and non-combatants as distant annoyances only, to be destroyed on the merest of whims. This in turn may lead to (more) violations of the requirements of *jus in bello*.

It has been suggested to me that, on the contrary, by reducing the risks to which their operators are exposed, UMS may also lower the levels of anger, fear and hatred among warfighters. The strong emotions that warfighters in combat feel towards their enemy are in part a product of the fact that that enemy often poses an immediate physical threat.[11] As the lives of operators of UMS are not at risk they may be less inclined to experience these passions. Insofar as anger, hatred, or fear are implicated in the commission of war crimes, reducing the level of these emotions amongst warfighters might also be expected to reduce the number of war crimes.

However, whether or not the operators of UMS are likely to develop more or less compassion and respect for their enemy or be more or less motivated by anger, fear and hatred seems to me an open question. Anecdotal evidence suggests that the operators of UMS become emotionally engaged in and experience strong emotions in response to events in the battlespace regardless of their geographical distance from it. Bender (2005) quotes one operator reporting that,

> . . . "the feeling of anger you get is pretty powerful" when American troops are seen or heard taking fire from insurgents. Others speak of the "adrenaline rush" in the room when the Predator destroys an enemy target. (p. A6)

Another report (Shachtman 2005a) quotes a Major Shannon Rogers describing his experience with a UAV.

> "We left their truck one big smoking hole", he remembers. "My heart was pumping as we were doing our business. It felt just as real to me, however many thousands of miles away, as if I were sitting right there in that cockpit".

These reports suggest that the operators of UMS *do* experience those emotions implicated in the commission of war crimes. Yet while these systems are capable of sustaining and generating these powerful negative emotions it is less clear that they are capable of generating the emotions and moral attitudes that might serve to prevent war crimes. Emotions such as compassion, joy, love, or empathy or moral attitudes such as respect are unlikely to develop or be sustained in a context where warfighters are thousands of miles away from their purported objects. Indeed, a likely consequence of increased use of UMS is a decrease in the number of military personnel involved in conflicts who have ever met or spoken with the people who inhabit the territory in which war is being fought. In the absence of any human relations with those who their actions will affect, warfighters may be less inclined to resist impulses arising out of fear, hatred, or anger where they arise.

As Mary Cummings (2004 & 2006) has argued, the alienation of the operators from the persons that their actions affect means that building ethics "into" the user interface represents a key challenge in the design of UMS. The interface is the primary means by which the operators gain access to information on the basis of which they must make life-and-death decisions; it is also the mechanism whereby the operators act on the basis of these decisions. The design of the interface can therefore be expected to exercise a significant influence on the actions of operators. This in turn suggests that the designers of the interfaces must take ethical considerations into account when designing them. The interface for a UMS should facilitate killing where it is justified and frustrate it where it is not. Obviously, it will not be possible for designers to make this discrimination at the level of individual actions; nor will it be possible to prohibit deliberate unethical use of UMS by an ill-motivated operator. However, it should be possible to take into account the morally relevant features of the circumstances in which a UMS is designed to be used and also those of its typical use and to design systems that promote ethical usage in these circumstances. In particular, the designers of UMS should work to discourage and counteract the alienation between operator and those whose lives they affect, noted above.

Perhaps the most important feature of systems in relation to this imperative is their sensors and the information that they provide to operators. "Good" sensors and good interfaces will present the operator with as much of the information that is morally relevant to the decisions that they must make as is possible. This might include information relevant to the identity, intentions, and history, of potential targets, as well as their current location and activities. This in turn is likely to require providing operators with access to available "human intelligence" and to any other relevant information available via other networks or systems. This information should help operators distinguish between legitimate and illegitimate targets according to LOAC and also distinguish situations where killing of (legally, rather than morally) legitimate targets is justified from situations where it may not be. Moreover, the sensors and information systems should facilitate the operators being able not only to reliably identify targets but also to comprehend what happens to them when lethal force is deployed. That is, as much as is possible, the system's sensors should communicate the moral reality of the consequences of the actions of the operator. It is essential that operators have a vivid awareness of what is at stake when they make decisions, so that they can learn to make them responsibly and well.

It must be acknowledged that these are demanding goals and that there are likely to be significant limits on designers capacity to achieve them, especially given the concerns expressed above about whether remote systems are capable of transmitting and representing the full range of moral and emotional information relevant to combat and also the budgetary and other design constraints the designers of UMS must operate under. Nevertheless, it is important to clarify and state them in this context in order that they may at least provide some direction in relation to ethical design. It is also worth noting that at least some of the imperatives arising out of a concern for ethical design align with those arising out of a concern with the operational demands on the systems.

Where possible, UMS should possess a range of capacities beyond the firing of deadly weapons. Lethal force should not be the first and only recourse available to operators. Thus, for instance, UGVs for operations in urban environments should have the capacity to communicate with other persons in the battle space, including non-combatants. Consideration should also be given to equipping such systems with "non"—or, more accurately, "sub"—lethal weapons. Providing operators with a larger range of options will allow them to respond more appropriately—and hopefully, more ethically—to each particular situation.

A possible *policy* response to the geographical and psychological distance between operators and their (potential) targets, with design implications, would be to return the operators of UMS to the theatre of operations in which the systems they operate function, so that they have some experience of the local culture and contact with the people whose lives they are affecting. This would have the obvious disadvantage of placing the operators at higher risk by virtue of being closer to the front line and would also involve expenses associated with the transport and supply of these personnel and associated systems.[12] However, it would go some way to addressing the concerns about "remote control" killing surveyed above.[13] Whether this trade-off is sufficient to justify putting the operators closer to the front line will depend on the details of the particular UMS and the roles for which it is intended, as well as the intensity of the particular conflict. Obviously, the range over which systems are intended to be used will have significant design implications. Armed Forces will therefore need to consider these issues early in the design of such systems.

Another important aspect of the project of ethical design will be working to avoid the creation of *other* types of what Cummings (2004 & 2006) describes as "moral buffers" between the operator and their actions. Many UMS have a good deal of automation built into them, into their sensors as well as into the operations of the system itself. Cummings suggests that the operators may come to over rely on the automation in these systems, to the detriment of the decisions they make. Moreover, Cummings argues, the presence of this automation may form a (further) moral buffer between the users of the system and their actions, allowing them to tell themselves that "the machine" made the decision. This, in turn, may encourage unethical choices by operators who are thereby able to distance themselves morally and emotionally from the consequences of their actions. Good design of UMS will therefore not only (as discussed above) ensure that we can *identify* those responsible for the consequences of the operation of the system, it will also ensure that those who *are* responsible *feel* responsible—and know precisely what they are responsible for.

A final, important, consideration relating to the ethical design of UMS is that because the operators of the UMS are themselves not in any danger while they are in combat, it seems as though they should err on the side of caution when it comes to making decisions about killing.[14] This means that there is some room in designing these systems for checks and balances, such as the gathering of more information outlined above, which would not be practical for warfighters actually present in the battlespace. Of course, importantly, the lives of *other* friendly forces in the battlespace may well be at stake, which means that many missions will still be time critical, such that it will still be necessary for the UMS to be capable of responding quickly as required. Nevertheless, the fact that the operators of UMS are safe from harm does alter what it is reasonable to expect from them by way of a concern for the requirements of jus in bello and therefore the requirements of ethical design of these systems.

The challenge of ethical design is a challenge that, arguably, it is yet to be adequately met. A number of articles on UMS report that the control units for these systems have deliberately been designed around the controls for the PlayStation game console or around a "Gameboy" controller in order to take advantage of potential operators existing familiarity with these controls (Graham 2006; Hambling 2007; Kenyon 2007; Thornton 2005). Unsurprisingly, this has led to reports that there is a tendency for the operators to mistake their activities for playing computer games.

According to Bender (2005),

For the Predator crews in Nevada, however, the main challenge is simply to remember they are not playing a video game when they step out of their air-conditioned office for a Wendy's hamburger.

"We have to impress upon them that they are not just shooting electrons," said Major Sam Morgan, a trainer of Predator pilots. "They're killing people."

Shachtman (2005b) also cites an analyst saying, of the operation of these systems

It's like a video game. It can get a little bloodthirsty. But it's fucking cool.

Presuming that we do not want warfighters making life-and-death decisions in the subconscious belief that they are playing a video game, these remarks suggest that much work remains to be done in promoting ethical behaviour through the design of UMS.

CONCLUSION

The development of UMS for military applications poses ethical as well as technical design challenges for roboticists, engineers, computer scientists, and others involved in the design of these systems.

I have argued that one set of ethical issues arises out of a concern for the safety of the operators of the system and of those who will work alongside them. While the development of UMS may keep some warfighters safe from harm, there are also circumstances in which it may place others at risk. Responding to this phenomenon will require negotiating a complex set of trade-offs regarding the capacities—and expense—of these systems. I have also highlighted the possibility that operation of UMS may expose the operators to unique psychological stresses.

There is also another, arguably more difficult, set of issues that arise out of the need for the operations of UMS to meet the requirements of the law of armed conflict. The profound difficulties involved in enabling fully autonomous weapons systems to distinguish between legitimate and illegitimate targets and assess the proportionate use of force suggest that it will be necessary to retain a "human in the loop" for the foreseeable future. A critical requirement for the ethical design and operation of UMS is that those responsible for each aspect of their design and operations can be clearly identified; this may require attributing responsibility if these systems are used in a "fully autonomous" mode. Finally, ethical design of UMS will require paying attention to the ways in which these systems may facilitate unethical behaviour by separating the operators from the consequences of their actions and working to overcome this and other "moral buffers" that may arise in the operation of robotic weapons.

Throughout, I have tried to suggest how these issues might begin to be addressed by appropriate design of UMS. My investigations suggest that some of these ethical issues can be "designed out" or at least "designed around". That is to say, with sufficient ingenuity and more sophisticated technology, engineers can avoid them and/or minimise their impacts. For instance, better neural networks, better sensors and better target recognition algorithms might mitigate some of the difficulties involved in the problem of discrimination and expand the number of roles in which it was appropriate to employ autonomous weapons systems. Sensors which make possible a more vivid appreciation of the battlespace might also reduce the psychological distance between operators and their targets and thus reduce the extent to which the distance between them acts as a "moral buffer".

However, it is important to note that there are real trade-offs involved in attempting to address some of these issues, such that efforts to address one will intensify another. Thus, for instance, technologies which make possible a larger scope for autonomous operations of robotic weapons systems exacerbate the problem of locating the responsibility for the consequences of the operations of these systems. Systems with sensors that make the battle more "real" for the operators will also increase the risk that they will suffer psychological stress as a result. Controlling UMS over long distances will decrease the risk to the operators but increase the "moral buffer" between them and their actions. Designers of UMS will therefore need to consider the relative priorities of these issues, the relationships between them, and the trade-offs involved in attempts to address them, in the pursuit of "ethical" design.

Unmanned systems are already playing a key role in contemporary conflicts. Given current enthusiasm for UMS and their obvious utility it seems likely that robotic systems will be used much more widely in military roles in the future (Featherstone 2007; Graham 2006; Hanley 2007; Hockmuth 2007; Office of the Under Secretary of Defense 2006; Peterson 2005; Scarborough 2005). It also seems likely that the scope of autonomous action allowed to UMS will increase as the technology improves.[15] These trends make the challenges of ethical design of unmanned systems that I have highlighted here all the more urgent.

NOTES

[. . .]

9. See Sparrow 2007 for further discussion.

10. A search for "Predator" AND " UAV" on YouTube on 27.6.07 produced at least four distinct pieces of footage purportedly taken by Predator UAVs.

11. It must also be acknowledged that military socialisation prior to combat may play a large role in producing these emotions. Whether this will affect the operators of UMS depends on the type of training they receive.

12. It is also worth observing that locating the operators of UMS in the nation in which a conflict is occurring, but confining them to a military base that is entirely isolated from the local culture, will *not* address the issue identified here. If security and/or other operational reasons mandate isolating military personnel from the local culture then it will make no difference whether the operators are isolated at a military base in their own country or isolated at a forward operating base.

13. It might also go some way towards reducing the stress associated with fighting a war in a country in which one has never set foot, discussed above.

14. This fact also has significant implications for the ethics of the return of fire from such systems when they come under attack. Klein (2003) suggests that UAVs and UCAVs need to be classified as "national assets" in order to ground a right to defend these systems if they come under enemy fire; presumably the same would be true of UGVs, UUVs, and USVs as well. While finessing the legal nomenclature may establish the legal right to fire upon enemy combatants who attack UMS, the fact that the life of the operator of UMS is not threatened when the system is attacked undercuts the moral justification for returning fire directed against them—at least insofar as this justification proceeds from the right to self-defence.

15. Because the communication infrastructure required to keep a "human in the loop" is a weakpoint in UMS, systems which dispense with a human operator will be more survivable. As the tempo of battle increases as a result of technological developments, including the development of UMS, systems which rely on human input may be at a substantial disadvantage in combat against fully autonomous systems. There is therefore a substantial incentive for designers of UMS to provide systems with a capacity for autonomous operations (Adams 2001; Blackmore 2005; Excell 2007; Featherstone 2007; Lerner 2006; Szafranski 2005).

REFERENCES

Adams, Thomas K. 2001. Future Warfare and the Decline of Human Decision-making. *Parameters: US Army War College Quarterly* (Winter, 2001–2): 57–71.

[...]

Arkin, Ronald C. 2007. Governing Lethal Behaviour: Embedding Ethics in a Hybrid Deliberative/Reactive Robot Architecture. Technical Report GIT-GVU-07-11 for US Army. Mobile Robot Laboratory, College of Computing, Georgia Institute of Technology. Available at http://www.cc.gatech.edu/ai/robot-lab/online-publications/formalizationv35.pdf at 25.10.07.

Asaro, Peter M. 2007. Robots and Responsibility from a Legal Prospective. *IEEE International Conference on Robotics and Automation*, Roma, Italy.

[...]

Bender, Bryan. 2005. Attacking Iraq, from a Nev. Computer. *Boston Globe*, April 3, A6.

Blackmore, Tim. 2005. Dead Slow: Unmanned Aerial Vehicles Loitering in Battlespace. *Bulletin of Science, Technology & Society* 25 (3): 195–214.

[...]

Canning, John S. 2005. A Definitive Work on Factors Impacting the Arming of Unmanned Vehicles, Washington, D.C.: Dahlgren Division Naval Surface Warfare Centre.

Canning, John S. 2006. A Concept of Operations for Armed Autonomous Systems, 3rd Annual Disruptive Technology Conference, September 6–7, Washington, DC.

[...]

Cummings, M. L. 2004. Creating Moral Buffers in Weapon Control Interface Design. *IEEE Technology and Society Magazine* 23 (3): 28–33, 41.

Cummings, M.L. 2006. Automation and Accountability in Decision Support System Interface Design. *Journal of Technology Studies* 32 (1): 23–31.

Dalton, Jane G. 2006. Future Navies—Present Issues. *Naval War College Review* 59: 17–39.

[...]

Dunlap, Jr., Charles J. 1999. Technology: Recomplicating Moral Life for the Nation's Defenders. *Parameters: US Army War College Quarterly* (Autumn): 24–53.

Excell, John. 2007. Unmanned Aircraft: Out of the Shadows. *The Engineer*, January 18.

Featherstone, Steve. 2007. The coming robot army. *Harper's Magazine*: 43–52.

Fielding, Marcus. 2006. Robotics in Future Land Warfare. *Australian Army Journal* 3 (2): 1–10.

Fitzsimonds, James R., and Thomas G. Mahnken. 2007. Military Officer Attitudes Toward UAV Adoption: Exploring Institutional Impediments to Innovation. *Joint Force Quarterly* (46): 96–103.

Fulghum, David A. 2003. Predator's Progress. *Aviation Week and Space Technology* 158 (9): 48–50.

Foster, Lt Col John. 2006. Ricochets and Replies: First Rule of Modern Warfare. *Air and Space Power Journal* (Spring).

Graham, Stephen. 2006. America's robot army. *New Statesman* 135 (4796): 12–15.

Gulam, Hyder, and Simon W. Lee. 2006. Uninhabited Combat Aerial Vehicles And the Law of Armed Conflict. *Australian Army Journal* 3 (2): 1–14.

Hambling, David. 2007. Military Builds Robotic Insects. *Wired Magazine*, 23 January. Available at http://www.wired.com/science/discoveries/news/2007/01/72543.

Hanley, Charles J. 2007. Robot-Aircraft Attack Squadron Bound for Iraq. *Aviation.com*, 16 July.

Hockmuth, Catherine MacRae. 2007. UAVs—The Next Generation. *Air Force Magazine*, February, 70–74.

Kainikara, Sanu. 2002. UCAVs probable lynchpins of future air warfare. *Asia-Pacific Defence Reporter* 28 (6): 42–45.

Kaplan, Robert D. 2006. Hunting the Taliban in Las Vegas. *Atlantic Monthly*. August 4.

Kenyon, Henry S. 2006. Israel Deploys Robot Guardians. *Signal* 60 (7): 41–44.

Kenyon, Henry S. 2007. Airborne Testbed Opens New Possibilities. *Signal* 61 (9): 47–9.

Klein, John J. 2003. The Problematic Nexus: Where Unmanned Combat Air Vehicles and the Law of Armed Conflict Meet. *Air and Space Power Journal Chronicles Online* (22 July). Available at www.airpower.maxwell.af.mil/airchronicles/cc/klein.html at 27.3.07.

[...]

Lazarski, Anthony J. 2002. Legal Implications of the Uninhabited Combat Aerial Vehicle. *Air and Space Power Journal* 16(2): 74–83.

[...]

Lerner, Preston. 2006. Robots Go To War. *Popular Science* 268 (1).

[...]

Marino, Dante and Tamburrini, Guglielmo. 2006. Learning Robots and Human Responsibility. *International Review of Information Ethics* 6:47–51.

[...]

Mustin, Jeff. 2002. Future Employment of Unmanned Aerial Vehicles. *Air and Space Power Journal* 16 (2): 86–97.

[...]

Office of the Under Secretary of Defense. 2006. *Development and Utilisation of Robotics and Unmanned Ground Vehicles: Report to Congress.* Washington D.C.: Office of the Under Secretary of Defense, Acquisition, Technology and Logistics, Portfolio Systems Acquisition, Land Warfare and Munitions, Joint Ground Robotics Enterprise.

Peterson, Gordon I. 2005. Unmanned Vehicles: Changing the Way to Look at the Battlespace. *Naval Forces* 26 (4): 29–38.

Royal Australian Air Force. 2004. *AAP 1003—Operations Law for RAAF Commanders.* 2nd. Ed. Canberra: Air Power Development Centre.

Schmitt, Michael N. 2005. Precision Attack and International Humanitarian Law. *International Review of the Red Cross* 87 (859): 445–466.

Scarborough, Rowan. 2005. Special Report: Unmanned Warfare. *Washington Times,* May 8.

Shachtman, Noah. 2005a. Attack of the Drones. *Wired Magazine* 13 (6). Available at http://www.wired.com/wired/archive//13.06/drones_pr.html, at 25.08.05.

Shachtman, Noah. 2005b. Drone School, a Ground's-Eye View. *Wired Magazine,* 27 May. Available at http://www.wired.com/science/discoveries/news/2005/05/67655 at 17.9.07

[...]

Shurtleff, D. Keith. 2002. The Effects of Technology on Our Humanity. *Parameters: US Army War College Quarterly* (Summer):100–112.

Sparrow, Robert. 2007. Killer Robots. *Journal of Applied Philosophy* 24 (1): 62–77.

Sullivan, Jeffrey M. 2006. Evolution or Revolution? The rise of UAVs. *IEEE Technology and Society Magazine* 25(3) (Fall): 43–49.

Szafranski, Col. Richard. 2005. The First Rule of Modern Warfare: Never Bring a Knife to a Gunfight. *Air and Space Power Journal* 19 (4): 19–26.

Thorton, Jr., Captain Robert L. 2005. The Case for Robots in the SBCTs (Now). *Infantry* 94 (1): 33–41.

Ulin, David L. 2005. When Robots Do the Killing. *Los Angeles Times,* January 30.

[...]

*Robert Sparrow is a visiting fellow at the Centre for Values, Ethics, and the Law in Medicine, at the University of Sydney.

With kind permission of Springer Science + Business Media: *Science Engineering Ethics* "Building a Better WarBot: Ethical Issues in the Design of Unmanned Systems for Military Applications," volume 15, 2009, 169–87, Robert Sparrow.